SECEDING FROM SECESSION

The Civil War, Politics, and the Creation of West Virginia

Eric J. Wittenberg,

Edmund A. Sargus, Jr., and Penny Barrick

Savas Beatie
California

Library of Congress Cataloging-in-Publication Data

Names: Wittenberg, Eric J., 1961- author. | Sargus, Edmund A., Jr., 1953- author.
    | Barrick, Penny L., author.
Title: Seceding From secession: The Civil War, Politics, and the Creation of West Virginia
    / by Eric J. Wittenberg, Edmund A. Sargus, Jr., and Penny L. Barrick.
Other titles: Civil War, politics, and the creation of West Virginia
Description: California: Savas Beatie [2020] | Includes bibliographical references and index.
    | Summary: "This book is the first modern study of the events that led to the creation
    of the State of West Virginia. It includes both historical and legal analysis and places
    those important events in their proper historical context"—Provided by publisher.
Identifiers: LCCN 2020007694 | ISBN 9781611215069 (hardcover) |
    ISBN 9781611215076 (ebook)
Subjects: LCSH: West Virginia—Politics and government—1861-1865. |
    West Virginia—History—Civil War, 1861-1865. | Statehood (American politics)
Classification: LCC F241 .W73 2020 | DDC 975.4/03—dc23
LC record available at https://lccn.loc.gov/2020007694

ISBN-13: 978-1-61121-506-9
eISBN: 978-1-61121-507-6

First Edition, First Printing

SB

Savas Beatie
989 Governor Drive, Suite 102
El Dorado Hills, CA 95762
916-941-6896 / sales@savasbeatie.com / www.savasbeatie.com

All of our titles are available at special discount rates for bulk purchases in the United States. Contact us for information.

Proudly published, printed, and warehoused in the United States of America.

"I believe the admission of West Virginia into the Union is expedient."

— President Abraham Lincoln, December 31, 1862

Table of Contents

Table of Contents (continued)

FOREWORD

by Frank J. Williams

SOMETHING like 65,000 books have been published on the Civil War, more than one a day since it ended, while 16,000 of those books are about Abraham Lincoln himself. Between all those books, their studied narratives and storytelling, those authors and the country as a whole has a tremendous lack of consensus about what the Civil War means.[1]

The Civil War "has invited more speculation about whether it could have been avoided, or turned out differently" than any event in American history. What if Lincoln had assented to Southern succession? What if, in the winter of 1860-61, Congress and the states had adopted a constitutional amendment assuring the perpetuity of slavery? What if one army, during one of the many battles of the Civil War, had destroyed the other army completely? What if President Lincoln had vetoed the bill creating the state of West Virginia? Yet, none of these questions tell us what the war was all about.[2]

Abraham Lincoln holds our nation's mind like no other president. "He lived at the dawn of photography, and his pine cone face made a haunting picture." "He was the best writer in all American politics, and his words are even more powerful than his images." His greatest trial, the Civil War, was the nation's greatest trial, and the race problem that caused it is still with us today. Lincoln's murder, a poignant and violent climax to the Civil War, allowed future generations, including our own, to consider the "what-ifs."[3]

---

1 Frank J. Williams, "A LOOK AT LINCOLN: Consensus is Hard to Find," *Civil War Book Review*, Vol. 16 (Issue. 3, 2014), Article 3.

2 Ibid.

3 Ibid.

Abraham Lincoln did great things, greater than anything done by Theodore Roosevelt or Franklin Roosevelt.[4] He freed the slaves and saved the Union, and because he saved the Union he was able to free the slaves. Beyond this, however, our extraordinary interest in him, and esteem for him, has to do with what he said and did. And much of this had to do with the Union—what it was and why it was worth saving.

He saved it by fighting and winning the war, of course. But his initial step in this was the decision to go to war—not a popular decision, and certainly not an easy one. His predecessor, the incompetent James Buchanan, believed that the states had no right to secede from the Union, but that there was nothing he could do about it if they did.[5] Thus, by the time Lincoln took office, seven Southern states had seceded, and nothing had been done about it. Led by South Carolina, they claimed to be doing only what the original colonies had done in 1776. To oppose them might bring on the war, and Buchanan had no stomach for this.[6]

After the southern states began seceding, Lincoln clearly understood "that the time had come when the only way to save the Union was to go to war." However, he was forced to consider whether he could say this and "retain the support of the people who had voted for him?" To his abolitionist supporters, "slavery was a sin, and the slaveholders sinners." Yet, William Lloyd Garrison, "was no friend of the Union." Garrison believed that the Constitution "was 'a covenant with death and an agreement with hell.'" Garrison even said, "[d]uring the Fort Sumter crisis . . . 'all Union saving efforts are simply idiotic.'"[7]

Demographic historian J. David Hacker, using a "sophisticated analysis of census records," estimated the death toll of the war at 750,000, twenty percent more than originally believed.[8] That number has gained "wide acceptance from

---

4 Eric Rauchway,. "Some Notes on Comparing Lincoln and FDR." *The Chronicle of Higher Education*, www.chronicle.com/blognetwork/edgeofthewest/2011/12/26/some-notes-on-comparing-lincoln-and-fdr/.

5 Jean H. Baker, "Learning From Buchanan." The New York Times, *The New York Times*, 26 Feb. 2011, opinionator.blogs.nytimes.com/2011/02/26/learning-from-buchanan/.

6 Walter Berns, "Why America Celebrates Lincoln." *American Enterprise Institute*, 17 Feb. 2009, www.aei.org/publication/why-america-celebrates-lincoln/.

7 Ibid.

8 Tony Horwitz, "150 Years of Misunderstanding the Civil War." *The Atlantic*, 2 July 2013, www.theatlantic.com/national/archive/2013/06/150-years-of-misunderstanding-the-civil-war/277022/.

Civil War scholars." Hacker's estimate, if accurate, would mean that "the Civil War claimed more lives than all other American wars combined, and the increase in population since 1860 means that a comparable war today would cost 7.5 million lives." Hacker's death toll "[does not] include the more than half million soldiers who were wounded and often permanently disabled by amputation, lingering disease, psychological trauma and other afflictions."[9]

President Lincoln confronted many challenges: the first conscription in America, defining war powers of the president, civil liberties in war time, martial law, plans for Reconstruction, and admission of new states including West Virginia.[10]

Lincoln was not keen on admitting West Virginia as it had "seceded" from Virginia—which was a state and Lincoln would never concede that it, and other "so called" Confederate states, had left the Union.[11] So, supporters of West Virginia created a legal fiction that what became West Virginia, was really the authentic Commonwealth of Virginia.[12]

West Virginia was created out of necessity in the midst of the Civil War, and admitted to the Union in 1863. Many maintain that the admission of West Virginia to the Union was completed on less than constitutional grounds. The North coveted the creation and admission of West Virginia to the Union, but Article IV, Section 3.1 of the Constitution required, and requires to this day, the approval of the original state legislature to create the state of the original state's boundaries.

The settlers in the counties west of the Alleghenies of the original Virginia had an uneasy relationship with the remainder of the state. The counties that make up the current West Virginia were insufficient to gain the prestige and prominence of planters and plantation slavery. Those in the western counties complained of a state government that overtaxed and underrepresented them.

These western counties shared miles of border with both Ohio and Pennsylvania. The river system that created natural borders also provided for the flow of population and commerce. The people of Virginia's western counties were

9 Ibid.

10 Thomas Mackhuin Owens, "Civil Liberties in Wartime." *National Review*, National Review, Jan. 7, 2015, www.nationalreview.com/2014/10/civil-liberties-wartime-mackubin-thomas-owens/.

11 Fred J. Martin, *Abraham Lincoln's Path to Reelection in 1864: Our Greatest Victory* 204. Author House, 2013.

12 Ibid.

more intimately connected with those Pennsylvanians and Ohioans, more so than their fellow Virginians.

And as Virginia took steps to secede from the Union, the people in the western counties opposed such secession. Virginia's January 1861 call for a state convention ignored precedent that required a popular vote to sanction such a call. That convention, from February into April, discussed the issue of secession. The new Confederacy was represented there, and its supporters packed the galleries, while also threatening delegates by hanging nooses from lampposts. Delegates from the western counties of Virginia, latter day West Virginia, voted against secession on April 4. But fifteen days later, the convention voted to secede.

Secessionists sought to impose what amounted to martial law throughout the state. However, those in the western counties clearly opposed secession and such further actions. Just hours after approval of secession, officials in Wheeling and other communities received orders from the state to seize Federal property. This led to western Virginians directly contradicting the state's authority. Over the next few weeks, Unionists sponsored public meetings at Wheeling, Parkersburg, and other Ohio River communities, as well as at Clarksburg and other interior towns. County conventions followed, leading to a loyalist state convention at Wheeling on the thirteenth of May. As other border states, both Unionist and Confederate recruiters worked to gain support for their cause, sometimes working in the same community at the same time. At a second convention on the eleventh of June, fifty-seven delegates established the Unionist "Restored Government of Virginia," which subsequently sanctioned the course of the western counties toward independence from Virginia.

Due to geography and circumstance, western Virginia was bound to be the first part of the state to suffer the full force of the coming war. Railroads crossed through West Virginia in the northern corner of the region. The Baltimore & Ohio Railroad ran up the Potomac River from Harper's Ferry to Grafton, then swung north to Wheeling before entering the valley, and the Northwestern Railroad went from Parkersburg on the Ohio River to Grafton. Three east-west roads connected the region to the Shenandoah Valley of Virginia. The Northwestern Turnpike ran along the rails from Parkersburg through Grafton before crossing into Winchester; the Parkersburg & Staunton Turnpike went southwest from Parkersburg through Beverly before continuing east into Staunton; and the James River & Kanawha Turnpike ran from Guyandotte through Charleston, then through Gauley Bridge and White

Sulphur Springs on the border. So, too, a network of roads formed a north-south route from Grafton down to Gauley Bridge, linking the three turnpikes. The war was fought primarily along these routes through the state.

In occupied Unionist communities like Wheeling and Parkersburg, Loyal Virginians were aided by troops from Ohio and elsewhere. However, the Confederate occupation of Grafton forced the Federals either to move into the interior or to accept the loss of the B & O linking Washington to the Ohio Valley. After their occupation of Grafton in late May, the Union won battles at Phillippi on June 3, 1861 and Rich Mountain on June 10, 1861 and secured the area near the railroad. As Union forces pushed south, another federal column battled up the Kanawha River, the two converging at Gauley Bridge late in the summer.

The Confederates, fearing that the Union's actions were a prelude to a Union drive across the mountains into the Shenandoah, secured the area around Sewell Mountain. There was a clash between these small forces at the top of Alleghany Mountain on December 13. However, because of the logistical problems of movement and supply, large-scale clashes were nearly impossible.

Union forces sought to hold the region with the least possible numbers, which led to several Confederate incursions that were unable to remain in the region for long. William E. Jones, John D. Imboden, and Albert Jenkins led such raids in 1861. Several small towns changed hands frequently during the war. Of these was the town of Romney, which changed hands fifty-three times throughout the war.

Although both sides were persistent in their efforts to negotiate large columns through the mountains, each failed. For example, the Union's attempt to push east into the Shenandoah Valley ended at White Sulphur Springs on August 26th-27th, 1863. Similar drives to the south against the Virginia & Tennessee Railroad ended at Droop Mountain on November 6, 1863. Through 1864, Federals made several additional raids against the railroad, and Confederates continued their incursions into the region. However, that year's Union victories in the Shenandoah Valley left the war in West Virginia to sputter into guerrilla fighting.

In the political arena, there was a similar fight over the separation of West Virginia to Virginia. However, due to low turnout, the plan backfired, leaving West Virginia with a number of counties that might well have preferred remaining in Virginia.

As internal dissenters within the United States, Virginia secessionists appealed to the ideals of self-determination implicit in the Declaration of Independence. But, West Virginia found that it too had its own internal dissenters eager to do the same against the authority of the state. Despite attempts otherwise, West Virginia's secessionist minority found themselves hostages to geography, their own ill-fated attempt to thwart the new state, and the fortunes of war. In the end, West Virginia became a standing monument to the role of power rather than ideals in the Civil War era.

Pragmatism won the day when West Virginia was admitted to the Union as the 35th state on June 20, 1863.[13] Despite its low number of slaves, West Virginia was the last slaveholding state admitted to the Union.[14] At Lincoln's demand, the new state's constitution, ratified in 1863, provided for long-term, gradual emancipation for the children of slaves. Two years after admission, the Thirteenth Amendment was passed, abolishing slavery throughout the country.[15]

Frank J. Williams is the former Chief Justice of Rhode Island and founding Chair of The Lincoln Forum. He is the author or editor of more than twenty books, including *Judging Lincoln.*

13 Spencer Tucker and Paul G. Pierpaoli. American Civil War: a State-by-State Encyclopedia, 891. ABC-CLIO, 2015.

14 Ibid.

15 Ibid.

PREFACE

THE state of West Virginia began in controversy and war. Abraham Lincoln wrestled with the constitutionality of the process used to create the new state. The question of whether West Virginia was lawfully carved from Virginia divided Lincoln's cabinet and the Congress. With this book, we offer a fresh look at the only division of a state without the expressed consent of its duly elected legislative assembly.

Article IV, Section 3 of the United States Constitution requires the consent of a state before a new state can be formed from its territory. This process has happened several times in American history, including the 1792 creation of the Commonwealth of Kentucky from the territories of Virginia and in 1820, when the State of Maine was created from lands of Massachusetts. Without controversy, the legislatures of both Virginia and Massachusetts approved the divisions, which Congress then affirmed.

The secession crisis of 1860-1861 opened the drama that led to the creation of the State of West Virginia. When Virginia seceded from the Union in April 1861, the majority of the state's population west of the Allegheny Mountains adamantly opposed this decision. A movement quickly formed in favor of creating a new, pro-Union state from that portion of Virginia. The struggle lasted two full years before the statehood drive came to fruition: West Virginia formally became the thirty-fifth state of the Union on June 20, 1863.

The federal government could ill afford to lose the all-important Baltimore & Ohio Railroad. For this reason alone, the burgeoning statehood movement drew the attention of Washington. The B&O passed through the eastern panhandle of West Virginia, and then through its heart to Wheeling, where it crossed the Ohio

River into Ohio. Two counties, through which the B & O ran, made up the new state's eastern panhandle, which was about the only part of the new state not located to the west of the Alleghany Mountains. While occupied by federal troops, both counties, Berkeley and Jefferson, were dragged into the Union in order to maintain control of the rail line. With public sentiment in doubt, the citizens of Berkeley and Jefferson Counties did not vote in the original plebiscites used in the creation of the State of West Virginia.

Consequently, in 1866, with the Civil War over and Reconstruction under way, the Commonwealth of Virginia sued the State of West Virginia in the United States Supreme Court, seeking the return of Berkeley and Jefferson Counties to Virginia. For five contentious years, the case languished before a deadlocked Supreme Court, with a final decision denying Virginia's claims issued in March 1871. In the end, the Supreme Court avoided the question of whether West Virginia's creation complied with the requirements of the Constitution.

We hope to provide a better understanding and appreciation of the process by which West Virginia joined the Union and the constitutional issues underlying those events. Our goal is to explain the role played by the B&O Railroad and the critical leadership provided by Abraham Lincoln, America's greatest president. Without Lincoln, there would be no State of West Virginia.

Eric J. Wittenberg is an award-winning Civil War historian who is also an attorney with more than thirty years of litigation experience. Edmund A. Sargus, Jr. is from southeastern Ohio, just across the Ohio River from Wheeling. He is also the Chief Judge of the United States District Court for the Southern District of Ohio. As such, questions of constitutional law are of great interest to him, as is the history of the Civil War and of Wheeling. Penny Barrick is a senior lawyer with the District Court where she has the opportunity to consider issues of constitutional law regularly in her role assisting Chief Judge Sargus. Collectively, we have more than 90 years of experience in the practice of law, and we hope that that experience gives us insights that help us to tell this fascinating story. We hope our combined interests and skills enable us to tell the story of the creation of the State of West Virginia fully and in an unprecedented way that addresses the military, political, and legal issues thoroughly.

As with every project of this type, we are grateful for the assistance that we have received from a variety of people during the course of researching and writing this book, and we are grateful to all of them. We hope to be forgiven if we forget anyone who contributed to this project; any omissions are unintentional.

Frank J. Williams, former chief justice of the Supreme Court of Rhode Island, and chairman emeritus of the Lincoln Forum, penned the foreword that follows. We appreciate Frank's support and willingness to help. We thank retired attorney Jack Decker of Columbus, Ohio, who provided the impetus to the writing of this book. Jon-Erik Gilot of Wheeling was of great assistance to our efforts to identify sources, as was Bob Arrington. Joe Geiger, the state archivist of West Virginia, provided much support. Hunter Lesser provided some suggestions as to sources. John Emond helped us to gather useful material from the collection of papers of Associate Justice Samuel Freeman Miller of the United States Supreme Court, who penned the majority decision for the Court in the case of *Virginia vs. West Virginia*. Edward Alexander drew the fine maps that appear in this book.

We are also grateful to Theodore P. Savas, managing director of Savas Beatie, for publishing this book. Eric has a long-standing working relationship with Ted, and we appreciate Ted's stewardship of this process. The capable staff at Savas Beatie made the labyrinthine process of publishing this book much easier than it otherwise could have been, and for that we are thankful.

Ed wishes to thank his wife, Judge Jennifer Sargus, whose patience and wisdom guides and encourages him. Penny wishes to thank her husband, Dave Barrick, for always supporting her endeavors. She also would like to thank Ed for igniting in her a love of Civil War history, and to both of her coauthors for sharing with her their passion for this topic. Once again, Eric wishes to thank his long-suffering wife, best friend, and travel companion, Susan Skilken Wittenberg, for her support and love. Without Susan's support, none of Eric's historical work would be possible, and he is extremely grateful to her for that.

Eric J. Wittenberg
Edmund A. Sargus, Jr.
Penny L. Barrick

Columbus, Ohio

INTRODUCTION

T HE United States Supreme Court convened for business on the morning of March 6, 1871. "The Honorable, the Chief Justice and the Associate Justices of the Supreme Court of the United States," intoned the Marshal of the Supreme Court, Richard C. Parsons of Cleveland, Ohio.[1] "Oyez! Oyez! Oyez! All persons having business before the Honorable, the Supreme Court of the United States, are admonished to draw near and give their attention, for the Court is now sitting. God save the United States and this Honorable Court."

The nine justices of the Supreme Court filed in and took their seats. The Court, long on tradition, arranged seating by seniority. Chief Justice Salmon Portland Chase, age 63 and from Cincinnati, Ohio, took his usual position in the center chair. Immediately to his right sat the senior Associate Justice, 80-year-old Samuel Nelson, who had been on the court for more than 25 years. To his left sat the next senior Associate Justice, 68-year-old Nathan Clifford. Noah Haynes Swayne, age 67, sat to the right of Nelson. Samuel Freeman Miller sat to the left of Clifford, and David Davis sat to the right of Swayne. Stephen Johnson Field sat to the left of Miller. William Strong sat to the right of Davis, filling the right side. Finally, James Philo Bradley, the most recent appointee to join the Court on March 23, 1870, took the last seat on the left.

---

1 "The West Virginia Case," *Alexandria Gazette and Virginia Advertiser*, March 7, 1871.

The case of *Virginia v. West Virginia*, first filed in 1866, vexed the Supreme Court for almost five years.[2] The parties first argued the case in the spring of 1867. The Supreme Court had tied, in a 4 to 4 vote, in its efforts to resolve such a significant case during the South's Reconstruction. After four years of deadlock, the Supreme Court, with two recently confirmed justices, was at last ready to decide the case.

The lawyers also took their seats. Benjamin Robbins Curtis of Massachusetts, the only member of the Whig Party to serve as an Associate Justice of the Supreme Court, who dissented in what historians generally consider to be the Court's worst-ever ruling, *Dred Scott v. Sanford* in 1857, represented the Commonwealth of Virginia.[3] Reverdy Johnson, a distinguished lawyer and U.S. Senator from Maryland, and Ambassador to Great Britain, represented the State of West Virginia. Both litigants were represented by two of the best lawyers then practicing in the United States, and both capably presented the cases of their respective clients before the bar.

Justice Samuel Freeman Miller, a physician and lawyer from Kentucky, cleared his throat, took a sip of water, and began reading the majority's opinion. Miller and five other Justices—Chief Justice Chase and Associate Justices Nelson, Swayne, Strong and Bradley—made up the 6-3 majority, and Miller's opinion represented the views of those six justices. When Miller finished reading the majority opinion, Associate Justice David Davis, a former U.S. Senator from Illinois who had served as Abraham Lincoln's campaign manager at the 1860 Republican Party convention, read the dissenting opinion. Associate Justices Clifford and Field joined Davis's dissent. At last, nearly five years after the lawsuit was filed, the important case of *State of Virginia vs. State of West Virginia* was finally over.

In the first detailed modern treatment of these events, this book comprehensively examines the historic events that led to the dismembering of Virginia. The new state of West Virginia was born in the middle of a devastating civil war. Then, once the agony of the Civil War ended, the legal drama played

---

2 *State of Virginia v. State of W. Virginia*, 78 U.S. 39, 63 (1870).

3 In the *Dred Scott* case, the Supreme Court held that "a negro, whose ancestors were imported into [the U.S.], and sold as slaves," whether enslaved or free, could not be an American citizen, and therefore had no standing to sue in federal court, and that the federal government had no power to regulate slavery in the federal territories acquired after the creation of the United States. *Dred Scott v. Sandford*, 60 U.S. 393, 403 (1857), *superseded* (1868).

out in the Supreme Court, where Virginia claimed that the division of the state violated the United States Constitution.

The story of West Virginia statehood includes a number of colorful, heroic figures. Governor Francis H. Pierpont is often called The Father of West Virginia. Sen. John S. Carlile was one of the earliest and most ardent supporters of the concept of statehood, a position he later renounced. As a result, his colleague, Sen. Waitman T. Willey, led the fight for the new state in the U. S. Senate by necessity. Archibald W. Campbell, the firebrand editor and publisher of the *Wheeling Intelligencer* newspaper, provided one of the most strident voices advocating for the dismemberment of Virginia, even though he was only 27 years old. President Abraham Lincoln and his cabinet played leading roles in the statehood drama. None played a greater role than did Salmon P. Chase of Ohio. Chase participated in the deliberations that led to the admission of the new state in his role as Lincoln's Secretary of the Treasury. Five years later, as Chief Justice of the Supreme Court, Chase sat in judgment of a statehood decision he had himself urged upon Lincoln.

This book contains four appendices. The first sets forth in their entirety the letters to Abraham Lincoln written by his six cabinet members in December 1862 where they provided the President their opinions as to the constitutionality and expediency of admitting West Virginia to the Union. The second appendix provides the complaint filed by the Commonwealth of Virginia to initiate the 1866 lawsuit. The majority decision and the dissenting opinion of the Supreme Court in the case of *State of Virginia v. State of West Virginia* make up the third appendix. The fourth appendix addresses a second lawsuit, filed in the Supreme Court in 1911, between Virginia and West Virginia. Virginia sought to recover the payments on certain public debt owed in 1861 by both states. In this later case, and unlike the 1871 decision, the Supreme Court conclusively sanctioned the constitutionality of the creation of the State of West Virginia. And, the fifth appendix addresses some current events, proving that this issue remains as relevant today as it was in 1861.

No other book addressing these events has taken the approach that this book takes. All three of the authors are lawyers, and all maintain a fascination with history and law. We hope to provide a new appreciation for these events.

CHAPTER ONE

Sectional Differences

LONG before the election of Abraham Lincoln as President of the United States in November 1860, tensions between the eastern and western portions of Virginia threatened the cohesiveness of the large state.

The differences dated back to the earliest days of Virginia. Before the Declaration of Independence, Members of the Continental Congress considered separating the western portion of Virginia from the eastern portion, including a proposal for a new state, to include those counties west of the Allegheny Mountains. The proposed State of Vandalia would have included nearly all of what is today West Virginia as far east as the boundary with Maryland, with a capital at Point Pleasant. After the signing of the Declaration, delegates to the Continental Congress considered establishing the State of Westsylvania, including lands west of the Alleghenies. The boundaries were the same as Vandalia, but included a part of Maryland and a section of Pennsylvania extending to about 50 miles north of Pittsburgh. Ultimately, the Continental Congress rejected this plan. These counties remained part of Virginia until the events of 1863.[1]

---

1 Richard Ellsworth Fast, *The History and Government of West Virginia* (Morgantown, WV: The Acme Publishing Co., 1901), 84-85.

Northwestern Virginia is much different in geography from the rest of Virginia. The Blue Ridge mountain chain separates northwestern Virginia from the eastern part of the state. Eastern Virginia is mostly level or rolling land, rising from the ocean or the Chesapeake Bay. By contrast, western Virginia rises rolling and hilly, with tall mountains marking the dividing line. Rivers in the northwest empty into the Ohio River while eastern rivers flow through the Tidewater region and ultimately empty into the Chesapeake Bay or the Atlantic Ocean. People in northwestern Virginia tended to align themselves with Pennsylvania and Ohio in political, financial and cultural matters, and not with the eastern part of the state: Pittsburgh is 60 miles from Wheeling, while Richmond is 320 miles away. These differences caused tension between the eastern and western portions of the state for decades prior to Lincoln's election.

Waitman T. Willey, then a United States Senator representing West Virginia, wrote in 1866: "Who carries anything from west of the Alleghenies to eastern Virginia to sell? Who brings anything from East Virginia to West Virginia to sell? There are and have been almost literally no business and no intercourse between the two sections for twenty-five years, excepting what was connected with matters of revenue and legislation at Richmond. There is no State in the Union, which has been admitted ten years ago, of which the people of East Virginia know less than they do of West Virginia; and excepting the capital of the State, the people of West Virginia are equally unfamiliar with East Virginia."[2]

"Now while the boundary lines of Virginia held us with Eastern Virginia," declared the editor of the *Morgantown Star* in 1861, "our intercourse has been principally with the people of Pennsylvania, Maryland and Ohio; and we know but little of the people of Eastern and the [Shenandoah] Valley of Virginia from personal intercourse, and they know so little of us that they never have properly appreciated our interests."[3]

"The interests of West Virginia, however, with less than four per cent of her population slave, were those of a northern state," wrote James Morton Callahan, an early West Virginia historian. "Her sons continued to attend schools in free states rather than the schools across the Blue Ridge. Her markets were in Pittsburgh, Baltimore and the Mississippi River towns rather than Norfolk. Her geographic conditions allied her interests with those of

2 Ibid., 86-87.

3 Quoted in the September 9, 1861 issue of the *Wheeling Intelligencer*.

Pennsylvania and Ohio and her industries were those which called for white rather than slave labor. Her natural destiny and future loyalty to the Union were forecasted by [Sen. Daniel] Webster in his speech at the laying of the corner stone of the addition to the capital at Washington (in 1851). 'And ye men of Western Virginia, who occupy the slope from the Alleghenies to the Ohio and Kentucky,' said he, 'what benefit do you propose to yourself by disunion? If you secede what do you secede from and what do you secede to? Do you look for the current of the Ohio to change and bring you and your commerce to the waters of Eastern rivers? What man can suppose that you would remain a part and parcel of Virginia a month after Virginia had ceased to be a part of the United States?"[4]

"The present-day West Virginia in 1860 had a white population of nearly 380,000, a Negro-slave population of approximately 18,000, and almost 3,000 persons of color," observed one authority.[5] The 1860 census indicated that there were 490,865 slaves in Virginia, constituting 31% of the state's entire population.[6] Berkeley and Jefferson Counties, in what became the eastern panhandle of West Virginia, lay to the east of the Allegheny Mountains and relied on slave labor to work the plantations that drove their economies. The mountains served as a physical dividing line between the plantation economy of the east and the more commercial and industrial economy of northwestern Virginia. The entire northern and western areas of Virginia bordered on free soil, not slave states.

Ironically, the dominance of the eastern portion of the state traced its roots to the slave economy. The east depended on slaves, "the possession of which could be guaranteed and secured only by giving to masters a voice in the government adequate to the protection of their interests," wrote Henry Dering of Morgantown in western Virginia to future U.S. Senator Waitman T. Willey in March 1861. "Talk about Northern oppression, talk about our rights being stolen from us by the North; it's all stuff and dwindles into nothing when compared, to our situation in Western Virginia. The truth is the slavery

4 James Morton Callahan, *Semi-Centennial History of West Virginia* (Charleston, WV: The Semi-Centennial Commission of West Virginia, 1913), 139-140, quoting "Mr. Webster's Speech," *National Intelligencer*, July 5, 1851.

5 Richard Orr Curry, "The Virginia Background for the History of the Civil War and Reconstruction Era in West Virginia: An Analytical Commentary," *West Virginia History* 20 (July 1989), 215-246.

6 1860 Census results, U.S. Census Bureau, Washington, D.C.

oligarchy, are impudent boastful and tyrannical. It is the nature of the institution to make men so; and tho I am far from being an abolitionist, yet if they persist, in their course, the day may come when all Western Virginia will rise up, in her might and throw off the Shackles, which thro this very Divine institution, as they call it, has been pressing us down."[7]

The ethnic makeup of the white population also differed. The eastern portion of Virginia consisted largely of English stock descended from the original settlers of the region. By contrast, the northwestern region had significant numbers of Scotch-Irish, Welsh, and German immigrants who came in the Eighteenth and Nineteenth Centuries and later as part of the large exodus of the 1840's. Further, migrants from other American states tended to settle in those areas that offered the best economic opportunity, which was found in the northwestern portion of the state and not the east.[8]

Northwestern Virginians were a perpetual minority in the Commonwealth's politics, if for no other reason than they had little in common with the wealthy slaveholding plantation owners of the Tidewater region who controlled the entire state from the state capital at Richmond. Voting restrictions also favored the east by limiting the franchise to male landowners. As one historian observed, when the 1830 constitution was drafted, "it was felt to be so partial to the 'eastern aristocrats' that every voting delegate from the west opposed it; and when submitted to the people it was condemned in the west by an impressive majority."[9]

Religion also played a role in these events. Ministers, missionaries, and laymen of the Methodist-Episcopal Church played an important role in the push for both emancipation of the slaves and statehood for northwestern Virginia. "I am certain in saying that the loyal status of the people of [northwestern Virginia] may be attributed more than to any other cause perhaps than to those Christian ministers traveling throughout these mountains denouncing in the early days of the rebellion from their pulpits the heresy of secession and caused the people to resist and place their lives in their hands,"

---

7 Henry Deering to Waitman T. Willey, March 16, 1861, Waitman T. Willey Papers, West Virginia & Regional History Collection, West Virginia University Libraries, Morgantown, West Virginia ("WVU").

8 Richard Orr Curry, *A House Divided: A Study of Statehood Politics and the Copperhead Movement in West Virginia* (Pittsburgh: University of Pittsburgh Press, 1964), 119.

9 James Garfield Randall, *Constitutional Problems Under Lincoln*, 2d ed. (Champaign: University of Illinois Press, 1951), 434-436.

wrote Chester D. Hubbard, the first West Virginian elected to Congress, to Lincoln in 1864. "But the ministers stood as a breakwater, holding back the tide of rebellion, before the soldiers of the Republic caused the rebels to flee,"[10] Hubbard wrote to Lincoln recommending a Methodist minister, Reverend James Drummond of Wheeling, for a presidential appointment.

In 1851, a new Virginia constitution took effect. Sections 22 and 23 of the 1851 constitution provided:

> Sec. 22. Taxation shall be equal and uniform throughout the commonwealth, and all property other than slaves shall be taxed in proportion to its value, which shall be ascertained in such manner as may be prescribed by law.
>
> Sec. 23. Every slave who has attained the age of twelve years shall be assessed with a tax equal to and not exceeding that assessed on land of the value of three hundred dollars. Slaves under that age shall not be subject to taxation . . .[11]

Those two clauses imposed a limit on the taxable value of slaves that worked to the favor of slaveholders in the eastern part of the state, but which provided no limitations on the taxable value of any other property. This provision ended up subsidizing slaveholders at the expense of those who did not own slaves. Since there were relatively few slaves in the western portion of the state, the low taxing of slaves was very unpopular in that section of Virginia.

In May 1861, James Paxton told the First Wheeling Convention that the west had suffered "political inferiority" and "unjust, oppressive, and unequal taxation," referring specifically to the taxation of slaves.[12] Granville Hall, another delegate to the convention, complained that "a slave worth . . . $1600 to $1800 was taxed the same as $300 value of land."[13]

10 Chester D. Hubbard to Abraham Lincoln, November 25, 1864, Abraham Lincoln Papers, Manuscripts Division, Library of Congress, Washington, D.C. (hereafter referred to as "Lincoln Papers").

11 1850 Constitution of Virginia, in Francis Newton Thorpe, *The Federal and State Constitutions, Colonial Charters, and Other Organic Laws of the States, Territories and Colonies Now or Heretofore Forming the United States of America* (Washington, DC: U.S. Govt. Printing Office, 1909), 3829-3852.

12 Virgil A. Lewis, State Archivist, comp., *How West Virginia was Made: Proceedings of the First Convention of the People of Northwestern Virginia at Wheeling, May 13, 14 and 15, 1861, and the Journal of the Second Convention of the People of Northwestern Virginia at Wheeling, which Assembled, June 11, 1861* (Charleston, WV: News-Mail Co., 1909), 87.

13 Granville Davisson Hall, *The Rending of Virginia. A History* (Chicago: Mayer & Miller, 1902), 62.

Reflecting upon the disparate treatment of slaves imposed by the 1851 constitution, the *Wheeling Intelligencer* ran an editorial in December 1860 that foreshadowed events to come the next year. "We have been treated and regarded as a separate people," wrote editor Archibald W. Campbell in making an argument in support of separating the western portion of the Commonwealth of Virginia from the eastern portion. "And such indeed we are. There is no affinity between Eastern and Western Virginia. There never was, and while geography and climate holds sway there never can be."[14]

This schism became increasingly obvious as the secession crisis of 1861 unfolded.

14 Editorial, *Wheeling Intelligencer*, December 25, 1860.

CHAPTER TWO

The Baltimore & Ohio Railroad: Catalyst to Statehood

THE Baltimore and Ohio Railroad began in 1828 as one of the first commercial railroads in the world. By 1853, the line connected Annapolis, Maryland to Wheeling in the far northernmost corner of antebellum Virginia. Charles Carroll of Carrollton, Maryland, a signer of the Declaration of Independence, then 90 years of age, remarked, upon the laying of the cornerstone in Baltimore in 1828, "I count this among the most important acts of my life, second only to my signing the Declaration of Independence—if even it be second to that!"[1] The B&O eventually expanded into thirteen different states.

By 1861, the B&O maintained 188 miles of track in Virginia and offered a direct connection to both eastern and western Virginia. It followed the course of the Potomac River and paralleled the National Road for most of its route, passing through the important logistics center of Harpers Ferry at the confluence of the Shenandoah and Potomac Rivers. Crossing the Allegheny Mountains proved to be an engineering challenge: "Such a stupendous undertaking was probably never before, or even since, recorded in the annals of

---

1 J. H. Newton, G. G. Nichols, and A. G. Sprankle, comps., *History of the Pan-Handle; Being Historical Collections of the Counties of Ohio, Brooke, Marshall, and Hancock, West Virginia* (Wheeling, WV: J. A. Caldwell, 1879), 201.

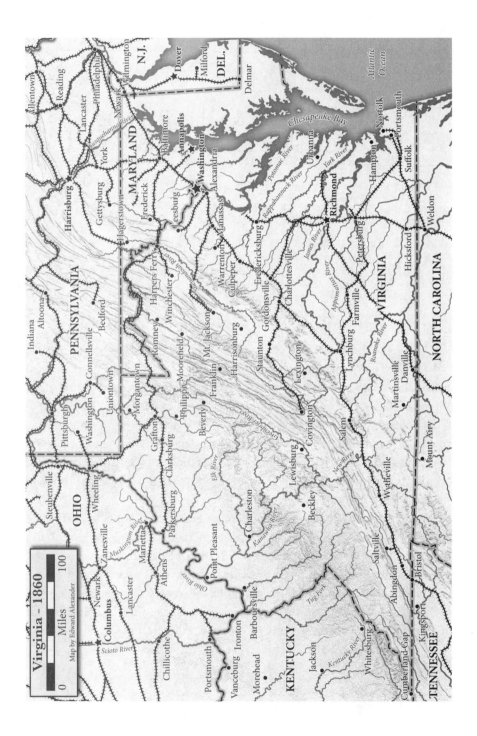

engineering, but the section in question, to this day, stands a noble example of American skill and enterprise," noted an early history of the northern panhandle of West Virginia.[2] In 1857, a speaker at the celebration honoring the completion of the B&O, marveled that the railroad "had, for all practical purposes of transit, obliterated the Alleghenies from the map of our country."[3]

At the outset of the Civil War in 1861, the B&O owned 236 locomotives, 128 passenger coaches, 3,451 rail cars, and 513 miles of railroad, all in states south of the Mason-Dixon Line.[4] It had one of the largest workforces in the United States, employing more than 2,300 laborers, 315 machinists, 268 carpenters, and a handful of women. It carried over 300 different job titles on its payroll.[5]

In 1858, John W. Garrett became president of the B&O. Garrett was born in Baltimore, Maryland on July 31, 1820 as the son of an Irish immigrant. Garrett attended, but did not graduate from Lafayette College in Easton, Pennsylvania, and then began working as a clerk and apprentice in his father's mercantile, banking and financial services firm. He learned the business from the bottom up. With the opening of the National Road, the company's operations expanded westward toward the Mississippi River and eventually to California and the Southwest. Garrett and his brother Henry gradually took over the company's operations. Henry joined the board of directors of the B&O in 1847, and John soon followed. In 1858, at the behest of board member Johns Hopkins (namesake of the eponymous Baltimore university), the largest stockholder since 1847, John Garrett became the B&O's new president. He held this position until the 1880's. Among his many contributions, Garrett organized and executed the funeral train that carried the body of the assassinated Abraham Lincoln home to Springfield, Illinois for burial.[6]

As an early West Virginia historian noted, Garrett "was as much a part of Mr. Lincoln's Cabinet as any man in it, and was often called to Cabinet councils

2 Ibid.

3 William Prescott Smith, *The Book of the Great Railway Celebrations of 1857* (New York: D. Appleton & Co., 1858), 96.

4 Kathleen Waters Sander, *John W. Garrett and the Baltimore & Ohio Railroad* (Baltimore, MD: Johns Hopkins University Press, 2017), 79-82.

5 William G. Thomas, *The Iron Way: Railroads, the Civil War, and the Making of Modern America* (New Haven: Yale University Press, 2011), 48.

6 Sander, *John W. Garrett.*

John W. Garrett, president of the Baltimore & Ohio Railroad during the Civil War.

(B&O Railroad Museum)

when questions of grave moment were to be discussed."[7] The colorful Garrett played an important role in the internecine drama that was about to unfold. Unlike many Marylanders who harbored Southern sympathies, Garrett was a strong Unionist. He was determined that his railroad would play an important part of the war to preserve the Union.

Radical abolitionist John Brown's October 1859 raid on the important logistics center of Harpers Ferry was the first hostile action against the B&O. Brown and 21 of his men stopped an express train of the B&O at Harpers Ferry. Brown and his followers then seized possession and control of the Harpers Ferry railroad bridge and the U.S. Army arsenal there. Ironically, an African-American train porter was mortally wounded during Brown's seizure of the train. This proved to be the first of many hostile events plaguing the B&O over the next six years.

The construction, maintenance and operation of the B&O represented one of the first instances of a national system of transportation connecting the United States. During the presidential election of 1860, more than 1,000 Baltimore voters cast their ballots for Abraham Lincoln, more than in any other county of Maryland, and more than in any of the southern states, where Lincoln's name did not even appear on the ballot. All along the B&O route through Maryland and western Virginia, where the railroad maintained its maintenance and repair shops, large numbers of voters turned out for Lincoln.

---

7 Theodore F. Lang, *Loyal West Virginia, 1861-1865* (Baltimore, MD: The Deutsch Publishing Co., 1895), 146.

It was no coincidence that the counties traversed by the B&O most strongly supported Lincoln's candidacy.[8]

With the coming of the Civil War, the B&O represented a strategic military asset, capable of moving troops and supplies for long distances in a short time. Construction and maintenance costs made it one of the most expensive railroads in the country to operate. All of its route and property lay to the south of the Mason-Dixon Line, and much of it passed through slave-holding territory.[9] Because of the significance of Garrett's railroad, the rail lines were the location of 143 raids, skirmishes, and battles during the Civil War. On April 18, 1861, retreating Union troops severed the B&O at Harpers Ferry. They burned the surrounding buildings and the rifle factory before abandoning the site. Later that evening, Virginia militia took control of the area and salvaged the ruins. Those Confederate troops soon formed the nucleus of the Army of Northern Virginia. During May of 1861, Confederate Col. (later Lt. Gen.) Thomas J. Jackson attacked that portion of the B&O that crossed the Shenandoah Valley, devastating the line, sequestering locomotives, burning freight cars, and tearing up rails.

"It is well-known that the granting of a charter for the extension of the Baltimore & Ohio Road through to the Ohio River was long resisted at Richmond as in line with the policy of discrimination against the western sector, to protect the slave-holding East against and undue increase of western power and influence—Richmond fearing also the commercial rivalry of Baltimore," noted an early historian of the events that led to the creation of West Virginia. "This hostility toward railroad facilities for the Northwest persisted down to the opening of the Rebellion; and the manifestation of it vindicating the wisdom of extending the borders of the new state eastward so as to take in the line of the Baltimore and Ohio"[10]

Beginning in 1856, Archibald W. Campbell served as editor of the *Wheeling Intelligencer* newspaper.[11] Campbell, an outspoken Unionist, described the

---

8 Thomas, *The Iron Way*, 62.

9 Festus P. Summers, *The Baltimore and Ohio in the Civil War* (New York: G. P. Putnam's Sons 1939), 43-44.

10 Granville Davisson Hall, *The Rending of Virginia. A History* (Chicago: Mayer & Miller, 1902), 61.

11 Archibald W. Campbell was born in Steubenville, Ohio on April 4, 1833. He graduated from Bethany College in 1852 and from the Hamilton College Law School in Clinton, New

Archibald W. Campbell, the publisher of the *Wheeling Intelligencer*, taken later in life.

(West Virginia State Archives)

dilemma that was the B&O in an editorial that ran in his newspaper on April 27, 1861:

This road in its geographical position, is to be deeply sympathized with . . . . The main stem runs through 379 miles of country, and through every kind of country, at that. And the public sentiment which it traverses, is not less varied than the soil it passes over. The terminus at one end is among the mobocracy; at the other end, here in Wheeling, among good, order-loving Union men. At Harpers Ferry it is completely under military despotism, and every train has to run the gauntlet of cannon and armed espionage. At Cumberland it passes through loyalty and Union, and from that point on West, it might be said to be all right.[12]

The economic importance of the B&O, as well as its strategic location, made the rail-line a flashpoint throughout the Civil War.

Concerned about the federal government's seeming lack of concern for the maintenance of the B&O, Wheeling resident George M. Hagans wrote to

York in 1855. He moved to Wheeling in 1856 and took a job with the *Wheeling Intelligencer* newspaper. That fall, he and a partner purchased the newspaper, and he became its editor. He was member of the fledgling Republican Party and was a strong advocate of the abolition of slavery. The *Intelligencer* was the only Republican daily paper in Virginia, and was the only newspaper in the state to endorse Abraham Lincoln for the presidency in 1860. Thereafter Campbell used the *Wheeling Daily Intelligencer* to argue that the interests of western Virginia and of democracy required the establishment of a new state. Campbell became one of the most influential leaders in the statehood movement, and strongly supported the abolition of slavery in the first West Virginia Constitutional Convention. In 1861, President Abraham Lincoln appointed him postmaster for Wheeling. He played an important role in the events that led to the birth of the new state of West Virginia. John T. Kneebone, et al., eds., *Dictionary of Virginia Biography*, 3 vols. (Richmond: The Library of Virginia, 1998), 2:553–554.

12 "The Baltimore and Ohio Road," *Wheeling Intelligencer*, April 27, 1861.

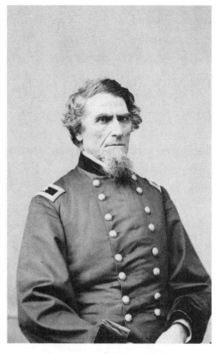

Brig. Gen. Benjamin F. Kelley, commander of
the so-called Railroad Division.

(Library of Congress)

Union general-in-chief Maj. Gen.
George B. McClellan in May 1861. "I
urge the immediate taking possession
of the B. & O. R. R. The opinion is that
the Confederates are now arranging for
such a step themselves," he urged.
"You need not fear of wounding the
State pride of West Va. The people will
welcome the presence of U.S. forces.
There is no doubt on this point for I
have talked with the leading men of
every county & this is their unanimous
judgment. The U.S. arms here at Wheeling ought to be instantly distributed
along the Rail Road; and decisive steps inaugurated at once. The people are with
the Federal Government, and instances are narrated to me of their spirit and
determination in this regard, as furnish incontestable evidence that they are now
ripe for a movement."[13]

The military situation in the eastern panhandle of what makes up today's
West Virginia was very unstable for most of 1861. Union and Confederate
forces jockeyed for position, with both sides recognizing the importance of the
B&O. In the fall of 1861, an independent military district was created to manage
that portion of the railroad between the western boundary of Alleghany
County, Maryland and the Ohio River. The district was headquartered in
Martinsburg, Jefferson County, with Brig. Gen. Benjamin F. Kelley in
command of the so-called "Railroad Division" assigned to protect the B&O
Railroad. Col. Dixon Miles commanded the region along the railroad to the east

13 Hagans to McClellan, May 13, 1861, George B. McClellan Papers, Manuscripts Division,
Library of Congress, Washington, D.C.

of that commanded by Kelley, including Harpers Ferry.[14] Kelley's district included Berkeley, Morgan, and Jefferson Counties, all of which were occupied by Union troops garrisoning the railroad. The Union effort to preserve and protect the B&O not only consumed significant amounts of vital resources and tied up thousands of soldiers, it also provided a major motivation for the secession crisis brewing in the northwestern counties of Virginia in 1861.

By the end of 1861, 23 B&O railroad bridges had been burned, 102 miles of telegraph wire had been cut down, 36.5 miles of track were torn up or destroyed, 42 locomotives were burned, 14 locomotives were captured, and 386 rail cars stolen or destroyed, shutting down the B&O for ten months.

When he penned his annual report for the year 1861, Garrett wrote, "On May 28, 1861, general possession was taken by the Confederate forces of more than one hundred miles of the Main Stem [of the B&O)], embroiling chiefly the region between Point of Rocks and Cumberland." He continued, "Occasional movements were also made, accompanied by considerable destruction up the roads between Cumberland and Wheeling, and Grafton and Parkersburg, during the fiscal year." He concluded, "The Protection of the Government was not restored throughout the line until March 1862, when this reconstruction was pressed with great energy, and the line reopened on the 29th of that month."[15]

Once service was restored, train movements were sporadic and subject to frequent stoppages, derailments, captures, and attacks. Prominent raids on the B&O during this period were:

The Great Train Raid of May 22-June 23, 1861

The Romney Expedition, January 1-24, 1862

Operations during the 1862 Maryland Campaign, September 8, 1862

Various raids of Brig. Gen. Albert G. Jenkins in western Virginia, Fall, 1862

"The Baltimore and Ohio railroad has been a positive nuisance to this state, from the opening of this war to the present," declared Virginia Governor John

14 The 14th New Jersey Infantry was garrisoned at Monocacy Junction just south of Frederick, Maryland, and was known as the Monocacy Regiment, providing just one example of the many Union units assigned to keep the B&O in business.

15 *Thirty-fifth Annual Report of the President and Directors to the Stockholders of the Baltimore and Ohio Railroad Company, for the Year Ending September 30, 1861* (Baltimore: William N. Innes, 1862), 6-7.

Letcher to the Commonwealth's legislature in September 1862, "and unless its management shall hereafter be in friendly hands, and the government under which it exists be part of the Confederacy, it must be abated."[16]

Once West Virginia joined the Union in June 1863, all of the B&O Railroad that had previously traversed Confederate territory between Harpers Ferry and Wheeling was entirely in Union hands. After the end of the Battle of Gettysburg on July 3, Secretary of War Edwin M. Stanton asked even more of Garrett and the B&O than he had previously. "You will please devote all energies and resources at the present to the exclusion of everything else," Stanton wrote to Garrett on July 5. "I know what you have done and expect you to surpass yourself."[17]

During 1862-1863, the B&O suffered additional destruction: 42 locomotives and tenders, 386 cars, 23 bridges, embracing 127 spans and a total length of bridge of 4,713 feet, 36 miles of track, and the telegraph and water stations for more than 100 miles of track were destroyed.[18] Despite this massive level of destruction, the B&O remained profitable. "It is gratifying and proper to inform the shareholders that the first six months of the fiscal year presented a large and profitable traffic, and that notwithstanding the interruption of its business and immense destruction of its property and the grave and varied embarrassments complicating the management, the board have been able to meet all the engagements of the company, and expect to continue to maintain its credit and financial position at that high and reliable standard so important to all the great interests involved," proudly declared Garrett in the company's annual report to shareholders.[19]

Large-scale Confederate efforts to cut the B&O largely ended after the Gettysburg Campaign. "We are now able to report positively that the crisis with the Baltimore and Ohio Railroad is past," declared the *New York Times* in October 1863. "The Confederates have all left, moving southward and our military forces, in great strength are following and endeavoring to intercept

---

16 Daniel Carroll Toomey, *The War Came by Train: The Baltimore & Ohio Railroad during the Civil War* (Baltimore, MD: B&O Railroad Museum, 2013), 134.

17 Stanton to Garrett, July 5, 1863, Box 72, Garrett Family Papers, Manuscripts Division, Library of Congress, Washington, D.C.

18 Lang, *Loyal West Virginia*, 153.

19 *Thirty-Seventh Annual Report of the President and Directors to the Stockholders of the Baltimore & Ohio R. R. Co. For the Year Ending September 30, 1863* (Baltimore, MD: J. B. Rose & Co., 1864), 7.

them."[20] While that was true, the B&O not only remained a target for the Confederates, the federal government also called upon Garrett and his railroad to do even more during the second half of the war.[21]

In 1863-64 and into 1865, the B&O was not only a target for Lt. Col. John S. Mosby's 43rd Battalion of Virginia Cavalry, it was also the target of numerous Confederate cavalry actions:

The Jones-Imboden Raid, April 24-May 22, 1863[22]

The Catoctin Station Raid, June 17, 1863

The First Calico Raid, June 19, 1863

The B&O Raid on Duffield Station, January 1864

The McNeill Raid, May 5, 1864

The Second Calico Raid, July 3, 1864

The Battle of Monocacy, July 9, 1864

The Johnson-Gilmor Raid, July 11, 1864

The Greenback Raid by Mosby's command, October 14, 1864

The B&O Raid on Duffield Station II, January 1865

Gilmor's B&O Raid, February 1865

The B&O Derailment Raid, March 1865

The western end of the B&O was shut down in 1864 when Confederate authorities tried to end the use of the B&O to transport Union soldiers to Washington, DC. The mayor of Charlestown, West Virginia, in Berkeley County, a Confederate sympathizer, threatened the B&O, declaring that if Union soldiers continued to use it, the railroad would be destroyed. When John Garrett refused to halt the use of the B&O for the transportation of Union

---

20 *New York Times*, October 3, 1863.

21 In the summer of 1864, Confederate forces commanded by Lt. Gen. Jubal A. Early invaded Maryland and advanced toward Washington, D.C. Garrett not only provided regular, detailed intelligence reports regarding the whereabouts of Early's army, the B&O also played a critical in carrying a division of Union soldiers to Monocacy Junction, near Frederick, Maryland. Those troops delayed Early's advance for an entire day, allowing time for major reinforcements to reach Washington. For more about the July 9, 1864 Battle of Monocacy, see Benjamin Franklin Cooling, *Monocacy: The Battle that Saved Washington* (Shippensburg, PA: White Mane, 2000).

22 The Jones-Imboden Raid is discussed in some detail in Chapter Six of this book.

soldiers, Virginia State Militia troops destroyed the Harpers Ferry railroad bridge, effectively cutting the B&O there until the bridge could be re-built.

Despite these determined efforts by Confederates to deprive the North of the use of the B&O, Garrett kept it open and running for the balance of the Civil War. By reliably carrying men and materiel to the theatre of war in Virginia, the B&O played an important role in tipping the balance in the Union victory in the Civil War. At the end of the Civil War, Lincoln described Garrett as "The right arm of the Federal Government in the aid he rendered the authorities in preventing the Confederates from seizing Washington and securing its retention as the Capital of the Loyal States." Confederate Vice President Alexander Stevens said that the South had been doomed from "the early months, after the fall of Fort Sumter, when the South was waiting for Maryland to act and Lincoln prevented that state from seceding—largely because of the overwhelming influence exerted by the Baltimore & Ohio in favor of the Washington government."[23]

Maintaining the B&O in the face of determined efforts by Confederate troops to cut it proved to be an expensive logistical challenge that reflected the road's importance to the efforts to preserve the Union. The railroad was so important, in fact, that it played a critical role in the formation of the new state of West Virginia. The story of the creation of West Virginia is inextricably intertwined with the ongoing struggle to control the B & O Railroad throughout the Civil War.

---

23 Both quoted in Sander, *John W. Garrett*, 173.

CHAPTER THREE

Western Virginia and the Response to the Secession of Virginia

T**HE** Southern states viewed the election of Abraham Lincoln as the last straw, the final act that drove them to secede from the Union. "The significant fact which menaces the South, is not that Abe Lincoln is elected president, but that the Northern people by a sectional vote, have elected a President for the avowed purpose of aggressions on the Southern rights," declared the editor of the *Richmond Enquirer* a few days after the election.[1] Consequently, many Southerners came to believe that war was inevitable.

"Some of our friends in Marshall county, and from one precinct in Brooke county, who were at our office on Saturday, apprehend trouble in voting for Lincoln and Hamlin, as their polls tomorrow," declared the *Wheeling Intelligencer* on November 5. "To our friends we would say, as we have everywhere counseled them on the stamp, vote your principles, if possible. Go to the polls in a mild, but determined spirit. We counsel no rashness, no violence, but only a firm, unarmed, determined defensive spirit. Go in numbers so far as you can, and stand by each other. See that the timid have your countenance and support. You that have leisure, remain at the polls as long as you can, and assist all who

---

1 *Richmond Enquirer*, November 10 and 19, 1860.

need assistance in preparing and voting their tickets. In this way, we believe, all difficulty can be avoided."[2]

As early as November 12, 1860, a public meeting occurred in Preston County for the purpose of expressing a determination to adhere to the Union. The men who attended that meeting unanimously composed a resolution declaring "that any attempt upon the part of the State to secede will meet with the unqualified disapprobation of the people of the county." Twelve days later, a similar meeting in Harrison County proclaimed, "The people will first exhaust all constitutional remedies for redress before they will result to any violent measures; that the ballot box is the only medium known to the Constitution for a redress of grievances, and to it alone we will appeal; that it is the duty of all citizens to uphold and support the lawfully constituted authorities."[3]

In January 1861, a resident of Wood County declared, "for every Secessionist there were one hundred Unionists who would accept a division of the state of Virginia as preferable to the dissolution of the Union."[4] A few days later, someone writing under the anonym "Democrat" wrote to the editor of the *Wellsburg Herald*, "We have no interest in a Convention whose object, and sole object…is to make us rebels and traitors to our country, to take us from under the stars and stripes and place us under the unprotected folds of the slimy serpent of South Carolina." He then proposed to use the Blue Ridge to sever the western portion of the state from the eastern portion. This would mean "we, of the West…sell them all our negroes, take up wheat culture, dairying and mining; join the North in commercial enterprise; . . . and build more rail-roads."[5]

John S. Carlile, a major figure in the events that followed, wrote a letter to the editor of *The Weekly National Intelligencer* newspaper, which was published in Washington, D.C. "Dissolve this Union and hitch Virginia to the tail of a Southern Confederacy to stand guard and play patrol for King Cotton! I drop the pen," he proclaimed. "I cannot contemplate the picture. Oh! for a Jackson

2 "To Lincoln Voters," *Wheeling Intelligencer*, November 5, 1860.

3 Virgil A. Lewis, *A History of West Virginia* (Philadelphia: Hubbard Brothers, 1889), 329-330.

4 *National Intelligencer*, January 9, 1861.

5 *Wellsburg Herald*, January 18, 1861.

John Letcher, war-time governor of Virginia. Letcher led Virginia out of the Union and was later supplanted by Francis H. Pierpont.

(Library of Congress)

to say and make good the saying 'The Federal Union; it must and shall be preserved.'"[6]

Because of the geographical split in the sentiments of the public, the secession crisis of 1861 hit the Commonwealth of Virginia harder than most states. Virginia did not secede during the initial wave of secessions after the election of President Abraham Lincoln, because the state was deeply divided on the question. In January 1861, despite having no pressing business pending, Governor John Letcher called a special session of the Virginia legislature, which convened on January 7, 1861 to consider Virginia's secession from the Union.[7] The next day, the legislature declared:

---

6 John S. Carlile to the editor, *National Intelligencer*, January 5, 1861.

7 John Letcher was born in Lexington, Virginia on March 29, 1813, attended private schools, and Randolph-Macon College. In 1833, he graduated from Washington Academy in Lexington (now Washington & Lee University). He studied law, was admitted to the Virginia bar in 1839, and opened a practice in Lexington. He was the editor of the *Valley Star* newspaper from 1840-1850, and was involved in politics. He served as a delegate to the 1850 Virginia constitutional convention, and served in Congress from 1851-1859. He was elected governor of Virginia in 1860. As governor, he helped organize the peace convention that met in Washington, DC on February 8, 1861. After the failure of that convention, he discouraged secession, but was active in sustaining the ordinance of secession, which was passed by the secession convention on April 17, 1861. Although Letcher scheduled a referendum on the ordinance of secession for May 23, 1861, Letcher took active steps to lead Virginia out of the Union that are set forth in the main text. After the referendum passed, Letcher appointed Col. Robert E. Lee as commander in chief of Virginia's army and navy forces on April 22, 1861 at the grade of major general. On April 24, 1861, Letcher agreed to place Virginia's forces under control of Confederate President Jefferson Davis. Col. John Brown Baldwin defeated Letcher for a seat in the Second Confederate Congress in May 1863. In 1864, Union troops under command of Maj. Gen. David Hunter burned Letcher's home to the ground. After the end of

Former United States President John Tyler of Virginia, who strongly supported the Ordinance of Secession.

(Library of Congress)

1. Resolved by the general assembly of Virginia, that the Union being formed only by the assent of the sovereign states respectively, and being consistent only with freedom and the republican institutions guaranteed to each, cannot and ought not be maintained by force.

2. That the government of the Union has no power to declare or make war against any of the states which have been its constituent members.

3. Resolved, that when any one or more of the states has determined, or shall determine, under existing circumstances, to withdraw from the Union, we are unalterably opposed to any attempt on the part of the federal government to coerce the same into reunion or submission, and that we will resist the same by all means in our power.[8]

Thirteen days later, on January 21, the legislature passed a resolution declaring, "if all efforts to reconcile the unhappy differences existing between the two sections of the country shall prove to be abortive, then, in the opinion of the general assembly, every consideration of honor and interest demands that Virginia shall unite her destiny with the slaveholding states of the South."[9] The legislature passed another resolution appointing three commissioners, including former U.S. President John Tyler, to go to Washington to engage in

the Civil War, Letcher resumed his practice of law in Lexington. He served in the Virginia House of Delegates 1875-1877 and served as a member and president of the Board of Visitors of the Virginia Military Institute 1866-1880. Letcher died on January 26, 1884 at age 70. He was buried in Presbyterian Cemetery in Lexington. For a full-length biography of Letcher, see F. N. Boney, *John Letcher of Virginia: The Story of Virginia's Civil War Governor* (Tuscaloosa: University of Alabama Press, 1966).

8 *Acts of the General Assembly of the State of Virginia, Passed in 1861, in the Eighty-fifth Year of the Commonwealth* (Richmond: W. F. Richie, 1861), 337.

9 Ibid.

direct negotiations with the Lincoln Administration.[10] With these resolutions as a backdrop, it became obvious that Letcher intended to lead the Old Dominion out of the Union.

A week later, Letcher called for a convention of delegates to determine whether Virginia should secede from the Union, which seemed like a foregone conclusion considering the recent enactments of the general assembly.[11] The citizens of Virginia elected one hundred fifty-two delegates from all corners of the state, including former President John Tyler and former Virginia Governor Henry A. Wise. The convention met in Richmond on February 13, 1861 to discuss whether to pass an ordinance of secession. Lincoln took office on March 4, intensifying the debate.

Delegates from western Virginia warned their brethren from the east that they would not be dragged into secession, and that ninety percent of the population of the western part favored giving Lincoln a chance. The western voters opposed taking up arms against the federal government.[12] A correspondent from the western part of the state showed remarkable foresight in the fall of 1860, even before the election of Abraham Lincoln, when he wrote, "It is evident from what I have seen and heard from Western Virginia that if John Letcher and the Richmond Junto attempt to drag Virginia into secession—Virginia will be two states before it is finished."[13] Francis H. Pierpont, a pivotal figure in the coming years, prophetically wrote to his fellow western delegate Waitman T. Willey on April 3, "This difficulty is not going to be settled without a fight." He concluded, "It ought to be as clear to you as to me."[14]

---

10 Ibid., 337-338.

11 Ironically, Letcher owed his election as governor in 1859 to strong support from the anti-slavery counties of northwestern Virginia. The *Richmond Whig* declared, "But the Yankeeism and Black Republicanism of the Pan Handle and other portions of the Northwest have carried John Letcher into the Gubernatorial chair, and we congratulate the eastern Democracy upon their abolition allies and the shameful triumph they have achieved." *Richmond Whig*, June 7, 1859. For a more detailed discussion, see Charles H. Ambler, *Sectionalism in Virginia from 1776 to 1861* (Chicago: University of Chicago Press, 1910), 320-327.

12 James C. McGregor, *The Disruption of Virginia* (New York: MacMillan, 1922), 98-99.

13 "Virginian," "Letter to the Editor," *National Intelligencer*, October 20, 1860.

14 Francis H. Pierpont to Waitman T. Willey, April 3, 1861, Francis H. Pierpont Papers ("Pierpont Papers"), West Virginia Historical Archives and Manuscripts Collection, State Archives, Charleston, West Virginia (hereinafter, "State Archives").

Willey's chief concern was for northwest Virginia. He feared that if Virginia followed South Carolina into secession, civil war was inevitable; Willey's half-brother, William J. Willey, ended up enlisting in the Confederate army. As Willey's biographer put it, "In that event he pictured the North and the South arrayed against each other with Virginia at the 'tag-end' of an insurrectionary government, and her northwest a victim of devastation and ruin." Under those circumstances, Willey believed that the only solution would be the dismemberment of Virginia as a means of protecting the northwest.[15]

Despite the dogged efforts of Letcher and the legislature to drag Virginia from the Union, the delegates did not favor it. On April 4, after plenty of long-winded speeches, the secessionist faction brought a motion to approve Virginia's secession. They lost, 90-45, in a surprising result. Delegate John Janney of Loudoun County in northern Virginia, a prominent former member of the Whig Party, told his wife that the secessionists were "without the slightest hope of success."[16] Unfortunately, that happy circumstance did not last long.

However, a crisis was then unfolding in Charleston harbor, in South Carolina. South Carolina forces threatened to open fire on Fort Sumter if the federal government tried to resupply the garrison there. Lincoln waffled over what to do for several weeks, and just a week before the failed secession vote, finally decided to send a supply ship to Fort Sumter, deepening the crisis and pushing the situation to the breaking point. Finally, on April 12, South Carolina forces commanded by Gen. P. G. T. Beauregard opened fire on Fort Sumter, initiating hostilities. On April 15, Lincoln responded by calling for 75,000 volunteers to come forward and enlist to put down the rebellion. Northern communities responded with a wave of patriotism and calls for the death of the Southern traitors, triggering defiance in the South. These events proved to be the catalyst that pushed things over the edge with respect to the secession of Virginia.

In the wake of the drama playing out in Charleston Harbor, the commissioners sent to negotiate with the Lincoln Administration returned to Richmond on April 15. Their futile meeting at the White House occurred on the same day that Lincoln issued his call for volunteers. Alexander H. H. Stuart of

---

15 Charles H. Ambler, *Waitman Thomas Willey, Orator, Churchman, Humanitarian* (Huntington, WV: Standard Print and Publishing Co., 1954), 35 and 43.

16 Nelson D. Lankford, *Cry Havoc! The Crooked Road to Civil War, 1861* (New York: Penguin Books, 2007), 59.

Staunton in the Shenandoah Valley, the lone Unionist among the three commissioners, acknowledged the provocative nature of Lincoln's proclamation and hoped that Unionists from the northern part of the state could fend off the secessionists. He uttered extremely prophetic words: "Secession is not only war," he declared to the delegates, "but it is emancipation; it is bankruptcy; it is repudiation; it is widespread ruin to our people." Despite this prophetic warning, secession fever grew once word of the events in South Carolina reached the convention.[17]

On April 17, Governor Letcher answered Secretary of War Simon Cameron's call for volunteers with the following proclamation, which was then presented to the secession convention:

Whereas, seven of the States formerly comprising part of the United States, have, by authority of their people, solemnly resumed the powers granted by them to the United States and have framed a Constitution and organized a Government for themselves, to which the people of those States are yielding willing obedience, and have so notified the President of the United States by all the formalities incident to such action, and thereby become to the United States a separate, independent and foreign power. And

Whereas the Constitution of the United States has invested Congress with the sole power "to declare war" and until such declaration is made, the President has no authority to call for an extraordinary force to wage offensive war against any foreign power; and

Whereas on the 15th instant the President of the united States, in plain violation of the Constitution, has issued a proclamation calling for a force of seventy-five thousand men, to cause the laws of the United States to be duly executed over a people who are no longer a part of the Union, and in said proclamation threatens to exert this unusual force to compel obedience to his mandates; and

Whereas the General Assembly of Virginia, by a majority approaching to entire unanimity, has declared at its last session, that the State of Virginia would consider such an exertion of force as a virtual declaration of war, to be resisted by all the power at the command of Virginia; and subsequently, the Convention now in session, representing the sovereignty of this State, has re-affirmed in substance the same policy, by almost equal unanimity; and

Whereas the State of Virginia deeply sympathises with the Southern States, in the wrongs they have suffered, and in the position they have assumed; and having made earnest efforts peaceably to compose the differences which have severed the Union, have failed in that attempt through this unwarranted act of the part of the President; and it is believed that the influences which operate to produce this proclamation

---

17 "Alexander Hugh Holmes Stuart," *The Alumni Bulletin*, Vol. I, No. 3 (Charlottesville: University of Virginia, November, 1894), 64.

against the seceded States will be brought to bear on this Commonwealth, if she should exercise her undoubted right to resume the powers granted by her people, and it is due to the honor of Virginia that an improper exercise of force against her people should be repelled:--

Therefore I, John Letcher, Governor of the Commonwealth of Virginia, have thought proper to order all armed volunteer regiments or companies within this State forthwith to hold themselves in readiness for immediate orders, and upon reception of this proclamation to report to the Adjutant General of the State their organization and numbers, and prepare themselves for efficient service. Such companies as are not armed and equipped will report that fact, that they may be properly supplied.

In Witness whereof, I have hereunto set my hand and caused the seal of the Commonwealth to be affixed, this 17th Day of April, 1861, and in the 85th year or the Commonwealth.

He then issued the following formal response to Secretary of War Simon Cameron's call for volunteers, which was also presented to the convention:

TO SECRETARY CAMERON

Executive Department,

Richmond, VA., April 16th, 1861.

Hon. Simon Cameron, Secretary of War:

Sir:--I received your telegram of the 15th, the genuineness of which I doubted. Since that time I have received your communication mailed the same day, in which I am requested to detach from the militia of the State of Virginia "the quota designated in a table," which you append, "to serve as an infantry or riflemen for the period of three months, unless sooner discharged."

In reply to this communication, I have only to say, that the Militia of Virginia will not be furnished to the powers at Washington, for any such use or purpose as they have in view.

Your object is to subjugate our Southern States, and a requisition made upon me for such object---an object, in my judgment, not within the purview of the Constitution, or the act of 1795---- will not be complied with. You have chosen to inaugurate civil war, and having done so, we will meet it, in a spirit as determined as the Administration has exhibited towards the South,

Respectfully,
JOHN LETCHER.[18]

18 "Governor Letcher's Proclamation; His Reply to Secretary Cameron—State of Affairs at Norfolk," *New York Times*, April 22, 1861.

Former Virginia Gov. Henry A. Wise, who led the push for Virginia's secession.

(Duke Univerity)

And with that, the Governor of Virginia threw down the gauntlet. Virginia would go to war with the federal government.

The same day, former Governor Henry A. Wise, who, ironically, hailed from the western portion of the state, gave a dramatic speech to the assembled delegates at the secession convention. He theatrically snapped open his pocket watch, laid a large pistol on the table in front of him, and declared that at that hour, and by his orders, Virginia was at war with the federal government. He then proclaimed that if anyone wanted to shoot him for treason, they would have to wrestle away the pistol. Former President Tyler turned his chair around, tears streaming down his face, as he cheered Wise's thunderous oration. Wise continued by telling the delegates "that armed forces are now marching upon Harpers Ferry . . . and there will be a fight or footrace before the sun sets this day."

"With his hair bristling and disheveled, and his eye standing out with a glare of excitement," Wise thundered on that events were then transpiring which caused a hush to cover over his soul, inciting the cheering delegates to vote for secession. Finally, he dramatically asked, "Why can't you realize that Lincoln's bloodthirsty proclamation makes waverers into traitors? The tyrant's troops now menace your folks. You must now decide whether to kill your kin. You must decide whether to return the murder weapons that I have ordered Virginia's patriots to seize." With a flourish, the former governor concluded, "You must now decide whether to secede from the tyrant or assassinate me."[19]

---

19 Fast, *The History and Government of West Virginia*, 101 and Callahan, *Semi-Centennial History of West Virginia*, 141.

With that fiery oration ringing, the time had finally arrived for the delegates to vote on the ordinance of secession.

"On Monday, April 17th, the convention passed the ordinance of secession, big with disaster to Virginia," recalled William H. Edwards, who attended the convention as a delegate from Kanawha County. "It was to be submitted to the voters a month later, but the managers proceeded as if the State were already out, as in fact it was."[20]

The Richmond convention passed the following ordinance, by a vote of 88 to 55:

AN ORDINANCE

To Repeal the ratification of the Constitution of the United States of America, by the State of Virginia, and to resume all the rights and powers granted under said Constitution:

The people of Virginia, in their ratification of the Constitution of the United States of America, adopted by them in Convention, on the 25th day of June, in the year of our Lord one thousand seven hundred and eight-eight, having declared that the powers granted them under the said Constitution were derived from the people of the United States, and might be resumed whensoever the same should be perverted to their injury and oppression, and the Federal Government having perverted said powers, not only to the injury of the people of Virginia, but to the oppression of the Southern slaveholding States.

Now, therefore, we, the people of Virginia, do declare and ordain that the Ordinance adopted by the people of this State in Convention, on the twenty-fifth day of June, in the year of our Lord one thousand seven hundred and seventy-eight, whereby the Constitution of the United States of America was ratified, and all acts of the General Assembly of this State, ratifying or adopting amendments to said Constitution, are hereby repealed and abrogated; that the union between the State of Virginia and the other States under the Constitution aforesaid, is hereby dissolved, and that the State of Virginia is in the full possession and exercise of all the rights of sovereignty which belong to a free and independent State. And they do further declare that the said Constitution of the United State of America is no longer binding on any of the citizens of this State.

This Ordinance shall take effect and be an act of this day when ratified by a majority of the votes of the people of this State, cast at a poll to be taken thereon on the fourth Thursday in May next, in pursuance of a schedule hereafter to be enacted.

20 William H. Edwards, "A Bit of History," *The West Virginia Historical Magazine Quarterly*, vol. 2, no. 5 (July 1902), 64.

Done in Convention, in the city of Richmond, on the seventeenth day of April, in the year of our Lord one thousand eight hundred and sixty-one, and in the eighty-fifth year of the Commonwealth of Virginia

JNO. L. EUBANK,

Sec'y of Convention.[21]

Forty-seven delegates from northwestern Virginia attended the secession convention. Thirty-two voted against secession, eleven voted for it, and four did not vote.[22] The western portion of Virginia rejected the secession movement.

On April 19, the editor of the *Richmond Dispatch* declared, "The announcement that the Convention of Virginia had passed an Ordinance of Secession was received with the most universal and profound satisfaction. There are no longer in Virginia two parties. The Union men and the Secessionists are arrayed in a solid bank of brotherhood under the Flag of Virginia." He continued, "The only rivalry is which shall do and suffer most in defence of our common honor against the monstrous despotism at Washington. Lincoln's Proclamation has accomplished the union of all parties in Virginia and the South. The ordinance of Secession is the answer of the Convention to that Proclamation, and the action of the Convention is but the echo of the people's will."[23] This may have been true east of the Allegheny Mountains, but those west of the mountains held a different opinion altogether.

"The East thought to browbeat the West as she always has done," keenly observed Laurane Boreman, the wife of the first governor of West Virginia.[24] Peter G. Van Winkle, a prominent railroad attorney and early advocate of statehood for western Virginia, sounded a similar note when he claimed that the eastern elite tried "to govern us by a centralized oligarchy."[25] A visitor to the

21 "The Virginia Secession Ordinance; An Ordinance," *New York Times*, April 28, 1861.

22 Homer F. Fansler, *History of Tucker County West Virginia* (Parsons, West Virginia: McClain Printing Co., 1962), 129.

23 "Secession of Virginia," *Richmond Dispatch*, April 19, 1861.

24 Laurane Boreman to Mr. Hill, April 18, 1861, Laurane Boreman Papers, State Archives.

25 *Address of the Delegates Composing the New State Constitutional Convention to Their Constituents, February 1863*, Peter G. Van Winkle Papers, West Virginia & Regional History Collection, West Virginia University Libraries, Morgantown, West Virginia.

area from Pittsburgh, Pennsylvania was convinced that if the Ordinance of Secession passed the electorate, western Virginia would be "free to take at once the course upon which they are determined . . . to separate from the seceding part of the State."[26] The passage of the Ordinance of Secession proved to be the last straw for the people of western Virginia.

While the Richmond convention passed the Ordinance of Secession, John S. Carlile visited President Abraham Lincoln at the White House. "Carlile was no antislavery zealot from the mountains of western Virginia. In the state convention, he had defended slavery as 'a social, political and religious blessing' that was (paradoxically) 'essential to the preservation of our liberties,'" as historian William C. Harris noted. "But, he told Virginians, the institution would not exist five years after the state's separation from the non-slaveholding states." After hearing what Carlile had to say, Lincoln instructed Carlile to go back home and rally his section of Virginia for the Union.[27]

Those delegates who opposed the Ordinance of Secession were not treated well by secessionists. Delegates from northwestern Virginia were threatened when they left the Convention on April 21. "About nine o'clock at night, and after you had retired to rest, I was in the office of the hotel conversing alone with the clerk, when a number of well-dressed and respectable-looking men entered hurriedly, and in an excited manner proceeded to scrutinize the names on the hotel register, of those who had arrived during the afternoon and evening; commenting variously, and in no very mild or flattering terms, upon the political status of several of our little party," a fellow delegate reported to Willey.

"When your name was reached the one who appeared to be the leader, and who was reading the names aloud, at once loudly and profanely denounced you as an enemy to Virginia and the South, and declared that you ought to be taken from your bed and thrown into the Potomac before morning. This proposition seemed to meet with general approval, as there was not the slightest objection or remonstrance interposed by any of the party. They were induced to leave the

---

26 *Wellsburg Herald*, May 13, 1861. The original article was published in the *Pittsburgh Chronicle* on May 11, 1861 and was reprinted in the *Herald*.

27 William C. Harris, *With Charity for All: Lincoln and the Restoration of the Union* (Lexington: University of Kentucky Press, 1997), 20.

hotel, however, without attempting to carry their murderous threat into execution," the delegate concluded.[28]

Even though a referendum was scheduled for May 23 to consider the Ordinance of Secession, on April 25, Letcher entered into a military alliance with the Confederacy and turned over control of Virginia's troops to the nascent Confederate armies. Two weeks later, Jefferson Davis formally admitted Virginia as the Confederacy's tenth state.[29] Ardent secessionists seized the U.S. arsenal at Harpers Ferry and the customs houses located in Richmond, Norfolk, and Portsmouth.

Also on April 25, Letcher forwarded a letter to Andrew Sweeney, the mayor of Wheeling, informing him of the passage of the Ordinance of Secession and ordering him to "seize at once upon the custom house of that city, the post office, and all public buildings and documents in the name of the sovereign State of Virginia." Sweeney shot back immediately, making Wheeling's position on the question of secession abundantly clear: "I *have* seized upon the custom house, the post office, and all public buildings and documents in the name of Abraham Lincoln, President of the United States, whose property they are."[30]

The outcome of the upcoming referendum seemed to be a foregone conclusion, or as the *Richmond Whig* correctly put it, the vote would be "but . . . a mere formality."[31] The line had been drawn in the sand.

28 Quoted in William P. Willey, *An Inside View of the Formation of the State of West Virginia with Character Sketches of the Pioneers in that Movement* (Wheeling, WV: The News Publishing Co., 1901), 52. William P. Willey was the son of Waitman T. Willey and, as such, had access to his father's personal papers.

29 For a detailed discussion of these events, see Ibid., 24-45.

30 Lang, *Loyal West Virginia*, 17.

31 *Richmond Whig*, April 23, 1861.

CHAPTER FOUR

The First and Second
Wheeling Conventions

A. Western Virginia's response to the Ordinance of Secession

Approximately 1,200 citizens of Harrison County met in the county seat of Clarksburg on April 22, 1861, led by John S. Carlile. This assembly passed following preamble and resolutions:

PREAMBLE.

WHEREAS, The Convention now in session in this State, called by the Legislature, the members of which had been elected twenty months before said call, at a time when no such action as the assemblage of a convention by legislative enactment was contemplated by the people, or expected by the members they elected in May, 1859, at which time no one anticipated the troubles recently brought upon our common country by the extraordinary action of the State authorities of South Carolina, Georgia, Alabama, Mississippi, Florida, Louisiana, and Texas, has, contrary to the expectation of a large majority of the people of this State, adopted an ordinance withdrawing Virginia from the Federal Union: and whereas, by the law calling said Convention, it is expressly declared that no such ordinance shall have force or effect, or be of binding obligation upon the people of this State, until the same shall be ratified by the voters at the polls,: and whereas, we have seen with regret that demonstrations of hostility, unauthorized by law, and inconsistent with the duty of law-abiding citizens, still owing allegiance to the Federal Government, have been made by a portion of the people of this State against the said Government: and whereas, the Governor of this Commonwealth, has, by proclamation, undertaken to decide for the people of Virginia, that which they have reserved to themselves, the right to decide by their votes at the polls, and has called upon the volunteer soldiery of this State to report to him and hold themselves in readiness to make war upon the Federal Government, which Government is Virginia's Government, and must in law and of right continue so to be, until the people of Virginia shall, by their votes, and through the ballot-box, that great conservator of a free people's liberties, decide otherwise: and whereas, the peculiar situation of Northwestern Virginia, separated as it is by natural barriers from the rest of the State, precludes all hope of timely succor in the hour of danger from other portions of the State, and demands that we should look to and provide for our own safety in the fearful emergency in which we now find ourselves placed by the action of our State authorities, who have disregarded the great fundamental principle upon which our beautiful system of Government is based, to wit: "That all governmental power is derived from the consent of the governed," and have without consulting the people placed this State in hostility to the Government by seizing upon its ships and obstructing the channel at the mouth of Elizabeth river, by wresting from the Federal officers at Norfolk and Richmond the custom houses, by tearing from the Nation's property the Nation's flag, and putting in its place a bunting, the emblem of rebellion, and by marching upon the National Armory at Harper's Ferry; thus inaugurating a war without consulting those in whose name they profess to act; and whereas, the exposed condition of Northwestern Virginia requires that her people should be united in action, and unanimous in purpose - there being a perfect identity of interests in times of war as well as in peace - therefore, be it

Resolved, That it be and is hereby recommended to the people in each and all of the counties composing Northwestern Virginia to appoint delegates, not less than five in number, of their wisest, best, and discreetest men, to meet in Convention at Wheeling, on the 13th day of May next, to consult and determine upon such action as the people of Northwestern Virginia should take in the present fearful emergency,

Resolved, That Hon: John S. Carlile, W. Goff, Hon. Chas. S. Lewis, J. Davis, Lot Bowen, Dr. Wm. Dunkin, W. E. Lyon, Felix Sturm, and James Lynch be and are hereby appointed delegates to represent this county in said Convention.

JOHN HURLEY, Pres.

J. W. Harris, Sec'y.[1]

Similar meetings occurred in other counties of western Virginia supporting the idea of a secession convention to be held in Wheeling.[2] The very idea of seceding from the Union was anathema to the citizens of western Virginia. As a modern historian wrote, "they believed in the Union and held firmly to it even

---

1 "Northwestern Virginia. Great Movement in Harrison County for a Separate Organization of the Northwest from the Seceders," *Wheeling Intelligencer*, April 25, 1861.

2 See, e.g., "Public Meeting at Guyandotte—Flag of Virginia Hoisted," *Kanawha Valley Star*, April 30, 1861.

during this period of calamity. To them it was a holding onto their faith and to the strength of their nationality."[3]

On May 3, 1861, Francis H. Pierpont addressed another assembly in Clarksburg. He warned eastern Virginia that "if secession is the only remedy offered by her for all our wrongs, the day is near when Western Virginia will rise in the majesty of her strength and patriotism and repudiate her oppressors and remain permanently under the stars and stripes."[4]

The next day, at a meeting at Kingwood in Preston County, the assembly declared that separation of western Virginia from the east was essential to maintain their liberties, and also resolved "to so far defy the insurgent rulers of the State as to elect a representative in the National Congress."[5] A wave of sentiment supporting the establishment of a new state built rapidly.

Wheeling was of vital importance to the Union in 1861. Founded by Ebenezer Zane in 1793, it was the largest city in the western portion of Virginia, and was a major center of transportation and commerce.[6] Its location at the head of low-water navigation on the Ohio River made it a nineteenth century boat-building center. There were also several significant nail and tobacco plants in the town. For the first half of the Nineteenth Century, Wheeling vied with Pittsburgh to be the center of commerce in that part of the country.

"For many years the centre of western population was in the Ohio valley, and good steamers were plying the Ohio when the National Road was first opened," as an early history of the city put it. "When the [National Road] was built to Wheeling its greatest mission was accomplished—the portage path across the mountains was completed to a point where river navigation was almost always available."[7] The westward expansion of the National Road to Wheeling was completed on August 1, 1818, and Wheeling was the terminus of the National Road for a number of years until it was extended into Ohio in the

---

3 Michael P. Riccards, "Lincoln and the Political Question: The Creation of the State of West Virginia," *Presidential Studies Quarterly*, vol. 27, no. 3 (Summer 1997), 552.

4 Charles H. Ambler, *Francis H. Pierpont: Union War Governor of Virginia and Father of West Virginia* (Chapel Hill: University of North Carolina Press, 1937), 83-84.

5 Lang, *Loyal West Virginia*, 122.

6 The city of Zanesville, Ohio was also named for Ebenezer Zane. The National Road also passes through Zanesville.

7 Archer Butler Hulbert, *The Old National Road: A Chapter of American Expansion* (Columbus, OH: F. J. Heer, 1901), 46-47.

1830's. The extension of the National Road into Ohio made the construction of a bridge across the Ohio River at Wheeling critical. A suspension bridge designed by Charles Ellet was built across the river at Wheeling Island in 1847, and was completed in 1849 at a cost of $250,000. The completed span was the longest suspension bridge in the world at 1,010 feet in length and 90 feet above the Ohio River. It carried the National Road into Ohio.[8] The B&O also passed through the city, meaning that it also featured good rail access to the east and to the west. Telegraph lines, a new method of transporting information almost instantaneously, ran along the B & O lines, adding to the strategic importance of the railroad.

Wheeling is situated 60 miles from Pittsburgh, 130 miles from Columbus and Cleveland, but is still 320 miles from Richmond, which meant that its primary commercial relationships were with Pennsylvania and Ohio, and not the eastern portion of Virginia. Wheeling had one of the few bridges across the Ohio River, it possessed a critical rail line, and it also had the Ohio River, which was needed for transportation. The city itself, a hub of pro-Union support, became an important strategic asset that the North was anxious to seize.

Virginia Southern Unionists called a convention in Wheeling for the purpose of repealing the ordinance of secession. Each dissident county was asked to send five delegates to the convention. When the time came to convene the meeting in Wheeling, over 400 men, some of whom were pursued by Confederate troops, flocked to the river town, "where amid great demonstrations, flags and banners flying, bands playing and people cheering, they assembled as a 'mass convention'. . . and promptly organized with all the machinery of a parliamentary body."[9]

"The Union men are rising in their strength. Letters are exhibited to us by friends here in the city from their friends, acquaintances and relatives in all the various counties of Western Virginia, and so far as we have read them they bring good news," wrote Archibald Campbell in an editorial in his *Wheeling Intelligencer*

---

8   Charles A. Wingerter, *History of Greater Wheeling and Vicinity* (Chicago: Lewis Publishing Co., 1912), 169-174. The Wheeling suspension bridge became the subject of Supreme Court litigation that found in favor of the bridge against river-boat interests. Pittsburgh interests were concerned that at 90 feet, it was low enough to interfere with the passage of steamboats. Edwin M. Stanton, who played a **significant** role in the events described in this book, represented the Pittsburgh interests opposed to bridge. The U.S. Supreme Court found in favor of the Wheeling bridge. *Pennsylvania v. Wheeling and Belmont Bridge Co.*, 59 U.S. 425 (1855).

9   Callahan, Semi-Centennial History of West Virginia, 142.

The Customs House in Wheeling, which is today known as West Virginia Independence Hall. *(Harper's Weekly)*

on May 10. "There is most unprecedented awakening on the subject of secession. The fact that we have been foully, treacherously and despotically dealt with has come upon the convictions of the people like a horrid fright. That fright has been succeeded by a most intense indignation, which is rapidly kindling into a towering and devouring flame of resentment and repudiation."[10]

The convention took place on May 13-15, prior to the Virginia referendum on the ordinance of secession scheduled for May 23, 1861. The delegates numbered 429, representing 29 counties attending this convention, some of whom had been elected by the voters of their respective counties, and some of whom chose to attend on their own initiative. William B. Zinn, who represented Preston County in the Virginia legislature for years, served as chairman. A debate ensued over whether all northwestern Virginians should be seated as delegates, or only those appointed by their constituencies. After much

10 *Wheeling Intelligencer*, May 10, 1861.

Judge John Jay Jackson, a cousin of Stonewall Jackson, who served as a delegate to the First Wheeling Convention.

(West Virginia State Archives)

discussion, the convention found a compromise: it appointed a committee on representation and permanent organization.[11]

The Convention vehemently denounced the Ordinance of Secession, and called upon the citizens of Virginia to reject it. The delegates wanted Unionists to claim Virginia's Congressional seats as well as seats in the state legislature. Some delegates, including prominent attorney John Jay Jackson, Jr. of Parkersburg, a cousin of an obscure but soon-to-be famous Professor Thomas J. Jackson of the Virginia Military Institute, wisely argued that it was imprudent to nullify the ordinance of secession before it was the voters of Virginia ratified it.[12]

John S. Carlile, a former Virginia legislator and one-term U.S. Congressman, of Harrison County, demanded that the Convention take immediate action in order to demonstrate the delegates' loyalty to Virginia and the Union. "Let us act," he proclaimed. "Let us repudiate these monstrous usurpations; let us show our loyalty to Virginia and the Union; and let us maintain ourselves in the Union at every hazard. It is useless to cry peace when there is no peace; and I will for one will repeat what was said by one Virginia's noblest sons and greatest statesmen, 'Give me liberty or give me death!'"[13]

11 Lewis, *How West Virginia was Made*, 36-41.

12 Ibid., 42-43. Thomas J. Jackson became famous in the summer of 1861 as the hero of the Battle of Bull Run, where Confederate Brig Gen. Barnard Bee proclaimed, "Look at Jackson standing there like a stone wall!" From that moment forward, Jackson was known as Stonewall Jackson, and became Gen. Robert E. Lee's principal lieutenant.

13 Ibid., 44. John S. Carlile was born in Winchester, Virginia on December 17, 1817. His father, a lawyer, was an abusive alcoholic who squandered his wife's inheritance. The family moved to Bedford, Pennsylvania. After Carlile's father abandoned his family, his mother obtained a

Senator John S. Carlile, an early advocate of statehood who later became an opponent. Carlile represented Virginia in the U.S. Senate through the Restored Government.

(Library of Congress)

Carlile was a "man of fine talents—a ready, keen, solid and impressive man." He was "somewhat singular looking, being very sallow and angular in his face, flat on his head, compact and well knit in his framework. He has a rich deep voice, fine power of expression, imperturbable coolness and a great deal of tact."[14]

On May 14, Carlile introduced the following resolution calling for the creation of a new state, to be called New Virginia:

> *Resolved,* That the committee on State and Federal Relations be instructed to report an ordinance declaring that the convention of the counties of the state composing the Tenth and Eleventh congressional district, to which shall be added the county of Wayne, with the other portions of the state is hereby dissolved, and that the people of the said counties are in full possession and exercise of all the rights of sovereignty which belong and appertain to a free and independent state in the United States and subject to the constitution thereof; and that the said committee be instructed to report a constitution and form of government for said state, to be called the state of New Virginia; and also that they report a declaration of the causes which have impelled the

---

divorce, and mother and son returned to Virginia, where his mother ran a school. At age 14, he moved out to work in a store, and eventually founded his own business, which failed. In 1840, he was admitted to the Virginia bar. He practiced in Beverly in Randolph County and Philippi in Barbour County during the 1840's. In 1847, he was elected to the Virginia Senate, and he served as a delegate to the Virginia constitutional convention of 1850. He then served one two-year term as a member of the United States House of Representatives, 1856-1857. He became one of the more prominent and more vocal leaders of the secession movement that led to the creation of West Virginia. www.encyclopediavirginia.org/Carlile_John_S_1817-1878# start_entry.

14 "The Movement in Harrison County," *Wheeling Intelligencer*, April 25, 1861.

Senator Waitman T. Willey, one of the strongest advocates of statehood. Willey represented Virginia in the U.S. Senate through the Restored Government.

(Library of Congress)

people of the said counties thus to dissolve their connection with the rest of the state, together with an ordinance declaring that such constitution and form of government shall take effect and be an act of this day when the consent of the congress of the United States and of the legislature of the state of Virginia is obtained, as is provided for by Section 3, Article 4, of the constitution of the United States.[15]

Debate grew heated after Carlile introduced this resolution. Waitman T. Willey, another prominent attorney from Parkersburg and a former member of the Whig Party, declared that doing so would constitute "triple treason" against the Commonwealth of Virginia, the Union and the Confederacy. "Termed the ablest lawyer of northwestern Virginia" by the *Philadelphia Inquirer*, Willey was a "tall, fine, spectacled specimen of the old Virginia gentleman."[16] Willey and his supporters condemned Carlile's proposal as revolutionary.

"During the 13th and 14th there was a great deal of excitement among the delegates and the people, both in and outside of the convention hall, the most excitable and revolutionary followers of Carlile making threats that Mr. Willey should be hung as a traitor to the cause on account of his constitutional, legal and conservative course of conduct," recalled a delegate. "Not being satisfied with the threats of hanging him, they posted notices throughout the city calling a meeting at the court house to condemn him as a traitor to the cause of the

15 R. H. Sayre, "An Important Contribution to the 'Missing Chapter' in the History of the Formation of West Virginia by an Eyewitness. Recollections and Narrative of a Member of the May Convention of 1861, the Restored Government and the New State, West Virginia," *The Bar* (October 1913), found at http://www.wvculture.org/history/statehood/sayre.html.

16 Allan G. Bogue, *The Earnest Men: Republicans of the Civil War Senate* (Ithaca, NY: Cornell University Press, 1981), 47.

Union." That delegate concluded, "If Mr. Carlile and his followers could have had full sway in the convention we would have had a counter-revolution, one that would have placed the loyal people of West Virginia at the mercy of the Rebel Government at Richmond, as the Federal Government could not and would not have recognized the Carlile revolt anything other than a counter-revolution."[17]

As Waitman Willey's son William observed years later, "Mr. Carlile's scheme for the formation of a new State was purely revolutionary in its entire conception. But this was a time of revolution. It was in the air. And doubtless he depended upon riding that wave, and being supported in the end by the plea of necessity, in any radical measure that might reach the result."[18]

Carlile himself recognized that having the First Wheeling Convention call for immediate statehood would have failed because the federal government "see in the Constitution of the United States, that it is only through it, and by virtue of its provisions, that a division can be had. They know another thing, too, that a separation is worth nothing without the perpetuity of the Government to which we desire to attach ourselves, and that they must first address themselves to maintaining the Government." He concluded, "In a short time the power of this Government may be established. Then we may be acknowledged as the Government of Virginia; then we can provide for that which is essential to our interest."[19]

Years later, George R. Latham, an attorney from Grafton who served as a delegate to the First Wheeling Convention, thanked Willey for opposing immediate statehood at that premature date. He told Willey, "your effort on that occasion saved us from anarchy, and placed the restoration of the Government of the State of Virginia upon a basis which secured it at once the respect of the thoughtful, and the confidence and recognition of the Government of the United States."[20]

17 Ibid.

18 Willey, *An Inside View*, 61.

19 "Virginia Convention Seventh Day," *Wheeling Intelligencer*, June 19, 1861.

20 Willey, *An Inside View*, 66. Latham was commissioned colonel of the 6th West Virginia Cavalry in May 1862. He was elected to Congress in 1865 and served a single term, replacing William G. Brown, who was one of the men selected to represent West Virginia by the Restored Government. See Chapter Four, infra.

Instead, the Convention adopted resolutions offered by its Committee on State and Federal Resolutions recommending that the voters of western Virginia should elect delegates to a Second Wheeling Convention to be convened on June 11 in the event that the voters of Virginia approved the ordinance of secession. It also appointed an emergency "central committee" of nine members to serve as the executive committee to organize Union sympathizers for the purpose of assembling a loyal government for Virginia. With that, the raucous First Wheeling Convention adjourned to await the outcome of the referendum on the Virginia Ordinance of Secession.[21]

"There is a punishment more severe for the Pan Handle than the usual punishment for treason," declared an indignant *Richmond Dispatch* editor on May 14. "Let the Pan Handlers depart in peace. Let Virginia sell out the Pan Handle to anyone who will have it. She would be willing to sell it cheap. Our only objection is, that there is still a gallant band of true patriots there, whom we dislike to offer up. Otherwise, there could be no qualification to our delight in getting rid of the Pan Handle. It has no interests, principles, sympathies, or instincts in common with Virginia. It is in it, but not of it. Oh happy day when Carlile & Co. shall no longer be Virginians even in name. Surely, Virginia can afford to say to such creatures, 'Go, poor devil, there is room enough in the world for me and thee.'"[22]

On May 18, Pierpont returned to his home in Fairmont, which was bitterly divided between those who favored secession and those who didn't. Those who favored secession concocted a plan to seize Pierpont and take him to Richmond as a prisoner of war, which would prevent him from participating in any further efforts to create a new state. However, Pierpont's business partner warned him of the nascent plot, and Pierpont escaped to Wheeling, leaving his wife and children behind. Such was the level of acrimony that developed between the two factions.[23]

The federal government assigned Maj. Gen. George B. McClellan to command Union troops sent to defend western Virginia. Determined to retain the western portion of Virginia as part of the Commonwealth, the Confederate government sent forces under command of Gen. Robert E. Lee to seize control

---

21 Lewis, *How West Virginia was Made*, 60-62.

22 "The Pan Handle," *Richmond Dispatch*, May 14, 1861.

23 Ambler, *Francis H. Pierpont*, 91.

of the region. After a series of engagements, McClellan's troops defeated Lee's army and drove it from western Virginia. "McClellan's invasion of Northwestern Virginia established the authority of the Reorganized Government of Virginia under Pierpont and made a separate State movement possible," observed modern historian Richard O. Curry.[24] Union troops occupied most of the region for the rest of the Civil War, with the North retaining control of the B&O Railroad. McClellan, himself a former president of a railroad, was appointed general-in-chief of all of the Union armies on the basis of his success in western Virginia, while Lee received the blame for the defeat and did not come to prominence for another year.[25]

The statewide referendum on the Virginia Ordinance of Secession occurred on Thursday, May 23, 1861. The outcome was almost a foregone conclusion. As Willey put it, "thirty thousand glittering bayonets surrounded the polls from the Chesapeake to the summit of the Alleghenies, and were menacing the lives and liberties of the people of northwest Virginia."[26] The final tally, as certified by Virginia Gov. John Letcher, was 125,950 for secession and 20,373 against. Twenty-five counties in the northwestern section of Virginia opposed secession and delivered majorities for Virginia remaining in the Union.[27] The passage of the referendum meant that Virginia seceded from the Union effective immediately. "The time for voting is past," declared Francis Pierpont, "the time for fighting has arrived."[28]

On May 25, reacting to the outcome of the plebiscite, a committee of politicians led by Carlile and Pierpont published a call to action in the *Kingwood Chronicle*. "People of North Western Virginia, why should we thus permit ourselves to be tyrannized over, and made slaves of, by the haughty arrogance and wicked machinations of would-be Eastern Despots," they asked. "Are we submissionists, craven cowards, who will yield to daring ambition . . . . The Union under the flag of our common country . . . causes our bosoms to glow

---

24 Curry, *A House Divided*, 68.

25 The details of military operations in West Virginia during 1861 stray far beyond the scope of this study. For a detailed narrative of those events, see W. Hunter Lesser, *Rebels at the Gate: Lee and McClellan on the Front Line of a Nation Divided* (Naperville, IL: Sourcebooks, 2004).

26 Ambler, *Waitman T. Willey*, 53.

27 "The Vote for Secession in Virginia," *New York Times*, June 1, 1861. This article breaks out the vote by county.

28 Ambler, *Francis H. Pierpont*, 92.

with patriotic heat, and our hearts to swell with honest love of country."[29] "The action of the Union men represented by Pierpont, Carlile and the rest was a very important factor in the history of the war, and has not attracted the attention it deserves."[30]

Outraged loyalists in Wheeling decided to ostracize those who voted for secession. They published a list of "Traitors in Wheeling," consisting of the names of "the Traitors and Rebels of Wheeling, Va., who voted May 23, 1861, for the infamous Ordinance of Secession, adopted by the usurpers in the Richmond, Va., Convention." They also published a second list of residents of the rest of Ohio County who voted for secession in an effort to shame anyone supporting secession.[31]

On May 26th, only three days after Virginia voters overwhelmingly supported secession, Carlile paid a visit to the White House to see Lincoln and his cabinet. He requested that Union troops be sent to the support the pro-Union western portion of Virginia. Two days later, Lincoln sent Brig. Gen. Benjamin F. Kelley and 10,000 troops "to hold possession of West Virginia and to coerce its loyal inhabitants into the secession movement." The troops also seized control of the B&O.[32]

Union Maj. Gen. Jacob B. Cox of Ohio, who commanded the troops, stated "I believe the occupation by the Confederates in 1861 would have wholly defeated the efforts to form a loyal state organization there, and that the present State would have been permanently to the fortunes and misfortunes of old Virginia."[33]

Union troops simultaneously dispatched from Parkersburg and Wheeling swept any Confederate troops out of northwestern Virginia, and made it possible for the delegates to the Second Wheeling Convention to travel to and safely gather in Wheeling.[34]

---

29 "To the People of North-Western Virginia," *Kingwood Chronicle*, May 25, 1861.

30 Ibid.

31 See "List of Traitors in Wheeling" and "List of Persons who Voted Direct for the Secession of the State of Virginia in Ohio County," Archives, Wheeling Jesuit University, Wheeling, West Virginia.

32 Ambler, *Francis H. Pierpont*, 92.

33 Ibid., 121.

34 Hall, *The Rending of Virginia*, 25.

B. The Second Wheeling Convention

A two-week-long Second Convention began in Wheeling on June 11, 1861. The delegates represented thirty-eight counties, five of which were east of the Allegheny Mountains. "The delegates to the June convention were chosen in various ways, sometimes by the county committee, sometimes apparently by self-appointment. There was no popular election in the true sense," recounted James Randall, an early chronicler of how constitutional issues were handled during the Lincoln Administration. Further, the process of choosing delegates was not designed to produce diverse representation, but rather was designed "to promote the selection of men actively interested in what the convention was expected to do—i.e., lay plans for a separate State."[35]

The delegates elected Arthur I. Boreman, a prominent attorney from Parkersburg, as president of the proceedings. He acknowledged, "in this Convention we have no ordinary political gathering. We have no ordinary task before us. We come here to carry out and execute, and it may be, to institute a government for ourselves. We are determined to live under a State Government in the United States of America and under the Constitution of the United States. It requires stout hearts to execute this purpose; it requires men of courage, of unfaltering determination; and I believe, in the gentlemen who compose this Convention, we have the stout hearts and the men who are determined in this purpose."[36]

That purpose was to separate northwestern Virginia from the rest of the Commonwealth and create a new state that remained loyal to the Union, prompting Carlile to say, "I find that even I, who first started the little stone down the mountain, have now to apply the rubbers to other gentlemen who have outrun me in the race, to check their impetuosity."[37]

The delegates prepared the following declaration to the people of Virginia:

---

35 Randall, *Constitutional Problems Under Lincoln*, 440-441.

36 Lewis, *How West Virginia Was Made*, 82-83.

37 Ibid., 125.

CONSTITUENT CONVENTION OF VIRGINIA, ASSEMBLED IN THE CUSTOM-HOUSE AT WHEELING, OHIO CO., JUNE, 1861.—SKETCHED BY JASPER GREEN, ESQ.—[SEE NEXT PAGE.]

The Second Wheeling Convention. *(Harper's Weekly)*

Declaration of the People of Virginia Represented in Convention at Wheeling

June 13, 1861

The true purpose of all government is to promote the welfare and provide for the protection and security of the governed, and when any form or organization of government proves inadequate for, or subversive of this purpose, it is the right, it is the duty of the latter to alter or abolish it. The Bill of Rights of Virginia, framed in 1776, reaffirmed in 1860, and again in 1851, expressly reserves this right to the majority of her people, and the existing constitution does not confer upon the General Assembly the power to call a Convention to alter its provisions, or to change the relations of the Commonwealth, without the previously expressed consent of such majority. The act of the General Assembly, calling the Convention which assembled at Richmond in February last, was therefore a usurpation; and the Convention thus called has not only abused the powers nominally entrusted to it, but, with the connivance and active aid of the executive, has usurped and exercised other powers, to the manifest injury of the people, which, if permitted, will inevitably subject them to a military despotism.

The Convention, by its pretended ordinances, has required the people of Virginia to separate from and wage war against the government of the United States, and against the citizens of neighboring State, with whom they have heretofore maintained friendly, social and business relations:

It has attempted to subvert the Union founded by Washington and his co-patriots in the purer days of the republic, which has conferred unexampled prosperity upon every class of citizens, and upon every section of the country:

It has attempted to transfer the allegiance of the people to an illegal confederacy of rebellious States, and required their submission to its pretended edicts and decrees:

It has attempted to place the whole military force and military operations of the Commonwealth under the control and direction of such confederacy, for offensive as well as defensive purposes.

It has, in conjunction with the State executive, instituted wherever their usurped power extends, a reign of terror intended to suppress the free expression of the will of the people, making elections a mockery and a fraud:

The same combination, even before the passage of the pretended ordinance of secession, instituted war by the seizure and appropriation of the property of the Federal Government, and by organizing and mobilizing armies, with the avowed purpose of capturing or destroying the Capitol of the Union:

They have attempted to bring the allegiance of the people of the United States into direct conflict with their subordinate allegiance to the State, thereby making obedience to their pretended Ordinance, treason against the former.

We, therefore the delegates here assembled in Convention to devise such measures and take such action as the safety and welfare of the loyal citizens of Virginia may demand, having mutually considered the premises, and viewing with great concern, the deplorable condition to which this once happy Commonwealth must be reduced, unless some regular adequate remedy is speedily adopted, and appealing to the Supreme Ruler of the Universe for the rectitude of our intentions, do hereby, in the name and on the behalf of the good people of Virginia, solemnly declare, that the preservation of their dearest rights and liberties and their security in person and property, imperatively demand the reorganization of the government of the Commonwealth, and that all acts of said Convention and Executive, tending to separate this Commonwealth from the United States, or to levy and carry on war against them, are without authority and void; and the offices of all who adhere to the said Convention and Executive, whether legislative, executive or judicial, are vacated.[38]

The convention also adopted an ordinance for reorganization of the state government on June 19:

An Ordinance for the Reorganization of the State Government
June 14, 1861

The people of the State of Virginia, by their delegates assembled in Convention at Wheeling, do ordain as follows:

1. A Governor and Lieutenant-Governor for the State of Virginia shall be appointed by this Convention to discharge the duties and exercise the powers which pertain to their respective offices by the existing laws of the State, and to continue in office until their successors be elected and qualified.

2. A Council, to consist of five members, shall be appointed by this Convention to consult with and advise the Governor respecting such matters pertaining to his official duties as he shall submit for consideration, and to aid in the execution of his official orders. Their term of office shall expire at the same time as that of the Governor.

3. The Delegates elected to the General Assembly on the twenty-third day of May last, and the Senators entitled, under existing laws, to seats in the next General Assembly, who shall qualify themselves by taking the oath or affirmation hereinafter set forth, shall constitute the Legislature of the State, to discharge the duties and exercise the powers pertaining to the General Assembly. They shall hold their offices for the terms for which they were respectively elected. They shall assemble in the city of Wheeling on the ____ day of ____ and proceed to organize themselves, as prescribed by existing laws, in their respective branches. A majority in each branch of the members qualified as aforesaid shall constitute a guarantee to do business. A majority of the members of each branch that qualified, voting affirmatively, shall be competent to pass any act specified in the twenty-seventh section of the fourth article of the Constitution of the State.

4. The Governor, Lieutenant-Governor, members of the Legislature, and all officers now in the service of the State, or of any county, city or town thereof, or hereafter to be elected or appointed for such service, including the Judges and Clerks of the several courts, Sheriffs, Commissioners of the Revenue, Justices of the Peace, officers of city and municipal corporations, and officers of militia and volunteers of the State not mustered into the service of the United States, shall each take the following oath or affirmation before proceeding in the discharge of the several duties:

---

38 *Journal of the Convention Assembled at Wheeling*, on the 11th of June, 1861 (Wheeling: Daily Press Book, 1861), 9-10.

I solemnly swear (or affirm) that I will support the Constitution of the United States, and the laws made in pursuance thereof, as the Supreme law of the land, any thing in the Ordinances of the Convention which assembled at Richmond on the 13th day of February, 1861, to the contrary notwithstanding; and that I will uphold and defend the Government ordained by the Convention which assembled at Wheeling on the 11th day of June, 1861, and the Legislature, Governor and all other officers thereof in the discharge of their several duties as prescribed by the last mentioned Convention.

5. If any elective officer who is required by the preceding section to take said Oath or Affirmation, fail or refuse so to do, it shall be the duty of the Governor, upon satisfactory evidence of the fact, to issue his writ declaring the office to be vacant, and providing for a special election to fill such vacancy, at some convenient and early day to be designated in said writ of which due publication shall be made for the information of the persons entitled to vote at such election, and such writ may be directed, at the discretion of the Governor, to the Sheriff or Sheriffs of the proper County or Counties, or to a special Commissioner or Commissioners to be ordered by the Governor for the purpose. If the officer who fails or refuses to take such oath or affirmation be appointed otherwise than by election, the writ shall be directed to the appointing power, requiring it to fill the vacancy.[39]

The majority of the delegates to the Second Wheeling Convention supported the idea of reorganizing the Virginia government out of the loyal counties of northwestern Virginia, vacating the elected offices, and seizing control of the levers of government. "By this method they controlled a state already recognized, and quite sure of the recognition of the Federal government in preference to that purporting to be the government of Virginia at the city of Richmond," observed West Virginia historian James Morton Callahan. "The state of Virginia could be legally dismembered only by its own consent. If the people west of the mountains were the state, they could easily get the consent for the division."[40]

"The officers and visible government of Virginia abdicated when they joined the Southern Confederacy. The people reclaimed and resumed their sovereignty after it had been abdicated by their regularly constituted authorities," observed an early West Virginia historian in explaining the motivations for establishing the Restored Government. "This right belongs to the people and can not be taken from them. A public servant is elected to keep

---

39 Ibid., 12-14.

40 Callahan, *Semi-Centennial History of West Virginia*, 143.

and exercise this sovereignty in trust, but he can do no more. When he ceases doing this the sovereignty returns whence it came—to the people."[41]

The delegates then developed plans for a new government. The almost unanimous convention elected Francis H. Pierpont as Governor, Daniel Polsey as Lieutenant Governor of Virginia, and James Wheat as Attorney General. The convention adjourned on June 26 with plans to reconvene on August 6.[42]

The 49-year-old Pierpont played a large role in establishing the newly formed government. "Probably no man supplied a larger proportion of the moral force in the resistance to secession in Northwestern Virginia than did Francis H. Pierpont," declared a contemporary.[43] "Frank Pierpont is one of those men well fitted for the stormy and revolutionary times that are upon us," wrote Archibald W. Campbell, the editor of the *Wheeling Intelligencer*, on May 6. "He has the moral, physical and mental power of a leader. A truer man to the cause of the Union does not live; and he has the vigor of apprehension, that incisiveness of speech and that indomitable will and courage that carries people with him."[44]

Often called "the Father of West Virginia," Francis Harrison Pierpont was born on June 25, 1814, in Monongalia County. He spent most of his life in Fairmont, south of Morgantown. As a boy, he worked on his father's farm and tannery, all while attending local schools. At age twenty-two, he enrolled in Pennsylvania's Allegheny College, graduating in 1840. He then went to Mississippi to teach school. He began reading law while teaching, enabling him to pass the bar examination.

The newly-minted attorney returned to Virginia and was admitted to the bar at Fairmont, Marion County. A gifted orator, Pierpont soon became prominent in the local bar and the local community. "Educated in Northern ideas and among northern people, Mr. Pierpont naturally became an outspoken abolitionist. His convictions were so intense he rarely allowed an opportunity to pass with opposition to the doctrine of human slavery. He took an active part, even before graduation from college, in the political discussions of the times,"

---

41 Cutright, *The History of Upshur County*, 113.

42 Otis K. Rice and Stephen W. Brown, *West Virginia: A History*, 2nd ed. (Lexington: University Press of Kentucky, 1993), 122.

43 Ambler, *Francis H. Pierpont*, 84.

44 "Frank Pierpont's Speech," *Wheeling Intelligencer*, May 6, 1861.

Daniel Polsley, Lieutenant Governor of
Virginia in the Restored Government.

(Portrait File, West Virginia State Archives)

noted a local newspaper. "In the differences which between the people of the Western and Eastern portions of the state, growing out of the grievances of the former on account of unequal taxation and other unjustness, Mr. Pierpont took a decided stand in favor of dividing the state and made active campaigns. When the war broke out the opportunity came."[45]

Pierpont served as governor of the so-called Reorganized Government of Virginia for about a year, and, in the meantime, was elected by the voters to complete the unfulfilled term of Letcher, who was declared to have abandoned his office. Pierpont was subsequently elected for a full term of four years, "and was recognized by President Lincoln as the legitimate governor of Virginia." His obituary noted, "He was one of the many war governors of the states who stood by the government in its darkest hours, and contributed a noble part in sending troops to the front to defend the flag. He was a true as steel in those solemn times that try men's souls."[46]

45 "Laid to Rest. Governor Pierpont's Funeral. The City Take a Half Holiday to Attend the Services. The People Were General Sad at the Death of the Grand Old Man Whom All Were Proud to Honor," *Fairmont Free Press*, March 30, 1899. For a full-length biography of Pierpont, see Ambler, *Francis H. Pierpont*.

46 Ibid. Pierpont remained governor of the "Restored Government of Virginia" for the rest of his term and never served as governor of West Virginia. The Restored Government maintained its capital at Alexandria until the end of the Civil War. President Andrew Johnson appointed him Provisional Governor of Virginia after the Confederate surrender, and he held office until 1868. Thereafter he served one term in the West Virginia legislature and served as Collector of Internal Revenue under Pres. James A. Garfield. He spent his last years with his daughter in Pittsburgh, PA., died on March 24, 1899, and was buried in Woodlawn Cemetery in Fairmont. One of the speakers at his funeral was 87-year-old former senator Waitman T. Willey of Morgantown.

Gov. Francis H. Pierpont, the leader of the Restored Government. Pierpont is often called "The Father of West Virginia." *(Ohio County Public Library, Wheeling, WV)*

When Pierpont accepted the governorship, he proclaimed, "they see treason rankling all of the State, with the Governor, Lieut-Governor and all the State officials, and four out of five of the Judges of the Court of Appeals, all the Judges of the Circuit Court, except one, and as far as I am advised, nearly all the prosecuting attorneys and Sheriffs engaged in this treasonable work."[47] Consequently, after taking office, Pierpont declared all offices open and began appointing people deemed loyal to these offices.

The ordinance passed by the Wheeling Convention "represents not only Western Virginia but the loyal citizens of several counties east of the Blue Ridge, and is unquestionably a genuine exponent of the Union sentiment in the State, so far as it has yet dared to manifest itself. It will, therefore, shrink from no just responsibility, and will interpose with the most positive measures to redeem the State from the treason which is hurrying it to destruction," declared an editorial in the *Wheeling Intelligencer*. "Its first step will be to declare that the present State government has in effect abdicated its functions, and is no longer in authority. No man who recognizes the supremacy of the federal Constitution can question the political or the moral right of the convention to do this.

---

47 Lewis, *How West Virginia Was Made*, 165. The one loyal judge mentioned by Pierpont was Judge George W. Thompson. While Thompson was a Unionist who opposed secession, he also was opposed to the Restored Government, which he viewed as unconstitutional. Pierpont probably came to regret calling Thompson loyal as events unfolded. After the Restored Government took office, Judge Thompson refused to take the oath of loyalty because of his belief that it was an unconstitutional act, so Pierpont removed him from office. Thompson eventually moved his family to Richmond, and Pierpont issued an arrest warrant for Thompson, apparently for purposes of effecting a prisoner exchange. Thompson was eventually arrested, and was released after the federal War Department intervened. Thompson swore out a complaint against Pierpont for false imprisonment. "A Wheeling paper says that Gov. Pierpont of West Virginia was arrested in Bridgeport by the Sheriff of Belmont County, [Ohio], and held to bail in the sum of $10,000 for his appearance in the next term of court held for that county," reported the *New York Daily Tribune*. "The charge preferred against him is the false imprisonment in Wheeling of Judge Geo. Thompson." See "General News," *New York Daily Tribune*, August 10, 1863. The Ohio court found against Thompson, but Thompson nevertheless caused Pierpont and his government great embarrassment. In 1866, Thompson sued Pierpont for false imprisonment while Pierpont was serving as the Reconstruction governor of Virginia. For further detail, see Robert Arrington, "Pierpont's Bastille—The Trials of Judge Thompson," https://sites.google.com/site/wvotherhistory/pierpont-s-bastille-the-trials-of-judge-thompson. Historian James C. McGregor noted that Thompson "was a most unsuccessful straddler. In Wheeling he was treated as a Secessionist sympathizer while the Richmond legislature refused to pay his salary because he had pronounced the ordinance of secession null and void." McGregor, *The Disruption of Virginia*, 222, n. 1.

Obedience to the State executive and Legislature, which are in league with rebellion, cannot be rendered without disloyalty to the Federal Government."[48]

Not all in western Virginia supported a new state. Parkersburg attorney John Jay Jackson, who had spoken forcefully at the First Wheeling Convention, declined to attend the Second Convention "because I ascertained by correspondence that the probable action of the Convention would be revolutionary and unconstitutional, and, in my judgment, unwise; that I would be powerless for any useful purpose, and therefore I deemed it inexpedient for me to attend it." Jackson believed that the Ordinance for the Reorganization of the State Government was unconstitutional: "This Ordinance . . . is palpably in conflict with the Laws and Constitution which it explicitly affirms. We then manifestly had two Governors and Governments, unless the Wheeling Government was irregular."

He also declared, "The Government of the United States has constitutionally and rightfully provided for the safety and protection of this section of the State. This was its duty; and if it had not regarded it as due to it, it still would have occupied Western Virginia as a strategic necessity, to protect Western Pennsylvania and Ohio. The protection was in no wise dependent on the Wheeling movement, but was independent of and before it. What good, then, has emanated from the Wheeling movement, I am at a loss to specify. But, has it not done harm? Has it not weakened the Union cause? Has it not alienated many of our Union friends, by imposing unnecessary shackles on their consciences?" He continued, "I thought by the recognition by the Government at Washington of the Wheeling Movement was not only a great error and wholly unproductive of good, but a gross violation of the Constitution of the United States." He explained some of his reasoning: "Is it not obvious that it is only the bayonets of the United States that can give it any respectability as a legislate body—nay, that can even rescue it from contempt? Is it not clearly a usurped Government—a Government founded in force?"[49]

The governors of Pennsylvania and Ohio supported the burgeoning separatist movement. "It was Ohio's Governor [William] Dennison who encouraged West Virginia's separatist movement," noted an observer. "When

---

48 "The Wheeling Convention," *Wheeling Intelligencer*, June 14, 1861.

49 John J. Jackson to William F. Peterson, February 17, 1862, published as "Letter from General J. J. Jackson," *The Crisis*, May 14, 1862. *The Crisis* was a so-called Copperhead newspaper published in Columbus, Ohio during the Civil War.

the leaders of Virginia's mountain counties, refusing to follow the eastern Virginians into the Confederacy, assembled at Wheeling, Dennison sent a messenger to promise military aid. Secretary of the Treasury [Salmon P.] Chase gave his blessing to this promise and urged Dennison to station Ohio troops just across the river from Wheeling. From Pennsylvania came [Governor Andrew G.] Curtin's approval and agreement to act with the Ohio executive in supporting western Virginians."[50]

On June 21, Pierpont asked Abraham Lincoln for help:

> Sir: Reliable information has been received at this department from various parts of this State that large numbers of evil-minded persons have banded together in military organizations with intent to overthrow the government of the State, and for that purpose have called to their aid like-minded persons from other States who in pursuance of such call have invaded this Commonwealth. They are now making war on the loyal people of the State. They are pressing citizens against their consent into their military organizations and seizing and appropriating their property to aid in the rebellion.
>
> I have not at my command sufficient military force to suppress this rebellion and violence. The legislature cannot be convened in time to act in the premises. It therefore becomes my duty as governor of this Commonwealth to call on the Government of the United States for aid to suppress such rebellion and violence. I therefore earnestly request that you will furnish a military force to aid in suppressing the rebellion and to protect the good people of this Commonwealth from domestic violence.[51]

He also sent Carlile to Washington to see about obtaining troops to drive the rebels from western Virginia.

When Carlile arrived in Washington, he went straight to the White House and demanded to see the President. He was told that Lincoln could not see him, as he was meeting with his cabinet. Carlile then demanded that his calling card be delivered to the meeting. The President summoned him. "Well," said Lincoln, "Mr. Carlile, what is the best news in West Virginia?"

Without answering Lincoln's question, Carlile declared, "Sir, we want to fight. We have one regiment ready, and if the Federal government is going to assist us, we want it at once."

---

50 William B. Hesseltine, *Lincoln and the War Governors* (New York: Alfred A Knopf, 1948), 212.

51 *The War of the Rebellion: A Compilation of the Official Records of the Union and Confederate Armies*, 128 volumes in 3 series (Washington, D.C.: United States Government Printing Office, 1889), Series 2, Vol. 2, 11, hereinafter referred to as *OR*.

"You shall have assistance," affirmed the President.[52]

Lincoln's first Secretary of War, Simon Cameron, responded a few days later. "The President . . . never supposed that a brave and free people, though surprised and unarmed, could long be subjugated by a class of political adventurers always adverse to them;" wrote Cameron, "and the fact that they have already rallied, reorganized their government, and checked the march of these invaders, demonstrates how justly he appreciated them." Cameron then advised Pierpont that significant military forces would soon be on their way to support him.[53]

"The world has not seen of late ages anything more amusing than Carlile & Co.'s parody of the Declaration of Independence—Who of them is the Jefferson of the new Revolution?" facetiously sneered the *Richmond Dispatch* on June 25. "Carlile must remind everybody of the Father of his Country in the dignity and grandeur of his character, as well as the majesty and purity of his personal deportment—There is no difficulty in discovering the parallel between George Washington and John S. Carlile, but who is the performer of Jefferson?"[54] The next day, the *Dispatch* described the leaders of the Wheeling Convention as "the traitors who have established a reign of terror" and swore revenge.[55]

The newspapers were not the only statements of outrage emanating from the eastern portion of Virginia. After the creation of the Restored Government, the Richmond-based legislature declared, "And whereas, the traitors there [western Virginia], contemplating a division of this time-honored commonwealth…therefore, Resolved by the Senate and House of Delegates that in no event will the state of Virginia submit to or consent to the loss of a foot of her soil."[56]

President Abraham Lincoln delivered his first Annual Message to Congress on July 1, 1861. He signaled his strong support of the efforts of the separatists of northwestern Virginia. After mentioning the status of the border states, Lincoln focused on Virginia. "The course taken in Virginia was the most

---

52 Lang, *Loyal West Virginia*, 127.

53 "Documents Accompanying the Governor's Message," *Wheeling Intelligencer*, July 3, 1861.

54 "Carlile's Declaration," *Richmond Dispatch*, June 25, 1861.

55 "The Northwest," *Richmond Dispatch*, June 26, 1861.

56 McGregor, *Disruption of Virginia*, 253.

remarkable—perhaps the most important," he declared. He pointed out that a number of loyal Union men had attended the secession convention in Richmond. After recounting the fact that some who had professed loyalty to the Union had also voted for secession, the President wrote, "Although they submitted the ordinance, for ratification, to vote of the people, to be taken on a day then somewhat more than a month distant, the convention, and the Legislature, (Which was also in session at the same time and place) with leading men of the State, not members of either, immediately commenced acting, as if the State were already out of the Union. They pushed military preparations vigorously forward all over the state. They seized the United States Armory at Harper's Ferry, and the Navy-yard at Gosport, near Norfolk. They received—perhaps invited—into their state, large bodies of troops, with their warlike appointments, from the so-called seceded States. They formally entered into a treaty of temporary alliance, and co-operation with the so-called 'Confederate States,' and sent members to their Congress at Montgomery. And, finally, they permitted the insurrectionary government to be transferred to their capital at Richmond."

The President concluded, "The people of Virginia have thus allowed this giant insurrection to make its nest within her borders; and this government has no choice left but to deal with it, *where* it finds it. And it has the less regret, as the loyal citizens have, in due form, claimed its protection. Those loyal citizens, this government is bound to recognize, and protect, as being Virginia."[57] Lincoln's support for the actions of the separatists was not lost on the leaders of the secession movement.

"The loyal people alone had the right to take full advantage of the forfeiture and re-produce and re-organize the Government," new state advocate Granville Parker, who later served as West Virginia Secretary of State from 1864-1866, wrote to both President Lincoln and the Congress in support of the Restored Government. "Full notice was given to all loyal people throughout the State, and who would and could be were represented…and caused to be elected and convened at Wheeling the present Legislature." He also pointed out that a

---

57 First Annual Message to Congress, July 1, 1861, included in Roy Basler, ed., *Collected Works of Abraham Lincoln*, 8 vols. (New Brunswick, NJ: Rutgers University Press, 1953), 4:426-428. The Annual Message to Congress is today called The State of the Union Address.

Granville Parker served as a delegate to the Constitutional Convention. He later served as Secretary of State of West Virginia and published *The Formation of West Virginia and Other Incidents in the Civil War.*

(Archive Collection, West Virginia State Archives)

number of eastern counties, including Northampton, Accomack, Fairfax, and Loudoun had elected representatives to the Restored Government.[58]

The August session of the Wheeling Convention continued the process begun in June. The key issue facing the August session was establishing the boundaries of the new state. A committee proposed that the new state would be named "Kanawha," which would consist of 39 counties. Greenbrier, Pocahontas, Hampshire, Hardy, Berkeley, Morgan, and Jefferson Counties would also join the new state if a majority of voters approved doing so. Other counties contiguous to them could also apply for admission if their voters approved.[59] The matter would be put to a referendum on the fourth Wednesday in October, at which time the voters would also choose delegates for a constitutional convention that would be convened.

Arthur I. Boreman, who served as the president of the second session of the convention, declared, "You have taken the initiative in the creation and organization of a new state." He continued, "This is a step of vital importance. I hope, and I pray God it may be successful; that it may not engender strife in our midst, nor bring upon us difficulties from abroad, but that its most ardent advocates may realize their fondest hopes of its complete success. So far as I am

58 Parker, *Formation of West Virginia*, 129.

59 The State of West Virginia eventually included a total of 55 counties.

personally concerned, I am content with the action of this Convention; I bow with submission to what you have done upon this subject."[60]

With that, the de facto partition of Virginia was completed. Passing the referendum placed before the voters was all that remained to conclude the dismemberment of the Old Dominion.

60 Proceedings of the Second Session of the Second Wheeling Convention, August 21, 1861, http://www.wvculture.org/history/statehood/wheelingconvention20821.html.

CHAPTER FIVE

Creating the
"Restored Government of Virginia"

SUPPORT for the Restored Government and the movement to establish a new state spread across the north. "The people of Western Virginia were the first of all the citizens from the seceded States to disclaim and resist the authority of the Confederate usurpers," declared the influential *New York Tribune* in September. "They led the way—set the example; and Eastern Tennessee, Missouri, and Kentucky have successfully followed . . . Western Virginia has claims—peculiar claims—upon the generosity of us all. The whole loyal country owes her a debt of gratitude."[1] Other northern newspapers followed suit, expressing their strong support for the efforts of the separatists.

On October 24, 1861, the referendum to approve the secession of thirty-nine counties from the rest of Virginia occurred. The *Wheeling Intelligencer* ran an editorial supporting the secession vote that morning:

> We can add nothing to what we have already said about the election that comes off to-day. The issue is plain, and the minds of those who have thought about the matter at all are made up. We have no idea there will be a full vote in this county. The people have had too much else to think about, important as is the election. The war has swallowed

1 "Western Virginia," *New York Daily Tribune*, September 14, 1861.

up all other subjects-even those of every day necessity. Out in the interior the vote will be larger and much more unanimous for division we expect, need we hardly think there will be any serious opposition to it where the matter has been properly presented and understood.

Our advice from Monongalia, Marion, Preston, Taylor, Harrison, Ritchie, Wood, &c., &c., lead us to believe that the vote will be pretty much all one way. We should regret to see any serious opposition. We ought to be all unified for division, for it is a matter that concerns us all vitally, and tough to band us together like brothers.

Discussion on the subject has ended. Division has been shown in all its advantages, we think, and we have yet to know that it has one single draw back or disadvantage. If ever there was a measure that appealed to every interest of a people for a united, enthusiastic and hearty support, it is the measure of division.

All that we have to say, then is, voters of Ohio County, consider only your own best interest, and improve to-day the golden opportunity for which you have to often longed, of organizing a separate state.[2]

Only 34% of the voters from the thirty-nine counties of the proposed state of Kanawha (plus the voters of Hampshire and Hardy) went to the polls to vote. When the ballots were counted, they showed that 18,408 had voted in favor of the new state, while only 781 opposed.[3] Only two counties east of the Allegheny Mountains took part in the plebiscite: Hampshire and Hardy, both of which were occupied by Union soldiers guarding the B&O. In Hampshire, the vote passed 195-18, and 150-0 in Hardy, likely reflecting intimidation of the voters by the soldiers garrisoned there.[4] Voters also elected delegates to a constitutional convention to be called in Wheeling the following month.

Although only twenty percent of the counties in Virginia voted in the election, they nevertheless represented a majority of the loyal counties. Statehood advocates justified this by claiming that only those who were loyal were entitled to vote and that those who supported the secession of Virginia were traitors who did not deserve to hold an equal position with the loyal voters of Virginia.[5] The process of creating a new state began almost immediately. The precise boundaries of the new state had to be established, and a constitution had to be drafted.

2   "The Election To-day," *Wheeling Intelligencer*, October 24, 1861.

3   Lewis, *History and Government of West Virginia*, 186.

4   Summers, *The Baltimore and Ohio in the Civil War*, 185.

5   *Speech of the Hon. P. G. Van Winkle, of West Virginia, Delivered in the Senate, April 21, 1864* (Washington, DC: Gibson Brothers Printers, 1864), 10-11.

The constitutional convention began on November 26, 1861. Delegates expressed disappointment that only a handful of the counties to the east of the Alleghenies sent delegates. Six of those counties—Jefferson, Berkeley, Morgan, Hampshire, Hardy, and Pendleton—ultimately were included within the boundaries of the contemplated new state. "As political units these counties were bound to the east by social and cultural ties," wrote historian Festus P. Summers, "while their geographic location and economic life made them one with the [Shenandoah] Valley." Although the population of these counties was primarily of non-English colonial stock, they held to the traditions of the Piedmont and Tidewater regions of the east. In 1860, Jefferson County counted 3,960 slaves, and supplied 1,600 recruits for the Confederate armies. Only Morgan, Hampshire, and Hardy Counties held strong Unionist sentiments.[6]

The passage of the B&O through some of these counties made them crucial to the new state. Waitman T. Willey said that the B&O "is the great artery that feeds our country. It conveys into our center, or by its ramifications of necessity infuses through the entire body politic of this new State the lifeblood of its existence. We cannot do without it." He continued, "unless this whole line of railroad is included in this new State its operations and its benefits will be embarrassed to the full extent of the power of eastern Virginia legislation; its utility will be crippled; it will be taxed as far as reason and decency—and further than there—will allow; and every influence of eastern Virginia will be arrayed against the successful working of this road."[7] And there it was: without the so-called "railroad counties" of the eastern panhandle, there could be no new state. Without a fully functional B&O, there could be no new state.

On December 9, one of the Richmond newspapers weighed in on the question of the secession of the western counties. "There can be no Virginia unless it includes both eastern and western Virginia," declared an editorial. "[Simon] Cameron, the execrable Secretary of War of the Lincoln despotism, has presented the servile Congress of that loathsome tyranny a map in which eastern Virginia is attached to Maryland....We can say that if we cannot hold

6 Ibid., 186.

7 *Debates and Proceedings of the First Constitutional Convention of West Virginia*, December 11, 1861, http://www.wvculture.org/history/statehood/cc121161.html.

West Virginia we can hardly defend the South."[8] Confederate President Jefferson Davis described the proposed partition of Virginia as "a monstrous usurpation."[9]

On December 10, the Special Committee on Boundary introduced the following resolution:

> RESOLVED, That the district comprising the counties of Frederick, Jefferson, Berkeley, Morgan, Hampshire, Hardy, Pendleton, Highland, Bath, and Alleghany shall also be included in and constitute part of the proposed new State, provided a majority of the votes cast within the said district, at elections to be held for the purpose on the third Thursday in April, in the year 1862, and a majority of the said counties are in favor of the adoption of the Constitution to be submitted by this Convention.[10]

Delegate Chapman J. Stuart of Doddridge County spoke in support of this resolution. "It is well known that in a majority of our northwestern counties all our trade and commerce and very near all our travel, is over the Baltimore and Ohio Railroad. Now, sir, unless we have the control of that road what is to become of us? Do you not see? The eastern portion of our State has always been disposed to unfriendly legislation towards us; and now when this excitement is up, and we are forming a new State, and cutting ourselves loose from the old state," he said. "I appeal to the members of this Convention, what they think will be the legislation of eastern Virginia towards us in regard to this great improvement, to which every vital interest we have is second. Now, sir, this resolution embraces some of the valley counties not exactly bordering on this Baltimore and Ohio Railroad; but their interests are so identified and interlocked with the counties bordering on the road that it is almost impossible to separate them."[11]

Thomas R. Carskadon of Hampshire County also voiced his support. "We lie there together. We have a community of interest; and if we are to be taken in without those other counties having the privilege of coming in, it as far as I am conversant with the views of the people, met with their disapprobation. They

---

8 *Richmond Dispatch*, December 9, 1861.

9 Jefferson Davis, *The Rise and Fall of the Confederate Government*, 2 vols. (New York: D. Appleton, 1881), 2:307.

10 *Debates and Proceedings of the First Constitutional Convention of West Virginia*, December 10, 1861, http://www.wvculture.org/history/statehood/cc121061.html .

11 Ibid.

wish to go to the Blue Ridge or to not go at all. We live together in a common interest, and the Baltimore and Ohio Railroad is our outlet to market, and if we are cut off there with but two counties, we know that then we can get no internal improvements from the government of West Virginia. They will not legislate for us on that side of the mountain. It is perfectly natural that there being but two counties we need never expect any legislation from them to our particular advantage," he declared.

"Our people, the Union citizens of Hampshire are desirous, almost to a man, to go into the new State; but they wish the same invitation and chance extended to the surrounding counties; and there are strong reasons why they should be," Carskadon continued. "If the counties of Hampshire and Hardy have delegates here, the counties of Morgan, Berkeley, and Jefferson certainly would have had if they had had the proper opportunity; from the fact that Berkeley gave something like 800 majority against secession, the county of Morgan as I said cast 300 and upwards, and Jefferson would have given a majority against the ordinance had it not been for the Confederate troops stationed in Harper's Ferry, some 7,000 or 8,000, at the time of the election." He concluded, "I believe the constituency which I represent would rather be out than in unless those counties lying along the Baltimore and Ohio Railroad and contiguous would have an opportunity to vote on the question."[12]

Opponents only wanted to include the four counties that the B&O passed through, and of the non-railroad counties, only Hardy County should be included. Alleghany County was deleted because it was much more closely aligned with eastern Virginia and was not a railroad county. Other counties from the Shenandoah Valley were also removed because they were pro-slavery and pro-secessionist, leaving only Hampshire, Hardy and Pendleton Counties.[13]

Willey spoke forcefully on the subject, declaring, "You might as well sever an artery in the human body as to cripple and cut off this great artery of trade and expect our bodies to live as expect this State to live and flourish unless we include in our boundary this Baltimore and Ohio railroad." He also opined that if the railroad counties were not included in the new state, "they will not care anything about the new State."[14]

12 Ibid.

13 Ibid., December 11, 1861.

14 Ibid.

Sen. Peter VanWinkle was a delegate to the Second Wheeling Convention who later played a prominent role in the Constitutional Convention. Van Winkle, who was one of the first two United States senators from West Virginia, voted against the impeachment of Andrew Johnson. *(Library of Congress)*

Peter G. Van Winkle now spoke up in support of the proposal. Van Winkle, of Parkersburg, was a 53-year-old prominent railroad attorney who had spent ten years as a lobbyist for the railroads in Richmond. In 1861, Van Winkle served as the president of the Northwestern Virginia Railroad, which the B&O controlled. As such, he did all that he could to make certain that he protected the interests of the B&O in these proceedings. He insisted that the B&O had to be removed entirely from Virginia's control, citing its importance to the commercial, industrial, and agricultural development of the new state. "Sir, there are numerous counties that under present circumstances, at any rate, cannot have a connection with their proper market unless it is by making use of this great line, lying below Wheeling and Parkersburg, on the Ohio river or back from the river; and every one of them has already felt the benefit of this great line," he said. "They send their produce to the river; it conveys it to Parkersburg or Wheeling; and the railroad takes it east."

He concluded, "I think then, sir, there is nothing in this objection to any of the counties even apart from this railroad. But when you bring it into competition with a great interest, when you remember everything is dependent on our material prosperity—and it is greatly dependent, I might say almost wholly dependent on keeping open a suitable avenue of communication—the objection, however formidable it may have appeared in the beginning, vanishes and becomes nothing."[15]

---

15 Ibid. Van Winkle was one of the first United States Senators elected from the new State of West Virginia in 1863.

Numerous other delegates weighed in on the question, all of whom focused on the importance of the B&O to the economic viability of the new state. The question became whether counties that had not voted on secession from Virginia could or should be included in West Virginia. Van Winkle ultimately solved the problem. On December 12, he introduced an amendment that the fate of the various counties would be decided by a plebiscite to be held in April 1862.[16]

After much debate, the convention chose the name "West Virginia" for the new state.[17] The leaders of the secession movement understood that the question of slavery would have to be addressed. They knew that the statehood movement in Kansas struggled mightily with this issue several years earlier, triggering bloodshed. Northern Congressmen made it clear that they would not accept another slave state into the Union, so a solution had to be found.[18] The *Wheeling Intelligencer* reprinted an article from the *Cincinnati Gazette* that reflected this attitude clearly: "If the people of western Virginia are sincere in their desire for a separation from the East, and if their desire is based on any just ground, it is because they want a free state."[19] But the convention avoided any question of abolishing slavery. The delegates voted to include the following provision in the new constitution: "No slave shall be brought, or free person of color be permitted to come into this State for permanent residence."

Despite these concerns, the delegates passed the new constitution by unanimous vote on February 18, 1862. The draft constitution was then submitted to the voters of West Virginia.[20]

On March 14, Pierpont wrote to Lincoln, "Owing to the favorable advance of the Federal troops into Virginia, and, I think, the certainty of the rebellion

16 Ibid. December 12, 1861, http://www.wvculture.org/history/statehood/cc121261.html.

17 The original proposal was to name the new state "Kanawha," which would consist of 39 counties. Greenbrier, Pocahontas, Hampshire, Hardy, Berkeley, Morgan, and Jefferson Counties would also join the new state if a majority of voters approved doing so. Rice and Brown, *West Virginia*, 123.

18 David R. Zimring, "'Secession in Favor of the Constitution': How West Virginia Justified Separate Statehood During the Civil War," *West Virginia History*, New Series, Vol. 3, No. 2 (Fall 2009), 24.

19 "West Virginia—Free or Slave," *Wheeling Intelligencer*, February 12, 1862.

20 Constitution of West Virginia, http://www.wvculture.org/history/statehood/constitution.html

being shortly put down in the State, I deem it important that I should issue a circular letter to the people. . . calling upon them to co-operate with me in restoring the government of the State in accordance with the Ordinance of the convention . . . at Wheeling on the 11th of June 1861."[21] The President responded a few days later with one of his famous quips. "Yours of the 14th received. Make haste slowly," said the President. "Things are improving by time. Draw up your proclamation carefully, and, if you please, let me see it before issuing."[22]

On April 3, 1862, the voters approved the new constitution by the lopsided count of 18,862 to 514.[23] Three counties—Jefferson, Berkeley and Frederick—did not participate in the vote. Jefferson and Berkeley Counties, viewed with suspicion by the Reorganized Government, were occupied by Union troops assigned to guard the B&O Railroad but held close ties to the eastern establishment by virtue of their slave-based agricultural economies. Because the B&O ran through these counties, the new government intended to incorporate them into West Virginia. Not trusting the outcome of the vote, these counties were simply excluded from participating in the election.[24]

Greenbrier County, located in the southeastern region of the area that made up the new state, held strong pro-secessionist sentiment. It did not send a single delegate to either Wheeling Convention, and was not represented in the Reorganized Government. It sent no delegates to the First West Virginia Constitutional Convention of 1861-1862, and reported no election returns from the referendum to approve the proposed constitution. Numerous residents of Greenbrier County enlisted in the Confederate army. Nevertheless, and despite not voting for its inclusion in the new state, Greenbrier County was also involuntarily pulled out of Virginia and dragged into West Virginia.[25]

Edward A. Pollard was one of the editors of the *Richmond Examiner* during this period. Pollard examined the cause of the loss of western Virginia in 1862. "We have already adverted to the causes which contributed to make the

21 Pierpont to Lincoln, March 14, 1862, Pierpont Papers.

22 Basler, *Collected Works of Abraham Lincoln,* 5:166.

23 Senate Misc. Doc. No. 98, 37th Congress, 2nd Session, 2-3.

24 *Virginia v. West Virginia,* 78 U.S. 39, 57, 11 Wall. 39 (1871). This important fact will be discussed at length, *infra.*

25 Otis K. Rice, *A History of Greenbrier County* (Lewisburg, WV: Greenbrier County Historical Society, 1986), 261.

[military] campaign in western Virginia a failure," he wrote in 1862. "The case which furnished the most popular excuse for its ineffectiveness—the disloyalty of the resident population—was, perhaps, the least adequate of them of them all. That disloyalty has been hugely magnified by those interested, in finding excuses in it for their own inefficiency and disappointment of public expectation. While Maryland, Kentucky, and other regions of the South, which not only submitted to Lincoln, but furnished him with troops, were not merely excused, but were the recipients of overflowing sympathy, and accounted a charitable stretch of imagination 'sister States' of the Southern Confederacy, an odium, cruelly unjust, was inflicted upon western Virginia, despite of the fact that this region was enthralled by Federal troops, and, indeed, had never given much evidences of sympathy with the Lincoln government as had been manifested both by Maryland and Kentucky in their State elections, their contributions of troops, and other acts of deference to the authorities in Washington. It is a fact, that even now, 'Governor Pierpont', the creature of Lincoln, cannot get one-third of the votes in a single county in western Virginia. It is a fact, that the Northern journals admit that in a large portion of this country, it is unsafe for Federal troops to show themselves unless in large bodies."[26] This was a remarkably clear-eyed analysis for so early in the war.

Article IV, Section 3, Clause 1 of the United States Constitution provides the mechanism for adding new states to the Union:

> New States may be admitted by the Congress into this Union; but no new State shall be formed or erected within the Jurisdiction of any other State; nor any State be formed by the Junction of two or more States, or Parts of States, without the Consent of the Legislatures of the States concerned as well as of the Congress.[27]

In order for the new State of West Virginia to be admitted to Congress, the legislatures of both Virginia and West Virginia had to approve the split. This proved to be an interesting bit of sophistry by the legislature of the so-called "Reorganized Government" of Virginia. The "Reorganized Government" evaded this requirement by claiming to represent all citizens of Virginia, and not just those seeking to secede from the rest of the Commonwealth. This legal

---

26 Edward A. Pollard, *The First Year of the War* (Richmond: West & Johnston, 1862), 177.

27 U.S. Constitution, Article. IV, Section 3, Clause 1.

sleight of hand provided the constitutional mechanism whereby West Virginia joined the Union.

On May 6, Governor Pierpont addressed the legislature. "The Constitution of the United States provides that 'no new State shall be formed or erected within the jurisdiction of any other State, without the consent of the Legislature of the State concerned, as well as of the Congress,'" he said. "Therefore, to complete the work which has been commenced, of the division of the State, it requires the consent of the Legislature of Virginia and the assent of Congress. Of course your honorable body will take such action in the premises as shall seem meet to you." He continued:

> It is urged by some that the movement is revolutionary - Those who urge this objection, do not understand the history, geography and social relation of our State. Geographically, the East is separated from the West by mountains which form an almost impassible barrier, as far as trade and commerce is concerned. The barrier is so great that no artificial means of intercourse have ever been made beyond a mud turnpike road. All the trade and commerce of the West is with other States, and not with Eastern Virginia. The two sections are entirely dissimilar in their social relations and institutions. While the East is largely interested in slaves, the West has none, and all the labor is performed by freemen. The mode and subjects of taxation in the State have been a source of irritation and indeed of strife and vexation, between the two sections for many years past, as well as that of representation in the Legislature. The subject of the division of the State has been agitated at one time and another ever since I can remember. I have no doubt but the rebellion has somewhat precipitated action on the subject at the present time, but of the ultimate division of the State I have not doubted for years. While I can see no possible advantage of the State remaining a unit, I can see many advantages to both sections by division.

Pierpont concluded with a flourish, "Gentlemen, if we could only get rid of the vast herd of the leaders in this rebellion in the State, and get their lands into the hands of honest, working men, I predict for the State a prosperity unexampled in its history. In ten years it would be more than a compensation for all that have gone, and all the slaves they have taken with them. I may have some other matters to submit to you, gentlemen, before you adjourn. If so I shall beg your indulgence and consideration."[28]

On May 13, 1862, with Pierpont's exhortations ringing in their ears, the legislature of the Reorganized Government passed this bill:

---

28 "Address to the Reorganized Government of Virginia, May 6, 181," Pierpont Papers.

An Act giving the consent of the Legislature of Virginia to the formation and erection of a new state within the jurisdiction of this state

§ 1. *Be it enacted by the General Assembly* that the consent of the Legislature of Virginia be, and the same is hereby, given to the formation and erection of the State of West Virginia, within the jurisdiction of this state, to include the Counties of Hancock &c. [forty-eight counties being named (being the forty-four first mentioned, with Pendleton, Hardy, Hampshire, and Morgan), but the Counties of Berkeley, Jefferson, or Frederick, not being included], *according to the boundaries and under the provisions set forth in the constitution for the said State of West Virginia and the schedule thereto annexed, proposed by the convention which assembled at Wheeling on the 26th day of November, 1861.*

§ 2. That the consent of the Legislature of Virginia be, and the same is hereby, given that the Counties of *Berkeley, Jefferson, and Frederick,* shall be included in and form part of the State of West Virginia WHENEVER the voters of said counties shall ratify and assent to the said constitution at an election held for the purpose, at such time and under such regulations as the commissioners named in the said schedule may prescribe.

§ 3. That this act shall be transmitted by the Executive to the senators and representatives of this Commonwealth in Congress, together with a certified original of the said constitution and schedule, and the said senators and representatives are hereby requested to use their endeavors to obtain the consent of Congress to the admission of the State of West Virginia into the Union.

§ 4. This act shall be in force from and after its passage.[29]

In short, a government created by the Unionist portion of Virginia—a minority of the total population—purported to speak for the entire state, including the majority of the state that supported secession. As one scholar put it, "To say that in this way, 'Virginia' gave her consent, is to deal in theory and fiction and to overlook realities."[30]

Citizens eligible to vote had to swear their fealty to the Reorganized Government. They were required to sign a form that stated, "I solemnly [affirm] that I will support the Constitution of the United States, and the laws made in pursuance thereof, as the supreme law of the land, anything in the Constitution and Laws of the State of Virginia, or in the Ordinances of the Convention, which assembled at Richmond on the 13th day of February, 1861, to the contrary notwithstanding: And that I will uphold and defend the Government of Virginia, as vindicated and restored by the Convention which

---

29 Quoted in *Virginia v. West Virginia, supra,* 78 U.S. at 42-43.

30 Randall, *Constitutional Problems Under Lincoln,* 453.

assembled at Wheeling on the 11th day of June, 1861."[31] Thus, each citizen was required to pledge his primary and unconditional loyalty to the U.S. Constitution first and then to the Reorganized Government as a condition of being able to cast a ballot.[32]

Judge John Jay Jackson, Sr., weighed in on the validity of these proceedings in a letter published in a Columbus, Ohio newspaper known for its Copperhead tendencies on May 17, 1862. "It was self-constituted, not called by authority of law, nor by the people, but only by a small fragment of the people. What legal authority could it, then, have?" he wrote. "Certainly none, and could only be regarded as a revolutionary movement on the part of those it purported to represent; and I think it questionable whether its proceedings are not repugnant to a majority of those in whose name it claimed to speak, for, as I am informed, the Ordinances, when submitted to the vote of the people did not receive one-third of the votes of the counties which purported to be represented." He concluded strongly, "Is it not obvious that it is only the bayonets of the United States that can give it any respectability as a legislative body—nay, that can even rescue it from contempt? It is not clearly a usurped Government—a Government founded in force?"[33]

Some thought that Pierpont was too zealous about suppressing opposition. Capt. Henry Lazelle, an inspector general officer, inspected Camp Chase in Columbus, Ohio, and reported to Col. William Hoffman, commandant of prisoners of war, about Joseph Darr of Wheeling, who conducted civilian arrests under the direction of Pierpont. "He is very zealous; perhaps too hasty and arbitrary," Lazelle wrote about Darr. "I have much to communicate to you of him and of the prisoners sent here by him. I have the official records of a number of prisoners sent herby him, seven of which state that the prisoner is charged with 'doing nothing.' One was taken from the almshouse where he had been nine years; another was a lunatic when arrested and is charged with being a lunatic. Many others have been sent here under equally slight charges whose cases I will soon submit to you, at least copies of their official records transmitted by him to Camp Chase, for I believe that it cannot be your desire that this camp should be filled to overflowing by political prisoners (made by

---

31 Oath of Loyalty, State Archives.

32 In 1862, only males could vote in West Virginia or Virginia. Judith Wellman, *The Road to Seneca Falls*, (Champaign: University of Illinois Press, 2010), 151-152.

33 "Letter from General J. J. Jackson," *The Crisis*, May 17, 1862.

half depopulating a section of country where the inhabitants are often compelled to expressions of apparent sympathy) arrested on frivolous charge, to be supported by the General Government and endure a long confinement. I have not expressed to him, however, a shade of any opinion upon this matter, or under any circumstances to other upon similar matters where there has been the possibility of doubt as to your action."[34] These were very serious charges, and if true, demonstrate a ruthless determination to bring about the desired result of creating a new state, no matter what the price.

Pierpont dispatched Van Winkle to Washington to press for admission to Congress of the representatives elected under the Restored Government. On July 6, after meeting with Van Winkle, Sen. Benjamin F. Wade of Ohio, a strong supporter of the new state movement and one of the leaders of the Radical Republicans, wrote to Pierpont, "Your Senators shall be admitted to their seats whenever they appear whether the old ones are vacated or not but I intend to have them vacated tomorrow."[35] Virginia Senators James M. Mason and Robert M. T. Hunter, who had cast their lot with the Confederacy, were formally expelled from the Senate on July 11, just as Wade had promised.

The legislature of the Reorganized Government then elected John Carlile and Waitman T. Willey as United States Senators from Virginia. "The first question of moment growing out of the Rebellion was the presentation of credentials by Messrs. Willey and Carlile, who claimed seats as senators from Virginia, the right to which was certified by the seal of the State with the signature of Francis H. Pierpont as governor," recalled Rep. James G. Blaine of Maine. "The credentials indicated that Mr. Willey was to take the seat vacated by Mason, and Mr. Carlile that vacated by Hunter. The loyal men of Virginia, especially from the western counties, finding that the regularly organized government of the State had joined the Rebellion, extemporized a government composed by the Union men of the Legislature which had been in session the preceding winter in Richmond."[36]

Sen. James A. Bayard, Jr. of Delaware opposed the seating of Willey and Carlile. "You are undertaking," he said, "to recognize a government of the State of Virginia which is not the regular State government. Even though the State

---

34 *OR*, Series II, 4:196.

35 Wade to Pierpont, July 6, 1863, Pierpont Papers.

36 James G. Blaine, *Twenty Years of Congress: From Lincoln to Garfield*, 2 vols. (Norwich, CT: The Henry Bill Publishing Co., 1884), 1:315.

Sen. James Bayard of Delaware,
who opposed statehood.

(Library of Congress)

may be in what you call a state of
rebellion, you are bound to take notice
of the fact that Mr. Letcher is the
Governor of Virginia . . . If you say he is
in rebellion, that does not authorize a
portion of the people of Virginia to
form a legislature for the purpose of
electing senators to take seats in this
body. You have no authority to create a
new state out of part of an existing State."[37]

After a great deal of contentious debate, Congress decided that the
Wheeling legislature spoke for the entire state of Virginia and seated Willey and
Carlile.[38] The motion to seat them passed 35-5.[39] Three men from the
northwestern part of the state were elected to the House of Representatives:
attorney Jacob B. Blair, attorney William G. Brown, and businessman Kellian V.
Whaley. Loyal members were also elected to the Virginia state legislature with
the understanding that they would not report to Richmond, but would instead
convene somewhere in northwestern Virginia at some later date as part of
Pierpont's Restructured Government.[40]

And with that, Restored Government set the wheels of statehood for West
Virginia into motion.

37 *Congressional Globe*, 37th Cong., 1st Sess., 103.

38 "The Election for Senators Yesterday," *Wheeling Intelligencer*, July 10, 1861.

39 *Congressional Globe*, 37th Cong., 1st Sess., 109.

40 Ambler, *Francis H. Pierpont*, 92.

CHAPTER SIX

Congress Debates Statehood

ONCE the Reorganized Government's legislature approved the split, West Virginia statehood required the consent of Congress.[1] Sen. Orville H. Browning, an Illinois Republican ally of Lincoln's, called it "a vast question" that he opposed.[2] On May 29, 1862, Senator Waitman T. Willey, from Morgantown, submitted a petition for the admission of West Virginia in the U. S. Senate in a speech setting forth the causes and conditions in Virginia that had led to the current state of affairs.[3] The Senate referred the legislation to the Committee on Territories, chaired by Sen. Benjamin F. Wade of Ohio. Wade, in turn, assigned Carlile, a member of the committee, to prepare

---

1 Art. IV, Sect. 3, United States Constitution.

2 Theodore Calvin Pease and James G. Randall, eds., *The Diary of Orville Hickman Browning*, 2 vols. (Springfield, IL: Illinois Historical Society, 1925), 1:550.

3 Willey was a 52-year-old lawyer from Morgantown who had been involved in local politics in the area for a number of years prior to these events. Although he was a slave owner, he was a staunch Unionist and was elected as a delegate to both Wheeling Conventions. He was then elected by the Reorganized Government to complete the term of Sen. James M. Mason, who had resigned his office to cast his lot with the Confederacy. He later won and served a full term as Senator for West Virginia. Mason was one of the targets of the Jones-Imboden Raid of April 1863, which is discussed *infra. Biographical Directory of the United States Congress, 1774-Present*, http://bioguide.congress.gov/scripts/biodisplay.pl?index=W000484. For a comprehensive biography of Willey, see Ambler, *Waitman Thomas Willey*.

Sen. Benjamin F. Wade of Ohio, one of the leaders of the Radical Republicans, who strongly supported statehood.

(Library of Congress)

a bill providing for the admission of the new state, a choice that proved problematic.

Although Carlile had been one of the earliest and most vocal proponents of the new state concept, "it became evident that he was an enemy to the same," observed an early historian. "His opposition was first made apparent by his delay in the preparation of the bill. Nothing was heard of it until the 23rd day of June, when it came from the committee. Carlile's proposed legislation removed any doubt as to his hostility to statehood."[4] A modern historian aptly described Carlile as the Senate's 'most eloquent Copperhead."[5] It was known as Senate Bill No. 365, and it shocked supporters of the secession movement.[6]

The original version of Carlile's bill called for the addition of more counties to the new state and the gradual emancipation of slaves, which would have alienated some of the additional slaveholding counties in the Shenandoah Valley that Carlile proposed to add. Granville Parker, originally from

4 Lewis, *A History of West Virginia*, 382-383.

5 Bogue, *The Earnest Men: Republicans of the Civil War Senate*, 47. Carlile apparently never elaborated on his reasons for his very abrupt flip-flop of his position on these events. It seems clear that he held Copperhead propensities, meaning he wanted peace with the South. He did not support the position of the abolitionists. In the end, he seems to have been what we could today call a strict constructionist when it came to his interpretation of the Constitution's requirements for creating a new state from an old one, and it appears that the mechanism employed in the process made him uncomfortable. He obviously did not advocate such a position during the early months of 1861, but he was also the object of a great deal of vitriol and verbal abuse at the Richmond Secession Convention. Perhaps he was angry at his treatment and sought retribution against Virginia, but then had second thoughts. At some point, he apparently became troubled by the process by which the new state was being created, realized that he had the power to do something about it, and took steps to do so.

6 *Congressional Globe*, 37th Cong., 2nd Sess., 2942.

Massachusetts and one of the delegates to the Second Wheeling Convention and to the constitutional convention, called on Senator Wade to encourage the passage of the bill with its original boundaries. Wade described Carlile's conduct as "very extraordinary" and observed, "that some of the Committee had begun to distrust the sincerity of Mr. Carlile. He requested we should see Mr. Willey, and ask him to call at his room next morning. Mr. [Ralph] Leete and myself called on Mr. Willey in the morning, and delivered the message. His manner was grave and reticent, but said, I think, he had prepared an amendment he intended to offer, when the Bill came up again."[7]

Carlile's incomprehensible change of position triggered outrage and numerous calls for his resignation from all around the proposed new state. "Judging from the position taken by Carlile, in the start of this matter, and his present strange somersault, we must conclude he has been bought over by the East," declared an angry editorial that appeared in the *Ritchie County Press*.[8]

When Wade called up the bill on June 26th, Sen. Charles Sumner of Massachusetts offered an amendment requiring immediate emancipation through compliance with the Ordinance of 1787, providing for the organization of the Northwestern Territory and which banned slavery.[9] Opponents of statehood knew a requirement that all slaves in West Virginia be freed immediately as a condition of statehood doomed a new West Virginia. "It was probably this blow between the eyes of their fraudulent, shallow subterfuge, by Mr. Sumner, that pleased its originators, and encouraged the remnant passing through Wheeling shortly after, on their way home, to pronounce the new State dead," sniffed Parker.[10] Sensing that such an amendment would kill statehood, the Senate rejected the amendment by a vote of 24-11. Republicans cast seventeen of the 24 votes against the amendment.[11]

---

7 Parker, *The Formation of the State of West Virginia*, 142. Ralph Leete was a prominent attorney, newspaper editor and publisher, and ardent free-soiler from Ironton, Ohio who was active in Republican Party politics.

8 "John S. Carlile and the New State," *Ritchie County Press*, reprinted in the *Wheeling Intelligencer*, July 28, 1862.

9 The Ordinance of 1787 provided: "Within the State there shall neither be slavery nor involuntary servitude other than in punishment of crime whereof the party is convicted."

10 Parker, *The Formation of the State of West Virginia*, 147.

11 Blaine, *Twenty Years of Congress*, 1:462. Many northern newspapers shared Sumner's view that West Virginia was only desirable as a free state. McGregor, *The Disruption of Virginia*, 302.

Sen. Charles Sumner of Massachusetts, who would not support statehood unless slavery in West Virginia was abolished in the process.

(Library of Congress)

On July 1, Willey again called up the bill and a heated discussion ensued, involving Senators Wade, John P. Hale of New Hampshire, and Jacob Collamar of Vermont. Willey then offered a compromise: an amendment that he hoped would garner support from Senator Sumner by calling for gradual emancipation within the state. Willey also hoped that a gradual emancipation would be acceptable to West Virginians. His amendment first required emancipation of all slave children born in the new state after July 4, 1863.[12] The bill then provided that slaves under the age of ten would be free upon reaching age twenty-one, while slaves over ten years of age but under twenty-one would be emancipated at age twenty-five. Slaves over age twenty-one would remain in bondage. Willey's historic amendment condemned many slaves to continued bondage, but nevertheless contained an explicit, ultimate end to slavery.[13]

Carlile openly opposed the Willey Amendment. Carlile urged the matter be referred for ratification only if it was approved by a majority of West Virginia's *registered* voters, not just a majority of those who voted. He charged that Willey knew that his amendment would not pass in such a referendum, and argued again that the people did not want a new state.[14]

The presence of a substantial delegations of citizens from western Virginia disproved Carlile's argument. Supporters of the new state flocked to Washington to lobby Congress. Senator Wade, in particular, observed that

12 Rice and Brown, *West Virginia*, 147.

13 Ibid.

14 Parker, *The Formation of the State of West Virginia*, 149.

western Virginia had sent its "population here *en masse* to urge it upon this Congress to pass this measure."[15] Sen. John C. Ten Eyck of New Jersey also expressed his amazement. "I understand and believe that a vast majority of the people of Western Virginia are looking here with tears in their eyes . . . anxiously hoping that Western Virginia will be admitted as a state."[16]

In the meantime, Rep. William G. Brown, who represented Virginia in the House, feared that the statehood bill would fail in the Senate. He prepared his own statehood bill, which he introduced on June 26, five days before Willey called up the Senate bill for the last time. Willey accepted the provisions of Brown's bill.[17] Brown's bill provided:

An Act for the admission of the State of West Virginia into the Union, and for other purposes

Whereas the people inhabiting that portion of Virginia known as West Virginia did by a convention assembled in the City of Wheeling, on the 26th November, 1861, frame for themselves a constitution with a view of becoming a separate and independent state; *and whereas*, at a general election held in the counties composing the territory aforesaid on the 3d of May last, the said constitution was approved and adopted by the qualified voters of the proposed state; and whereas, the Legislature of Virginia, by an act passed on the 13th day of May, 1862, did give its consent to the formation of a new state within the jurisdiction of the said State of Virginia, to be known by the name of West Virginia and to embrace the following named counties, to-wit [the forty-eight counties mentioned in the above-quoted Virginia Act of May 13, 1862, were here set forth by name, and not including Berkeley or Jefferson]; *and whereas*, both the convention and the legislature aforesaid have requested that the new state should be admitted into the Union, and the constitution aforesaid being republican in form, Congress doth hereby consent that the *said forty-eight counties* may be formed into a separate and independent state; therefore,

Be it enacted &c., that the State of West Virginia be, and is hereby declared to be one of the United States of America, and admitted into the Union on an equal footing with the original states, in all respects whatsoever &c.[18]

Carlile, still determined to defeat any attempt to bring West Virginia into the Union, proposing that further action on the subject be postponed until the first Monday of the following December, after the fall recess. Both Senators

---

15 *Congressional Globe*, 37th Cong., 2d Sess., 3319.

16 Ibid., 3036-3038.

17 Parker, *The Formation of the State of West Virginia*, 149.

18 2 Stat. at Large, 633.

Rep. William G. Brown served in the Virginia
House of Delegates and was elected to the
United States House of Representatives in
1844. He was a delegate to both the 1850-51
constitutional convention and the Richmond
Convention in 1861. Brown was later a
congressman for the Reorganized
Government of Virginia and West Virginia.

(Library of Congress)

Wade and John C. Ten Eyck of New
Jersey opposed the delaying tactic.
Carlile's motion to postpone
discussion of the statehood bill failed
by a vote of 23-17.[19]

After the rejection of Carlile's
proposed delay failed, the Senate passed Brown's bill on July 10 by an identical
23-17 vote. Only one Democrat voted for the bill, Sen. Henry M. Rice of
Minnesota. Willey's gradual emancipation proposal worked as he had hoped.
Ironically, Carlile voted against the bill because of the emancipation provision.
Sen. Charles Sumner of Massachusetts also opposed the bill because it did not
call for the immediate emancipation of all slaves in West Virginia. Sumner saw
West Virginia as a new slave state, despite the relatively small number of
enslaved persons in the forty-eight counties. Sen. Lyman Trumbull of Illinois, a
Republican ally of Lincoln, voted against the bill for the same reason. He also
feared that the passage of the act would weaken Pierpont's Restored
Government.

The next day, July 11, William Hickey, chief clerk of the Senate, "appeared
at the bar of the House of Representatives, and informed that body that the
Senate had passed Senate Bill No. 365, and requested the concurrence of the
House therein."[20] Rep. John A. Bingham of Ohio, whose district bordered on

19 Lewis, *A History of West Virginia*, 385.

20 Sylvester Myers, *Myers' History of West Virginia*, 2 vols. (Wheeling, WV: Wheeling News
Lithograph Co., 1913), 1:433.

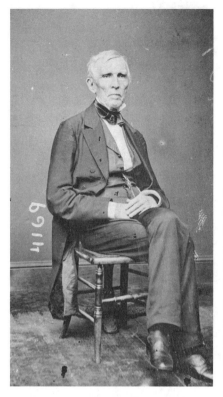

Rep. John Crittenden of Kentucky, who opposed statehood. One of Crittenden's sons was a major general in the Union army, and another was a major general in the Confederate army.

(Library of Congress)

northwestern Virginia, served as chairman of the House Committee on the Judiciary. Bingham made a motion that the bill be considered immediately, but Rep. Joseph E. Segar of Accomac County, Virginia, countered with a motion to table the bill. The motion to table failed by a vote of 70-44. Rep. Roscoe Conkling of New York then moved to delay consideration of the bill "until the second Tuesday in December next," which passed by a vote of 63-53. The statehood bill, therefore, languished until December.[21]

Carlile's betrayal of the cause frustrated and infuriated supporters of the new state. The General Assembly of the Restored Government unanimously passed a joint resolution asking Carlile to resign his position as Senator for "having failed to not only sustain the legitimate efforts of the federal government to suppress the insurrection, but having opposed by his votes in the senate and public speeches in and out of the senate opposed the bill for the admission of West Virginia into the Union."[22] Not surprisingly, Carlile refused to resign.

On December 9, 1862, the legislature at Wheeling passed a joint resolution, declaring, "That feeling the greatest anxiety and interest in the successful issue

---

21 *Congressional Globe*, 37th Congress, 2nd Session, 3397.

22 *Ordinances and Acts of the Restored Government of Virginia, Prior to the Formation of the State of West Virginia with the Constitution and Laws of the State of West Virginia, to March 2d, 1866* (Wheeling: John Frew, 1866), 71-72.

of the movement for a new State in West Virginia, we earnestly request the House of Representatives of the United States to take up and pass without alteration or amendment, the bill which passed the Senate of the United State on the 10th of July last."[23] This entreaty did the trick: the House of Representatives called up the bill on December 9 and began debating its merits in earnest.

Rep. John J. Crittenden of Kentucky, a respected conservative Whig, was a two-time former Attorney General of the United States. Crittenden had worked hard to fend off the secession crisis in 1861 while a member of the Senate. He now served as a member of the House of Representatives. "If Virginia were to-morrow to lay down . . . arms . . . and ask to be admitted," Crittenden asked, "what would you say to her if you had created a new State out of her territory?" He argued that because the Commonwealth of Virginia still existed, it should be restored to the Union whole and not dismembered once the rebellion ended.

He criticized the inherent conflict of interest. The drivers of statehood had also consented to the admission of the new state. "It is the party applying for admission consenting to the admission," he complained. "That is the whole of it." He continued, "This Legislature is here applying to be admitted as a new State, and at the same time and in the same character consenting that they themselves shall be so admitted! What does it amount to but that here is an application to make a new State at the instance of the parties desiring to be made a new State, and nobody else consenting, and nobody else left to consent to it?"[24]

Rep. Thaddeus Stevens of Pennsylvania, one of the leaders of the Radical Republicans in the House, viewed the division of Virginia as a consequence of the rebellion. In his view, the question of constitutionality was "a forced argument to justify a premeditated act." To Stevens, the citizens of Virginia who supported secession committed treason. He believed that West Virginia could be admitted to the Union "under our absolute power which the laws of war give us in the circumstances in which we are placed. I shall vote for this

23 Ibid., 71.

24 *Congressional Globe*, December 9, 1862, 37th Congress, 3rd Session, 46-47. Crittenden authored and offered the Crittenden Compromise in 1860 in an effort to prevent civil war from breaking out, a noble effort that failed. Crittenden's family history embodies the schisms that divided Kentucky during the Civil War: one son was a major general in the Confederate army, and another was a major general in the Union army.

Rep. Thaddeus Stevens of Pennsylvania, who felt that the war provided sufficient justification for adding West Virginia to the Union.

(Library of Congress)

bill," he thundered on the floor of the House, "upon that theory, and upon that alone; for I will not stultify myself by supposing that we have any warrant in the Constitution for this proceeding." Admitting the new state, therefore, was necessary to achieve the Union's war ends, with the means and the constitutional concerns of no consequence.[25]

In contrast, Rep. Martin F. Conway, a staunch abolitionist from Kansas and a supporter of the Free State movement in the 1850's, questioned the constitutionality of the legislation. "I have no objection to the erection of a new State in Western Virginia. I believe the inhabitants of that section are thoroughly loyal; that they are opposed to Slavery, and would make a prosperous and powerful State," he claimed in the floor debate. "I would be most happy to vote for their admission, if their application came to us in a proper and constitutional form. I wish we had organized a territorial government in Western Virginia at the outset of the rebellion. We could then have passed an enabling act, and the Territory could now come forward and ask to be admitted as a State in a manner to admit of no exception or dispute."

Conway firmly believed that the creation of the new state—which he facetiously referred to as the "Pierpont State"—was an unconstitutional act. "This Pierpont State is an institution of very recent origin. It started into existence about two years ago, and is a spontaneous production of the soil," he continued. "A number of individuals met at Wheeling, and, without any legal

25 Ibid., 50.

Rep. Joseph E. Segar of Virginia. While loyal to the Union, Segar opposed the dismemberment of Virginia.

(Library of Congress)

authority whatever, arranged a plan for a Government. Several persons have since been holding themselves out as officials of this organization, including Pierpont, the Governor; but to what extent it executes the actual functions of a Government does not satisfactorily appear."

He went on: "The argument in favor of the validity of the Wheeling Government is that the original State of Virginia fell into treason and became null and void, and caused a vacuum which could only be filled in this way. Now this is entirely unsatisfactory to me; for, in the first place, I do not see how a State can fall into treason: and secondly, if it should, what right would Mr. Pierpont have to assume the office of Governor over any other individual who might wish it? Where did the law come from which gave him his warrant? From a mob or a mass meeting? Neither mobs nor mass meetings make laws under our system."

Conway concluded: "In my judgment, a State can only be out of the Union (unless through a constitutional amendment) when its people have accomplished a revolution, or, in other words, have, by force of arms, become either a belligerent Power or absolutely independent. In my opinion, the situation with regard to our seceded States is that they are out of the Union by having acquired at least a belligerent character, thus securing an international status incompatible with their Federal relations. This places them to us in the position of a foreign Power with whom we are at war, and makes their territory subject to our sovereign will whenever we take it from them."[26]

---

26 "Making New States: Speech of Hon. Martin F. Conway, of Kansas, Delivered in the House of Representatives, Tuesday, Dec. 9, 1862," *New York Times*, December 16, 1862.

Rep. Jacob B. Blair was selected to fill a congressional seat before the outbreak of the Civil War, was re-elected in 1863, and was instrumental in convincing President Lincoln of the necessity of signing the statehood bill.

(Portrait File, West Virginia State Archives)

Even two members of Congress elected under the authority of the Restored Government opposed West Virginia statehood. Rep. Joseph Segar, a loyalist who represented a portion of Virginia under Union control near Hampton Roads, passionately argued against the bill. He claimed that a majority of voters in those counties proposed to make up the new state had not voted for the split. The disputed counties included 48,000 voters. Only 19,000 voted for the secession of northwestern Virginia. Although he was loyal to the Union, Segar begged, "Let there not be two Virginias; let us remain one and united. Do not break up the rich cluster of glorious memories and associations which gather over the named and the history of this ancient and glorious Commonwealth."[27]

"It is not within the power of a State to secede," insisted Representative Jacob B. Brown, one of the representatives appointed by the Restored Government. "The Constitution has prescribed the only mode in which a State can be relieved from all the obligations assumed by her; and although the State of Virginia could not commit treason, her functionaries might, and leave the legislative and executive power with the people, to whom they originally and primitively belonged." Brown also complained that every branch of the federal government recognized the Restored Government as the legitimate government of Virginia, citing letters to Governor Pierpont offering military support and addressing him as the governor of the state as evidence.[28]

27 *Congressional Globe*, 37th Cong., 3d Sess., 54-55.

28 Ibid., 39.

Rep. John Bingham of Ohio, one of the strongest advocates of statehood in the House of Representatives.

(Library of Congress)

Rep. Schuyler Colfax of Indiana pointed out that Secretary of the Treasury Salmon P. Chase gave the Restored Government the sum of $40,000, representing the proceeds of public land sales that could only be transferred to the legitimate government of Virginia. Therefore, the Restored Government acted as the legitimate representative of the people of Virginia.[29]

Rep. John A. Bingham of Ohio presented the strongest arguments for admitting the new state. He disputed Stevens' contention that a state must be understood as the majority of residents of that state, saying that this was only true insofar as "the majority act in subordination to the Federal Constitution, and to the rights of every citizen of the United States guarantied thereby."[30]

Bingham continued:

> [W]here the majority become rebels in arms, the minority are the State; and the minority, in that event, have a right to administer the laws, and maintain the authority of the State government, and to that end to elect a State Legislature and executive, by which they may call upon the Federal Government for protection "against domestic violence," according to the express guarantee of the Constitution. To deny this proposition is to say that when the majority in any State revolt against the laws, both State and Federal, and deny and violate all rights of the minority, that however numerous the minority may be, the State government can never be reorganized, nor the rights of the minority protected thereby so long as the majority are in the revolt.[31]

29 Ibid., 43-44.

30 Ibid., 57.

31 Ibid.

Bingham then quoted James Madison's words in *The Federalist* No. 43 as support for his interpretation of the Article IV, Section 4 of the U.S. Constitution, which guarantees each state a republican form of government (sometimes called the "Guarantee Clause"): "Why may not illicit combinations, for purposes of violence, be formed as well by a majority of a State as by a majority of a county or a district of the same State? And if the authority of the State ought, in the latter case, to protect the local magistracy, ought not the Federal authority, in the former, to support the State authority?"[32]

He noted that this was "precisely" the situation in the troubled state of Virginia. "I do recognize, in the language of Mr. Madison, even the rights of a minority in a revolted State to be protected, under the Federal Constitution, both by Federal law and by State law,'" he said. Bingham maintained, "the legislative powers, incapable of annihilation, have returned to the people at large for their exercise." In this instance, the people meant the loyal Unionists of the new state. "I say that the power remained with the loyal people of that State to call a convention and create a provisional government, which they did."[33]

Bingham then referred to the 1849 U.S. Supreme Court decision in *Luther v. Borden*, where the Court held that Congressional action regarding representation determined whether a given form of state government satisfied the Guarantee Clause.[34] "The ultimate power to decide that question, 'which of these bodies is the Legislature of Virginia?' is in the Congress of the United States." He concluded, "It has been affirmed by every branch of this Government, legislative, executive, and judicial, and more than once, that when the storm of revolution shakes the civil fabric of a State of the Union, the ultimate and final arbiter to determine who constitute the legislative and executive government of

32 Ibid., quoting Clinton Rossiter, ed., *The Federalist Papers* (New York: New American Library, 1961), 276. Article IV, Section 4, of the Constitution provides: "*The United States shall guarantee to every state in this union a republican form of government*, and shall protect each of them against invasion; and on application of the legislature, or of the executive (when the legislature cannot be convened) against domestic violence." (emphasis added)

33 Ibid., 58.

34 48 U.S. 1 (1849).

that State, and hold its great trust of sovereignty, is the Congress of the United States, or the President acting by authority of an act of Congress."[35]

After so much passionate debate, the statehood bill passed the House by a vote of 96-55 on December 10, 1862. Congress then sent the bill to Lincoln for his signature, a matter that remained unresolved in the President's mind.[36]

35 *Congressional Globe*, 37th Cong., 3d Sess., 57.

36 Ibid., 37th Cong., 2nd Sess., 3320.

CHAPTER SEVEN

Lincoln and the Cabinet Debate the Constitutionality and Expediency of Admitting the New State

On December 15, Sen. Orville H. Browning, who voted against the statehood bill, went to the White House to visit President Abraham Lincoln. He brought the statehood bill with him and handed it to Lincoln. "He [Lincoln] was distressed at its passage," observed Browning in his diary, "and asked me how long he could retain it before approving or vetoing. I told him ten days. He wished he had more. I replied I would give him a few days more. That I would not now lay it before him, but would retain it and furnish him a copy to examine, which I did."[1]

At the behest of Attorney General Edward Bates, Lincoln asked the six members of his cabinet for their written opinions regarding the constitutionality and political expediency of admitting West Virginia to the Union.[2] Relations between Lincoln and his cabinet were strained. According to

---

1 Pease and Randall, *The Diary of Orville Hickman Browning*, 1:596.

2 Lincoln to his cabinet, December 23, 1862, included in John G. Nicolay and John Hay, eds., *Abraham Lincoln Complete Works Comprising His Speeches, Letters, State Papers and Miscellaneous Writings*, 2 vols. (New York: The Century Co., 1894), 2:283. Caleb B. Smith had served as Secretary of the Interior from March 5, 1861 until December 31, 1862, when he resigned in order to accept an appointment as a United States District Judge in his home state of Indiana.

Sen. Orville Browning of Illinois, a Republican friend of Abraham Lincoln. Browning personally delivered the statehood bill to Lincoln.

(Library of Congress)

Doris Kearns Goodwin, Lincoln's cabinet was a "team of rivals." Several of the cabinet officers were Lincoln's primary rivals for the leadership of the Republican Party. In particular, Secretary of the Treasury Salmon P. Chase held presidential ambitions, and even considered challenging Lincoln for the Republican nomination in 1864. Secretary of State William H. Seward was Lincoln's primary rival for the nomination in 1860.[3]

Cabinet meetings were, as Secretary of the Navy Gideon Welles noted, "infrequent, irregular, and without a system." Seward was often absent from the few meetings that were held, but there was "a reluctance to discuss and bring to a decision any great question without him," although, as Welles observed, Seward somehow managed to spend "a considerable portion of every day with the President, patronizing and instructing him, hearing and telling anecdotes, relating interesting details of occurrences in the Senate, and inculcating his political party notions." On the occasions when Secretary of War Edwin M. Stanton appeared, it was only to "whisper to the President, or take dispatches or the papers from his pocket and go into a corner with the President."[4] The team of rivals was dysfunctional.

He had already left Washington to return to Indiana when Lincoln called for the opinions of his cabinet, and did not participate in the discussions. No replacement for Smith had yet been appointed, leaving only six cabinet officers to opine on the constitutionality and expediency of admitting West Virginia to the Union.

3 For more on the tumultuous relationship between Lincoln and his cabinet officers, see Doris Kearns Goodwin, *Team of Rivals: The Political Genius of Abraham Lincoln* (New York: Simon & Schuster, 2005).

4 Edgar T. Welles, ed., *The Diary of Gideon Welles, Secretary of the Navy Under Lincoln and Johnson*, 3 vols. (Boston: Houghton-Mifflin, 1911), 1:124 and 136 and 2:58.

Consequently, Welles and Secretary of the Treasury Chase were left wondering whether they should even bother to attend cabinet meetings. "We...are called members of the Cabinet," complained Chase to his fellow Ohioan, Sen. John Sherman, "but are in reality only separate heads of departments, meeting now and then for talk and whatever happens to come uppermost, not for grave consultation on matters concerning the salvation of the country. . . . No regular and systematic reports of what is done are made, I believe, even to the President: certainly not to the so-called Cabinet."[5]

Chase, in particular, was problematic.[6] Welles described Chase as having "a good deal of intellect, knows the path where duty points, but in his calmer moments, resolves to pursue it. But . . . He has inordinate ambition, intense selfishness for official distinction and power to do for the country, and considerable vanity. These traits impair his moral courage; they make him a sycophant with the truly great, and sometimes arrogant towards the humble . . . .

5 Robert Bruce Warden, *An Account of the Private Life and Public Services of Salmon Portland Chase* (Cincinnati: Wilstach, Baldwin & Co., 1874), 484.

6 Salmon Portland Chase was born in Cornish, New Hampshire on January 13, 1808. His father died when he was nine years old, leaving his mother with ten children. Young Salmon went to live with his uncle, Bishop Philander Chase, an important figure in the Episcopal Church. He studied in the schools of Windsor, Vermont, Worthington, Ohio, and Cincinnati College before enrolling at Dartmouth University. He graduated from Dartmouth with distinction in 1826, earning membership in Phi Beta Kappa. He then moved to Washington, D.C., where he opened a classical school and studied law under U.S. Attorney General William Wirt. He was admitted to the bar in 1829. In 1830, he moved to Loveland, Ohio and opened a law practice in Cincinnati. He became committed to the cause of abolitionism and defended escaped slaves in court. He was elected to Cincinnati City Council in 1840 as a member of the Whig Party. He left the Whig Party and became the leader of the Liberty Party in Ohio for seven years. In 1848, he became one of the founders of the Free-Soil Party, and worked for the election of Martin Van Buren as president. From 1849-1855, he served in the United States Senate, where he opposed the Compromise of 1850 and the Kansas-Nebraska Act of 1854. He helped found the Republican Party and was elected Governor of Ohio in 1855, serving until 1860. He ran for the Republican nomination for president in 1860, but received only 49 votes at the convention. He threw his support to Lincoln, and remained one of the leaders of the Republican Party. He was elected to the Senate in 1860, but two days later, Lincoln appointed him as Secretary of the Treasury. He served as Secretary of the Treasury until his resignation in June 1864. That October, after the death of Chief Justice Roger B. Taney, Lincoln appointed Chase as the Supreme Court's Chief Justice. The Senate approved him that day, and he immediately took office. As Chief Justice, he presided over several important Supreme Court cases as well as the impeachment trial of President Andrew Johnson. Chase died of a stroke on May 7, 1873, was buried in Oak Hill Cemetery in Washington, D.C. and was reinterred in Cincinnati's Spring Grove Cemetery in 1886. For a comprehensive biography of Chase, see John Niven, *Salmon P. Chase: A Biography* (New York and London: Oxford University Press, 1995).

That he is irresolute and wavering, his instinctive sagacity prompting him rightly, but his selfish and vain ambition turning him to error is unquestionably true."[7] In 1864, Chase described himself as "too earnest, too antislavery, and, say, too radical."[8] These traits created a great deal of tension in the operations of the cabinet.

Only a day after Lincoln met with Senator Browning about West Virginia statehood, a group of more than thirty Republican Senators convened to express their frustration and anger with the administration, and in particular, with Lincoln's refusal to relieve Maj. Gen. George B. McClellan of command of the Army of the Potomac until November 1862. Seward was the primary target of their frustration, as they blamed him for Lincoln's conservative approach to ending the rebellion. Concerned, Lincoln met with a delegation of nine of the Republican Senators on the nights of December 18 and 19 to listen to their complaints and to defend his administration.

The remaining cabinet members also attended the December 19 meeting. They heard Lincoln admit that, while the cabinet did not meet regularly, he kept them informed of the most important issues. According to Lincoln, the cabinet usually agreed with the decisions that Lincoln made. Lincoln believed that Chase, who was one of the leaders of the Radical Republican movement, was responsible for "all the mischief" and put him on the spot. Lincoln asked Chase directly whether he supported Lincoln's description of the cabinet. Chase reluctantly agreed, but told the senators that the cabinet was not asked to discuss many important issues. The other cabinet members had little to say, and the meeting ended about midnight.

On the morning of December 20, Lincoln summoned Chase, Welles, and Stanton. He told them that he had summoned them because the "matter was giving me great trouble," prompting Chase to say that he had prepared a letter of resignation. "Where is it?" asked Lincoln.

"I brought it with me," responded Chase. "I wrote it this morning."

"Let me have it," said the President, snatching the letter of resignation from Chase's hand. He opened the letter. "This," declared Lincoln, "cuts the Gordian knot" as a look of satisfaction spread across his face. "I can dispose of this subject now without difficulty. I see my way clear."

---

7 Welles, *The Diary of Gideon Welles*, 2:121.

8 David Herbert Donald, ed., *Inside Lincoln's Cabinet: The Civil War Diaries of Salmon P. Chase* (New York: Longmans, Green & Co., 1954), 231.

Chase was shocked, as he had not expected such a response from Lincoln. Stanton also offered to resign.

"You may go to your department," Lincoln said to Stanton. "I don't want yours." He then turned to Chase. "This," he said, as he held out Chase's letter, "is all I want; this relieves me; my way is clear; the trouble is ended. I will detain you no longer." The three cabinet officers left the Oval Office. Lincoln ultimately declined to accept Chase's resignation, but he retained the letter of resignation for future use.[9]

Three days later, in the midst of tumult, Lincoln asked his cabinet for their opinions on West Virginia statehood. The six sitting cabinet officers split three to three on the questions of whether the act of admitting West Virginia to the Union was constitutional and expedient, prompting a frustrated Lincoln to say, "[a] President is as well off without a Cabinet as with one."[10] The written opinions of the six cabinet officers are presented in their entirety in Appendix A to this book.

Attorney General Bates outspokenly opposed the idea of dismembering Virginia.[11]In August 1861, while the constitutional convention proceeded in Wheeling, he responded to a letter from one of the delegates.[12] "The formation

---

9 Welles, *The Diary of Gideon Welles*, 1:196-204.

10 Lewis, *History of West Virginia*, 399.

11 Edward Bates was born on his family's plantation in Goochland County, Virginia on September 4, 1793. He was tutored at home as a boy and then attended the Charlotte Hall military academy in Maryland. He served in the War of 1812 before moving to St. Louis in the Missouri territory with his brother James in 1814. James immediately began practicing law there while Edward studied law with the judge for the Louisiana Territory. Bates practiced law in Missouri once he gained admission to the bar. In 1820, he was elected as a delegate to Missouri's first constitutional convention, and wrote the preamble to the state's new constitution. He was appointed as Missouri's first attorney general. He was a Whig who shared the political views of Kentucky Senator Henry Clay. After flirting with the Know-Nothing Party in the early 1850's, Bates joined the Republican Party and was one of its primary candidates for the 1860 presidential nomination. Lincoln appointed him attorney general in 1861, and he held that position until he resigned in 1864. He returned to St. Louis and continued to be involved in political matters and the practice of law until his death on March 25, 1869. Bates was the first cabinet member from a state west of the Mississippi River. He was buried in Bellefontaine Cemetery in St Louis. For a full-length biography, see Marvin R. Cain, *Lincoln's Attorney General: Edward Bates of Missouri* (Columbia: University of Missouri Press, 1965).

12 For example, on December 27, 1862, the *Alexandria Gazette* reported, "It is reported that Attorney General Bates regards the admission of West Virginia as unconstitutional. His

Attorney General Edward Bates, who strongly believed that the statehood bill was unconstitutional. *(Library of Congress)*

of a new State out of Western Virginia is an original, independent act of revolution. I do not deny the power of revolution. I do not call it right, for it is never prescribed, it exists in force only, and has and can have no law but the will of the revolutionists," he declared. "Any attempt to carry it out involves a plain breach of both the Constitutions—of Virginia and of the Nation."[13]

Bates candidly expressed his opinions about the statehood bill in his personal diary. He believed that the statehood bill "was forced thro' Congress rapidly and secretly," and that it was unconstitutional. He felt that "extremists" rammed the legislation through both houses of Congress, and called the bill "monstrous."[14] Hence, he came out strongly against the bill in his opinion letter to Lincoln.

Bates believed that the act was unconstitutional because the Wheeling government's actions in consenting to the split were a sham. First, he pointed out that the Restored Government represented only a fraction of the population of Virginia, perhaps 25%. More importantly:

[T]he Legislature which pretends to give the consent of Virginia to her own dismemberment is (as I am credibly informed) composed chiefly if not entirely of men who represent those forty-eight counties which constitute the new State of West Virginia. The act of consent is less in the nature of a law than of a contract. It is a grant

opinion, it is thought, will have considerable influence in preventing the President from signing the bill."

13 Quoted in Parker, *The Formation of the State of West Virginia*, 49.

14 Howard K. Beale, ed., *The Diary of Edward Bates 1859-1866* (Washington, DC: U.S. Government Printing Office, 1933), 271.

Secretary of the Navy Gideon Welles, who opposed statehood. *(Library of Congress)*

of power, an agreement to be divided. And who made the agreement, and with whom? The representatives of the forty-eight counties with themselves! Is that fair dealing? Is that honest legislation? Is that a legitimate exercise of constitutional power by the Legislature of Virginia? It seems to me that it is a mere abuse, nothing less than attempted secession, hardly veiled under the flimsy forms of law.

He concluded:

I consider this proceeding revolutionary, all the more wrong, because it is needlessly begun at a moment when we are strained to the uttermost, in efforts to prevent a far greater revolution. If successful, it will be "at once an example and fit instrument" for tearing into pieces the regions further south, and making out of the fragments a multitude of feeble communities. And, for what good end? We may thereby stimulate the transient passions and prejudices of men in particular localities, and gratify the personal ambition and interest of a few leaders in those little sections. We may disjoint the fabric of our national government, and destroy the balance of power in Congress, by a flood of senators representing a new brood of fragmentary States.

And now, Sir, I give it as my opinion, that the bill in question is unconstitutional; and also, by its own intrinsic demerits, highly inexpedient.

And I persuade myself that Congress, upon maturer thought, will be glad to be relieved by a veto, from the evil consequences of such improvident legislation.[15]

Bates was one of three cabinet officers to oppose the bill.

Secretary of the Navy Gideon Welles also opposed the bill.[16] Like Bates, Welles candidly expressed his opinion in his diary. "The House has voted to

---

15 Bates to Lincoln, December 27, 1862, Lincoln Papers.

16 Gideon Welles was born in Glastonbury, Connecticut on July 1, 1802, the son of a shipping merchant and ardent Jeffersonian. The Welles family was prominent and his ancestors included both politicians and seafarers. His father was a delegate to the convention that drafted Connecticut's first post-Revolutionary constitution. He was educated at the Episcopal

create and admit Western Virginia as a State," he wrote on December 11. "This is not the time to divide the old Commonwealth. The requirements of the Constitution are not complied with, as they in good faith should be, by Virginia, by the proposed new State, nor by the United States. I find that [Postmaster General Montgomery] Blair, with whom I exchanged a word, is opposed to it." Welles noted that Lincoln "thinks the creation of this new State at this time is of doubtful expediency."[17]

On December 26, he related a conversation he had had with Secretary of War Edwin M. Stanton, who served as the final Attorney General of the United States during the administration of President James Buchanan. Stanton favored the bill, and could not understand why Welles opposed it. Welles explained his position clearly:

> I thought our duties were constitutional, not experimental, that we should observe and preserve the landmarks, and that mere expediency should not override constitutional obligation. This action was not predicated on the consent of the people of Virginia, legitimately expressed; was arbitrary and without proper authority; was such a departure from, and an undermining of, our system that I could not approve it and feared it was the beginning of the end. As regarded a Free State south of the Ohio, I told him the probabilities were that pretty much all of them would free by [January 1, 1863] when the Proclamation emancipating slaves would be published. The Rebels had appealed to arms in vindication of slavery, were using slaves to carry on the War, and they must be content with results of that issue; the arbitrament of arms to with they had appealed would be against them. This measure, I thought, we were justified in

---

Academy in Cheshire, Connecticut, and then earned a degree from the American Literary, Scientific and Military Academy at Norwich, Vermont (now Norwich University). He was admitted to the bar, but became a journalist, founding, publishing and editing the *Hartford Times*. From 1827-1835, he served as a Democratic representative to the Connecticut House of Representatives. He held several other appointed offices in Connecticut, and, like his father, was an ardent Jacksonian Democrat who worked closely with Martin Van Buren and James K. Polk. However, in 1854, he joined the Republican Party. Lincoln appointed him Secretary of the Navy in 1861, and Lincoln fondly referred to him as "Father Neptune." Andrew Johnson retained him as Secretary of the Navy after Lincoln's assassination, but he and Seward helped to found the National Union Party in 1866 to support the reconciliation policies espoused by Johnson. Welles remained loyal to Johnson, supporting the President through his impeachment order. When Welles left politics, he spent the rest of his life supporting the Navy and writing and editing. He died at the age of 75 on February 12, 1878 and was buried in Cedar Hill Cemetery in Hartford, Connecticut. For a full-length biography of "Father Neptune," see John Niven, *Gideon Welles: Lincoln's Secretary of the Navy* (New York and London: Oxford University Press, 1973).

17 Welles, *The Diary of Gideon Welles*, 1:191.

adopting on the issue presented and as a military necessity, but the breaking up of a State by the General Government without the prescribed forms, innate right, and the consent of the people fairly and honestly expressed, was arbitrary and wrong.

"Stanton attempted no defense," he concluded.[18]

In his formal opinion to Lincoln, Welles wrote:

> Were Virginia, or those parts of it not included in the proposed new State invaded and held in temporary subjection by a foreign enemy instead of the insurgents, the fragment of territory and population which should successfully repel the enemy and adhere to the Union would doubtless, during such temporary subjection, be recognised, and properly recognised, as Virginia. When, however, this loyal fragment goes farther, and not only declares itself to be Virginia, but proceeds, by its own act, to detach itself permanently and forever from the commonwealth, and to erect itself into a new State within the jurisdiction of the State of Virginia, the question arises whether this proceeding is regular, legal, right, and, in honest good faith, conformable to, and within the letter and spirit of, the Constitution.

He pointed out that the primary duty of the federal government is to maintain the integrity of the states, and that:

> It would be no trivial act to break up, even in the most regular and formal manner, and in time of peace, an ancient commonwealth; and unless the people themselves, in the mode prescribed by the Constitution, deliberately and voluntarily consent to the formation or erection of a new State within the jurisdiction of an old one, Congress should not, by any exercise of questionable authority, attempt to enforce a division or separation. An observance of the rights of the States is conducive to the union of the States, and a regard for both should prevent such hasty action as will seriously affect either. The Federal government is not authorized to divide or dismember a State; and yet there is no denying the fact that on the approval or rejection of this act, presented to the Executive at this unfortunate time for calm and deliberate action, depends the division or integrity of the State of Virginia. Can it be said to be the wish of the people of Virginia that a new State shall be erected within its jurisdiction, or that they have duly signified their consent to it?

He concluded:

> Believing as I firmly do in the restoration of the Union and the establishment of the Government on a basis more enduringly satisfactory and correct than ever heretofore, I also anticipate a state of things that will, in the progress of events, make north-western Virginia serviceable in promoting the great cause of State and national

18 Ibid., 208-209.

Postmaster General Montgomery Blair, who opposed statehood. *(Library of Congress)*

regeneration. The loyal spirit of West Virginia will, I trust and believe, infuse itself into the disloyal section, and render the whole united people of that great commonwealth, which has unsurpassed natural advantages, as conspicuous in the future as in the past in support of the Union, the Constitution, and the rights of man. It is undoubtedly the true policy of Virginia to preserve its territorial integrity; and the day cannot be distant when, under an improved dispensation, the people beyond the mountains, no less than those of the valley and of the tide-water section, will be converts to that policy, and satisfied that a division would be unwise and inexpedient.

I do not therefore deem it expedient that West Virginia should be erected into a State, nor advise that the bill be approved.[19]

Welles did not consider himself to an authority on constitutional law. but his analysis drew strength from the precise text of the document.

Postmaster General Montgomery Blair was the third member of the cabinet to oppose the admission of West Virginia to the Union.[20] Blair drew a

---

19 Welles to Lincoln, December 29, 1862, Lincoln Papers.

20 Montgomery Blair was born in Franklin County, Kentucky on May 10, 1813 as the son of Francis Preston Blair, editor of the *Washington Star*, and a prominent figure in Democratic Party politics during the era of Andrew Jackson. Blair graduated from the United States Military Academy in 1835, and served in the Seminole War in Florida for one year before resigning his commission. He went to St. Louis, where he studied law. He was admitted to the bar in 1830 and opened a law office there. He served as U.S. Attorney from 1839-1843 and as a judge for six years. He moved to Maryland in 1852, and devoted most of his law practice to arguing cases before the United States Supreme Court, including arguing for the plaintiff in the Dred Scott case. Blair abandoned the Democratic Party in the wake of the Kansas-Nebraska Act and became one of the founders of the Republican Party in 1854. Four years after changing parties, Pres. James Buchanan removed him from his post as United States Solicitor in 1858. In 1861,

distinction between recognizing the representatives sent to Congress by the Restored Government of Virginia, and finding that the same government had consented to the creation of West Virginia. The "circumstances of the case" excused the irregularity of of the representatives from the Restored Government of Virginia, but not so the formation of the new state.

> But whilst it was just to the people of Western Virginia, whose country was not overrun by the rebel armies, to allow this representation, and for this purpose, and for the purposes of local government to recognize the State government instituted by them, it would be very unjust to the loyal people in the greater part of the State…to permit the dismemberment of their State without their consent.

Blair also asked, what of

> the loyal people in the greater part of the State, who are now held in subjection by rebel armies, and who far exceed in number the twenty thousand who have voted on the constitution for Western Virginia, to permit the dismemberment of their state without their consent. It is no fault of the loyal people of Virginia that they are not in condition to be heard on this question according to the forms of law. The State is held by armies which they could not resist, and which so far the Federal Government itself has not been able to eject from the State. If these armies were driven from the State, and the people still refused to recognize their obligations to the General Government, their wishes might be properly disregarded in the action of that government with respect to the question before us. But until that is done, I think a measure which affects them so greatly should be postponed. If hurried through now, it will probably be the source of lasting irritation between the people of the two sections of the State—and it will I am sure form the only obstacle, but a most serious one to an immediate restoration of the proper relations of the State to the General Government after the rebel armies are driven from it.

Lincoln appointed him postmaster general with the expectation that his hardline position on the Southern states would counterbalance the more conciliatory positions of other cabinet members. In July 1864, troops of Lt. Gen. Jubal A. Early's command burned Blair's handsome home in Silver Spring, Maryland. He resigned his post in September 1864 after implementing significant reforms in the postal service. Disagreeing with Republican policy regarding Reconstruction, he reverted to the Democratic Party. His brother Francis Blair, Jr. was the Democratic nominee for vice president in 1868. Blair resumed practicing law and made an unsuccessful run for Congress in 1882. Blair died on July 27, 1883 and was buried in Rock Creek Cemetery in Washington, D.C. For a full-length biography of Blair, see Madison Davis, *The Public Career of Montgomery Blair, Particularly with Reference to His Services as Postmaster General of the United States* (Washington, DC: Columbia Historical Society, 1910).

He concluded:

> The subject is one which will engage public attention hereafter if not immediately so that our action on it will characterize the administration in the annals of the country—It is with the rights of the States we are dealing—we have heard indeed something too much of such things lately and some persons may therefore be disposed at this moment to ignore them altogether—But this will be found to be a great error.—The people of all the States have always manifested a wise solicitude for the just rights of the States & have never tolerated the slightest invasion of them—This arises not from mere State pride or vanity so ostentatiously displayed by Coxcombs—It is founded on the knowledge possessed by the thinking & controlling minds that the excellence of our system of government depends on carefully guarding those rights.—In dismembering the State which has still a hold on the hearts of our people as the land of Washington, Jefferson, Madison, Monroe and other immortal names, there should therefore be no room for debate on the legality of the act.[21]

The gist of Blair's objection—which was well-founded—was that the people of eastern Virginia, some of whom remained loyal, were not properly represented in the process of creating the new state.

Seward, Stanton, and Chase represented the hard line, Radical Republican wing of the cabinet. Not surprisingly, all three supported the admission of the new State. Stanton, a former Attorney General of the United States, was remarkably brief in his comments. Stanton saw no constitutional problem.[22]

---

21 Blair to Lincoln, December 26, 1862, Lincoln Papers.

22 Edwin McMasters Stanton was born in Steubenville, Ohio on December 19, 1814. He was descended from Quaker settlers from Massachusetts. He was educated at a private school and seminary behind his mother's home until he was 10, when he transferred to a school run by a Presbyterian minister. He had his first asthma attack at age 10 and realized that the asthma would prevent him from a life of physical activity, so he developed an interest in books and poetry. His father, a physician, died suddenly in 1827, when Edwin was 13, leaving his widow destitute. Edwin's mother opened a shop in the family house, and Edwin was forced to leave school to work in a local bookshop. Stanton enrolled at Kenyon College in 1831, but was forced to leave at the end of three semesters for financial reasons. While there, he converted to Episcopalianism and became an ardent abolitionist. He worked as a bookseller in Columbus, Ohio for a time to try to earn sufficient money to return to Kenyon, but failed. He then returned to Steubenville, where he studied law. He practiced law in Cadiz, Ohio, where he became involved in local politics, including the anti-slavery movement, and was elected county prosecutor. When his law partner was elected to the U.S. Senate, Stanton moved to Steubenville, and ran the law practice there. In 1847, he was admitted to the Pennsylvania bar and relocated to Pittsburgh. In 1856, he relocated to Washington, DC, where he established contacts with the Buchanan Administration. In 1858, Stanton went to California to represent the administration's interests there. He returned to Washington in 1859, and was the lead

Secretary of War Edwin M. Stanton, a former U.S. attorney general who supported statehood. *(Library of Congress)*

"The Constitution expressly authorizes a new State to be formed or erected within the jurisdiction of another State," he wrote. "I have been unable to perceive any point on which the act of Congress conflicts with the Constitution." Given that Stanton was not only a former Attorney General, but was also considered to be one of the foremost attorneys in the United States, such a simplistic approach is somewhat surprising.

As to the question of the expediency of admitting the new state, Stanton said:

By the erection of the new state, the Geographical boundary heretofore existing between the free and slave states will be broken, and the advantage of this upon every point of consideration surpasses all objections which have occurred to me on the question of expediency. Many prophetic dangers and evils might be specified, but it is safe to suppose that those who come after us will be as wise as ourselves and if what we deem evils be really such, they will be avoided. The present good is real and substantial, the future may safely be left in the care of those whose duty and interest may be involved in any possible future measures of legislation.[23]

defense counsel in the murder trial of Congressman Daniel E. Sickles. He then served as Attorney General of the United States for the last several months of the Buchanan Administration. Lincoln appointed him Secretary of War in 1862, and he held that position until 1868, when he resigned after his scheme to lead to the impeachment and removal of President Andrew Johnson failed. He resumed his law practice until his death on December 24, 1869 at age 55. President Ulysses S. Grant, Vice President Schuyler Colfax, the entire cabinet, the entire Supreme Court, Congressmen and prominent Army officers such as Gen. William T. Sherman all attended his funeral. He was buried in Oak Hill Cemetery in Washington, D.C. For a full-length biography of Stanton, see William Marvel, *Lincoln's Autocrat: The Life of Edwin Stanton* (Chapel Hill: University of North Carolina Press, 2015).

23 Stanton to Lincoln, December 26, 1862, Lincoln Papers.

Secretary of State William H. Seward, who supported statehood. *(Library of Congress)*

In short, the ends of the war effort justified the rendering of Virginia, regardless of the constitutionality of the issue. "Time would reveal that his opinions arose from situational motivation rather than legal principle," wrote Stanton's biographer, William Marvel, "at the close of hostilities, the same Radicals who had recognized the rump legislature's authority to approve the partition of Virginia ignored its legitimacy as a state government, and Stanton would be the first to reveal the inconsistency when it became politically convenient."[24]

Seward felt that the act of admitting the new state was not only constitutional, but also expedient.[25] On the question of constitutionality, he wrote:

---

24 Marvel, *Lincoln's Autocrat*, 269.

25 William H. Seward was born in Florida, Orange County, New York on May 16, 1801. His father was a wealthy landowner and slave owner. A bright student, Seward attended local schools and then enrolled in Union College at the age of 15. He was elected to Phi Beta Kappa, but did not graduate due to a quarrel with his father over money. He and a friend went to Putnam County, Georgia, where he served as the principal of a new private academy. His family persuaded him to return to New York in 1819, where he studied law for a year before returning to Union College to receive his degree with highest honors in 1820. He was admitted to the New York bar in 1822 and established a practice in Goshen, Cayuga County. He established a relationship with newspaper publisher Thurlow Weed and immersed himself in local politics. He joined the Anti-Mason Party in 1826, and opposed the candidacy of Andrew Jackson, a Mason, for president in 1828. In 1830, he was elected to the New York State Senate and joined the Whig Party in 1832. He was defeated in a race for governor in 1834, and returned to his law practice. In 1838, he was elected governor and served as governor of New York, where he became involved in the anti-slavery movement. He left office in 1842 after two terms and resumed his law practice in Auburn. In 1849, he was elected to the U.S. Senate, and served two terms there. In 1854, he became one of the founders of the Republican Party. He was one of the leading candidates for the Republican presidential nomination in 1860, but lost to Lincoln. He

Western Virginia is organized unquestionably with all the constitutional elements and faculties of a State, and with a republican form of government. It, therefore, has a title to be a candidate for admission into the Federal Union. Congress has power to admit new States, but it is a power restricted within certain limitations. One of these limitations is that no new State shall be formed or erected within the jurisdiction of any other State without the consent of that State as well as the consent of the new State and the consent of Congress. It is an undisputed fact that the new state of Western Virginia has been both formed and erected within the jurisdiction of the State of Virginia. Has the consent of the State of Virginia to the formation and erection of the State of West Virginia been given, or has it not been given? Upon this point the constitutionality of the Act of Congress now before me turns. The constituted and regular authorities of a State called the State of Virginia sitting at Wheeling, within the jurisdiction of that State, claiming to be the State of Virginia, and acting as such, have in a due and regular manner declared and given the consent of the State of Virginia to the formation and erection of the State of West Virginia within the jurisdiction of the State of Virginia. Thus far the case seems simple and clear. But it is just at this point that a complication begins. If we would unfold it successfully we must first state the existing facts in regard to the constitutional position of the State of Virginia, as well as those which belong to the formation and erection of the new state of West Virginia.

He believed the people of eastern Virginia forfeited any right to object by virtue of their decision to secede from the Union.

About the month of April, 1861, an insurrection against the Federal Union broke out within the State of Virginia. The constituted authorities, with the seeming consent of a majority of the People of the State, inaugurated a revolutionary war which they have carried to the extreme points of pronounced independence and the setting up of a pretended revolutionary and belligerent government. The organized political body which has committed this treason, having broken and trampled under its feet the Constitution, and even the Union, of the United States, is still standing in that treasonable attitude within the jurisdiction of the State of Virginia, but it has been dislodged from that portion of that jurisdiction which is contained within the new state of West Virginia. This organization has not given its consent to the formation and erection of the state of Western Virginia, and in its present attitude it is clear that it neither can nor will give that consent. The State of Virginia having thus fallen into revolution, the people living within that part of its jurisdiction which is embraced

---

threw his support behind Lincoln, and was rewarded when Lincoln appointed him Secretary of State on September 28, 1860. He was severely wounded by an assassination attempt on the night of Lincoln's assassination, but survived and returned to duty. During the Johnson Administration, he arranged for the United States to purchase Alaska from Russia. He left office at the end of Johnson's presidency and returned to New York. He died on October 10, 1872 and was buried in Fort Hill Cemetery in Auburn. For a full-length biography of Seward, see John M. Taylor, *William Henry Seward: Lincoln's Right Hand* (Washington, DC: Brassey's, 1991).

Secretary of the Treasury Salmon P. Chase, who supported statehood. *(Library of Congress)*

within the new state of West Virginia, adhering in their loyalty to the State of Virginia and also to the United States, availed themselves of the fortune of the civil war to discard the treasonable authorities of Virginia, reorganized the State, and with all needful forms and solemnities chose and constituted the public functionaries for the state as nearly in conformity with the constitution of Virginia as in the revolutionary condition of that State was practicable. The State of Virginia, thus reorganized, appeared in Congress by its representatives in both Houses, and was then deliberately acknowledged and recognized by the Executive, as well as by the Legislature of the United States, as the State of Virginia, one of the original members of the Federal Union. This State of Virginia, thus constituted and acknowledged, has given its consent to the formation and erection of the State of West Virginia, within the jurisdiction of the State of Virginia. Why is not this consent an adequate one?

As to expediency, he declared:

Upon the question of expediency I am determined by two considerations. First. The people of Western Virginia will be safer from molestation for their loyalty, because better able to protect and defend themselves as a new and separate State, than they would be if left to demoralizing uncertainty upon the question whether, in the progress of the war, they may not be again reabsorbed in the State of Virginia, and subjected to severities as a punishment for their present devotion to the Union. The first duty of the United States is protection to loyalty wherever it is found. Second. I am of opinion that the harmony and peace of the Union will be promoted by allowing the new State to be formed and erected, which will assume jurisdiction over that part of the valley of the Ohio which lies on the South side of the Ohio river, displacing, in a constitutional and lawful manner, the jurisdiction heretofore exercised there by a political power concentrated at the head of the James river.[26]

26 Seward to Lincoln, December 26, 1862, Lincoln Papers.

Finally, Chase adopted the same position argued by John Bingham during the debate in the House of Representatives. He drew a sharp distinction between the overall population of a state and its loyal population. In times of insurrection, only those who were loyalists should be considered to represent the population of the state for purposes of the national government. His opinion foreshadowed the holding of the U.S. Supreme Court in *Virginia v. West Virginia* nine years later:

> And, in my judgment, no other course than this was open to the National Government. In every case of insurrection involving the persons exercising the powers of State Government, when a large body of the people remain faithful that body, so far as the Union is concerned, must be taken to constitute the State. It would have been as absurd as it would have been impolitic to deny to the large loyal population of Virginia the powers of a State Government, because men whom they had clothed with Executive or Legislative or Judicial powers had betrayed their trusts and joined in rebellion against their country.

> It does not admit of doubt, therefore, as it seems to me that the Legislature which gave its consent to the formation and erection of the State of West-Virginia was the true and only lawful Legislature of the State of Virginia. The Madison Papers clearly show that the consent of the Legislature of the original State was the only consent required to the erection and formation of a new State within its jurisdiction. That consent having been given, the consent of the new State, if required, is proved by her application for admission.

> Nothing required by the Constitution to the formation and admission of West-Virginia into the United States is, therefore, wanting; and the Act of admission must necessarily be constitutional.

> Nor is this conclusion technical as some may think. The Legislature of Virginia, it may be admitted, did not contain many members from the Eastern Counties. It contained, however, Representatives from all Counties whose inhabitants were not either rebels themselves, or dominated by greater numbers of rebels. It was the only Legislature of the State known to the Union. If its consent was not valid, no consent could be. If its consent was not valid, the Constitution as to the People of West Virginia has been so suspended by the rebellion that a most important right under it is utterly lost.

> It is safer, in my opinion to follow plain principles to plain conclusions, than to turn aside from consequences clearly logical because not exactly agreeable to our views of expediency.

For these reasons, and in order to protect the interests of the loyal population of Virginia, Chase believed that it was expedient to admit the new state.[27]

---

27 Chase to Lincoln, December 28, 1862, Lincoln Papers.

The evenly-divided cabinet provided Lincoln with little guidance with which to make a decision as a result of its inability to come to a consensus. The President agonized over the decision whether to sign the bill. "The division of a state is dreaded as a precedent," he told his friend, Sen. Orville Browning of Illinois. A Congressman told him, "Mr. Lincoln, you must veto this bill." Lincoln, always quick with a quip, said, "I'll tell you what I'll do. I'll split the difference and say nothing about it."[28]

Left to his own resources, Lincoln composed his own well-reasoned opinion to justify his decision to admit West Virginia to the Union:

> The consent of the Legislature of Virginia is constitutionally necessary to the bill for the admission of West-Virginia becoming a law. A body claiming to be such Legislature has given its consent. We can not well deny that it is such, unless we do so upon the outside knowledge that the body was chosen at elections, in which a majority of the qualified voters of Virginia did not participate.
>
> But it is a universal practice in the popular elections in all these states, to give no legal consideration whatever to those who do not choose to vote, as against the effect of the votes of those, who do choose to vote. Hence it is not the qualified voters, but the qualified voters, *who choose to vote*, that constitute the political power of the state. Much less than to non-voters, should any consideration be given to those who did not vote, *in this case*: because it is also matter of outside knowledge, that they were not merely neglectful of their rights under, and duty to, this government, but were also engaged in open rebellion against it. Doubtless among these non-voters were some Union men whose voices were smothered by the more numerous secessionists; but we know too little of their number to assign them any appreciable value. Can this government stand, if it indulges constitutional constructions by which men in open rebellion against it, are to be accounted, man for man, the equals of those who maintain their loyalty to it? Are they to be accounted even better citizens, and more worthy of consideration, than those who merely neglect to vote? If so, their treason against the constitution, enhances their constitutional value! Without braving these absurd conclusions, we can not deny that the body which consents to the admission of West-Virginia, is the Legislature of Virginia. I do not think the plural form of the words "Legislatures" and "States" in the phrase of the constitution "without the consent of the Legislatures of the States concerned &c" has any reference to the new State concerned. That plural form sprang from the contemplation of two or more old States contributing to form a new one. The idea that the new state was in danger of being admitted without its own consent, was not provided against, because it was not thought of, as I conceive. It is said, the devil takes care of his own. Much more should a good spirit---the spirit of the Constitution and the Union---take care of it's own. I think it can not do less, and live.

---

28 Both quoted in Carl Sandberg, *Abraham Lincoln: The War Years*, 4 vols. (New York: Harcourt, Brace & Co., 1939), 1:656.

Abraham Lincoln, the sixteenth President of the United States. *(Library of Congress)*

But is the admission into the Union, of West-Virginia, expedient. This, in my general view, is more a question for Congress, than for the Executive. Still I do not evade it. More than on anything else, it depends on whether the admission or rejection of the new state would under all the circumstances tend the more strongly to the restoration of the national authority throughout the Union. That which helps most in this direction is the most expedient at this time. Doubtless those in remaining Virginia would return to the Union, so to speak, less reluctantly without the division of the old state than with it; but I think we could not save as much in this quarter by rejecting the new state, as we should lose by it in West-Virginia. We can scarcely dispense with the aid of West-Virginia in this struggle; much less can we afford to have her against us, in congress and in the field. Her brave and good men regard her admission into the Union as a matter of life and death. They have been true to the Union under very severe trials. We have so acted as to justify their hopes; and we can not fully retain their confidence, and co-operation, if we seem to break faith with them. In fact, they could not do so much for us, if they would.

Again, the admission of the new state, turns that much slave soil to free; and thus, is a certain, and irrevocable encroachment upon the cause of the rebellion.

The division of a State is dreaded as a precedent. But a measure made expedient by a war, is no precedent for times of peace. It is said that the admission of West-Virginia, is secession, and tolerated only because it is our secession. Well, if we call it by that name, there is still difference enough between secession against the constitution, and secession in favor of the constitution.

I believe the admission of West-Virginia into the Union is expedient.[29]

On December 30, as the President weighed his decision, Governor Pierpont dashed off a telegram to Lincoln. "The union men of West Va were not originally for the Union because of the new state," he wrote. "But the sentiment for the two have become identified. If one is stricken down I don't know what is become of the other."[30] Lincoln later told Pierpont that his telegram was "the turning point in my mind in signing the Bill. I said to myself, this is not a constitutional question, it is a political question. The government has been fighting nearly two years for its existence. But friends of the Bill say that it will strengthen the Union cause and weaken the cause of the Rebels. It is a step and is political. I will not trouble myself further about the constitutional point, so I determined to sign the bill and am satisfied with the conclusion."[31]

The next day, as Lincoln continued weighing his decision, Archibald Campbell, the publisher of the *Wheeling Intelligencer* newspaper, wrote to Lincoln to encourage him to sign the statehood bill. He said:

29 Basler, *Collected Works of Abraham Lincoln*, 6:26-28.

30 Francis Pierpont to Lincoln, December 30, 1862, Lincoln Papers.

31 Ambler, *Pierpont*, 185.

I wish simply to call your attention to the present feeling and the future danger connected with a veto of the bill that has passed Congress. No people were ever more united in a wish than are our people for a new state. South Carolina, in my opinion, was never as much united for Secession. Not a citizen of prominence in all our forty eight counties, with the single exception of Senator Carlile, opposes it. He, for his opposition in the Senate, together with his defection from the Union cause, has been more thoroughly and universally repudiated by our people than any public man ever was before by his constituency, so far as I can recall. Some twenty five large county meetings have requested his resignation, and at the same time have endorsed the bill for the new state as it had passed the Senate & has since passed the House. Numberless smaller meetings have done the same thing. Not a meeting, however insignificant, held anywhere for months past in any of the counties of the proposed State have neglected to endorse the bill. In addition, the legislature have endorsed it, & have formally requested the House to pass it while it was pending there in the early part of this month.

He continued:

A veto of the bill would be a disaster, the consequences of which I dread to contemplate. I verily believe that it would be a death blow to our Union sentiment. I can not see that there would be any coherency in it in the future. It would have lost the central magnet. It would be utterly disintegrated and demoralized. With our people the Union and the new State are convertible terms. Crush the one and you, as certain as death, in my opinion, crush the other. In the present prospects of our national affairs the expectation of a new state keeps thousands from falling away, and I see in a veto the sure melting away of our Union strengths. Destroy the hope of a new state and our people see themselves remanded again to Eastern Va & again identified and committed to her fortunes. A crushed minority sentiment, thoroughly disloyal, would soon warm into life and prestige. Mr Carlile with all his better and worse affiliations, now under ban, would rise and ride the wave.

Campbell concluded with a flourish, eloquently making the case for the citizens of West Virginia: "To sum up all, Mr President, I will say that a veto of the bill, in my earnest and most deliberate opinion, will be the death warrant of Unionism in Western Va."[32]

Lincoln summoned several West Virginia Congressmen to come see him at the White House on December 31. They were seated, and Lincoln told them that his cabinet had split 3-3 on the questions of the constitutionality and expediency of admitting West Virginia to the Union. Without telling them who had written it, he then read his opinion to them, as well as those of several of his

---

32 Archibald W. Campbell to Lincoln, December 31, 1862, Lincoln Papers.

cabinet members. When he finished, Lincoln told the visitors which was the opinion he had written. The President pulled out a drawer in the table by which he was sitting, with the remark: "Now gentlemen, I will give you the odd trick."

Rep. Jacob B. Blair, one of his visitors, remarked, "that is the trick we hope to take." They agreed that Lincoln's opinion "was the clearest, most pointed, and conclusive of all that was read to us. Above all it was the most satisfactory to us." They returned to the White House on January 1 to find out what Lincoln had decided to do. "I was there early in the morning, and he kept his promise as he always did," recalled Blair. "He brought the bill to me and holding it open before my eyes, he said: 'Do you see that signature?' I read–'Approved, Abraham Lincoln.'"[33]

The wives of Governor Pierpont and two other state officials expressed their gratitude to Lincoln in a January 1 letter: "God bless you—you have signed the Bill. In the name of the loyal Ladies of West Va, we thank you, for our blessed New Year's Gift—As the wives of our State Officers, we are doubly grateful—You have saved us from contempt and disgrace. The wildest enthusiasm prevails—The people are running to and fro, each one anxious to bear the 'Glad Tidings of this great Joy.'"[34]

The entire matter was in doubt until Lincoln signed the legislation. "It may be then, to the honest hard sense and wisdom of Abraham Lincoln, that we are indebted for the new State," observed a grateful Granville Parker, "for if he had vetoed, we could not have hoped to command a two-thirds vote of Congress."[35]

The legislation signed by Lincoln included the Willey Amendment as a condition of statehood. Before West Virginia could take its place among the states, Congress required the new state to amend its constitution and provide for gradual emancipation of slaves. The final hurdle for statehood journey now returned to West Virginia.

33 "A Chapter of Inside History in Regard to the Admission of West Virginia Into the Union. Letter from Ex-Congressman Blair to Ex-Senator Willey," *Wheeling Intelligencer*, January 22, 1876.

34 Mrs. Samuel Crane, Mrs. Francis H. Pierpont, and Mrs. L.A. Hagans to Abraham Lincoln, January 1, 1863, Lincoln Papers.

35 Parker, *The Formation of the State of West Virginia*, 185.

CHAPTER EIGHT

Establishing the New State

ON January 31, 1863, the legislature of West Virginia adopted the following act pertaining to Berkeley County, which did not vote in the October 24, 1861 election on West Virginia statehood:

An Act giving the consent of the State of Virginia to the County of Berkeley's being admitted into, and becoming part of the State of West Virginia

Whereas, by the Constitution for the State of West Virginia, ratified by the people thereof, it is provided that additional territory may be admitted into and become part of said state with the consent of the legislature thereof, and it is represented to the General Assembly that the people of the County of Berkeley are desirous that said county should be admitted into and become part of the said State of West Virginia, now, therefore,

1. *Be it enacted by the General Assembly* that polls shall be opened and held on the fourth Thursday of May next, at the several places for holding elections in the County of Berkeley for the purpose of taking the sense of the qualified voters of said county on the question of including said county in the State of West Virginia.

2. The poll books shall be headed as follows, *viz.*: "Shall the County of Berkeley become a part of the State of West Virginia?" and shall contain two columns, one headed "Aye" and the other "No", and the names of those who vote in favor of said county becoming a part of the State of West Virginia shall be entered in the first

column, and the names of those who vote against it shall be entered in the second column.

3. The said polls shall be superintended and conducted according to the laws regulating general elections, and the commissioners superintending the same at the courthouse of the said county shall, within six days from the commencement of the said vote, examine and compare the several polls taken in the county, strike therefrom any votes which are by law directed to be stricken from the same, and attach to the polls a list of the votes stricken therefrom, and the reasons for so doing. The result of the polls shall then be ascertained, declared, and certified as follows: the said commissioners shall make out two returns in the following form, or to the following effect:

"We, commissioners for taking the vote of the qualified voters of Berkeley County on the question of including the said county in the State of West Virginia, do hereby certify that polls for that purpose were opened and held the fourth Thursday of May, in the year 1863, within said county, pursuant to law, and that the following is a true statement of the result as exhibited by the poll books, *viz.*, for the County of Berkeley becoming part of the State of West Virginia, _____ votes; and against it _____ votes. Given under our hands this ___ day of _____, 1863;"

which returns, written in words, not in figures, shall be signed by the commissioners; one of the said returns shall be filed in the clerk's office of the said county, and the other shall be sent, under the seal of the secretary of this commonwealth, within ten days from the commencement of the said vote, and the governor of this state, if of opinion that the said vote has been opened and held, and the result ascertained and certified pursuant to law, *shall certify the result of the same under the seal of this state, to the governor of the said State of West Virginia.*

4. If the governor of this state shall be of opinion that the said polls cannot be safely and properly opened and held in the said County of Berkeley, on the fourth Thursday of May next, he may by proclamation postpone the same, and appoint in the same proclamation, or by one to be hereafter issued, another day for opening and holding the same.

5. If a majority of the votes given at the polls opened and held pursuant to this act be in favor of the said County of Berkeley's becoming part of the State of West Virginia, then shall the said county become part of the State of West Virginia when admitted into the same with the consent of the legislature thereof.

6. This act shall be in force from its passage.[1]

Four days later, February 4, the legislature passed this act with respect to Jefferson and several other counties:

An Act giving consent to the admission of certain counties into the new State of West Virginia upon certain conditions

---

1 *Ordinances and Acts of the Restored Government of Virginia*, 38.

1. Be it enacted by the General Assembly of Virginia that at the general election on the fourth Thursday of May, 1863, it shall be lawful for the voters of the district composed of the Counties of Tazewell, Bland, Giles, and Craig to declare by their votes whether said counties shall be annexed to and become a part of the new State of West Virginia; also, at the same time, the district composed of the Counties of Buchanan, Wise, Russell, Scott, and Lee, to declare, by their votes, whether the counties of the said last-named district shall be annexed to and become a part of the State of West Virginia; also, at the same time, the district composed of the Counties of Alleghany, Bath, and Highland to declare by their votes whether the counties of such last-named district shall be annexed to and become a part of the State of West Virginia; also, at the same time, the district composed of the Counties of Frederick and *Jefferson*, or *either* of them, to declare by their votes whether the Counties of the said last-named district shall be annexed to and become a part of the State of West Virginia; also, at the same time, the district composed of the Counties of Clarke, Loudoun, Fairfax, Alexandria, and Prince William, to declare by their votes whether the Counties of the said last-named district shall be annexed to and become a part of the State of West Virginia; also, at the same time, the district composed of the Counties of Shenandoah, Warren, Page, and Rockingham to declare by their votes whether the Counties of the said last-named district shall be annexed to and become a part of the State of West Virginia; and for that purpose, there shall be a poll opened at each place of voting in each of said districts headed 'For annexation' and 'Against annexation.' And the consent of this General Assembly is hereby given for the annexation to the said State of West Virginia of such of said districts, or of either of them, as a majority of the votes so polled in each district may determine, provided that the Legislature of the State of West Virginia shall also consent and agree to the said annexation, after which all jurisdiction of the State of Virginia over the districts so annexed shall cease.

2. It shall be the duty of the *governor of the Commonwealth to ascertain and certify the result as other elections are certified.*

3. In the event the state of the country will not permit or from any cause said election for annexation cannot be fairly held on the day aforesaid, it shall be the duty of the governor of this Commonwealth, as soon as such election can be safely and fairly held and a full and free expression of the opinion of the people had thereon, to issue his proclamation ordering such election for the purpose aforesaid, and certify the result as aforesaid.

4. This act shall be in force from its passage.[2]

In an election held on May 24, 1863, Berkeley County voters favored West Virginia statehood by a margin of 645 to 7. In Jefferson County, an actual vote count was never forthcoming, but the reported results indicated majority

---

2 *Id.* at 103-104.

support for the new state.[3] Pierpont's Restored Government in Alexandria certified the results of these plebiscites. On August 5, 1863, Berkeley County was declared to be a part of West Virginia. On November 2, 1863, Jefferson County was incorporated into the new state by legislative act.[4] Several years later, on March 10, 1866, the Thirty-Ninth Congress of the United States expressly authorized the transfer of Berkeley and Jefferson Counties to the State of West Virginia by joint resolution, setting the stage for the 1866 lawsuit that is the subject of the second part of this book.[5] Thus, the railroad counties of the eastern panhandle formally became a part of West Virginia. Nonetheless, statehood faced more hurdles.

Sen. John Carlile was not finished. After his efforts to block the statehood bill failed, Carlile still refused to resign. He remained in the Senate, determined that if he could not defeat statehood, he would delay the process as long as possible. On February 14, he introduced a supplementary bill in the Senate providing that Lincoln's Proclamation conditionally admitting West Virginia into the Union would not take effect until the "counties of Boone, Logan, Wyoming, Mercer, McDowell, Pocahontas, Raleigh, Greenbrier, Monroe, Pendleton, Fayette, Nicholas, and Clay, now in possession of the so-called Confederate Government, and over which the Restored Government of the State of Virginia have not been extended, have noted on and ratified the condition contained in said act."[6] This bill required the citizens of thirteen counties of Virginia to vote to join the new state even though the legislature of the Restored Government had not consented to their inclusion. The Senate defeated Carlile's last-ditch attempt to delay the admission of the new state on February 26 by a vote of 28 to 12. The vote removed the last remaining Congressional barrier to the admission of the new state.[7]

The final condition of admitting West Virginia to the Union was incorporating the Willey Amendment and gradual emancipation into the new state constitution. The constitutional convention met in Wheeling on February

3 Senate Misc. Doc. No 98, 37th Cong. 2nd Sess., 2-3.

4 Summers, *The Baltimore and Ohio in the Civil War*, 201.

5 *Congressional Globe*, 39th Cong., 1st Sess., Appendix, 426.

6 Ibid., 38th Cong., 3rd Sess., 951-952.

7 Lewis, *A History of West Virginia*, 392.

12, 1863. That day, Senator Willey addressed the delegates. "Why should we hesitate to accept the great advantages before us? We have complied with every requisition of the law. We have fulfilled every constitutional obligation," he asserted. "And now wealth and popular education, and material and moral progress and development, and political equality and prosperity in every department of political economy, so long withheld from us, are all within our grasp."[8]

The convention wrestled with the issue of compensation for slave owners affected by the emancipation of their slaves. The convention appointed a Special Committee on the Question of Slaves Emancipated, chaired by Peter G. VanWinkle. The committee reported that the U.S. Constitution required that slaveowners receive compensation for the value of the freed slaves. The convention ultimately approved a measure that required such compensation. The state legislature was directed to appropriate $500,000 for that purpose, with the federal government asked for reimbursement.[9]

With compensation for slave owners included, the delegates unanimously approved the new constitution on February 18, 1863. The proposed state constitution placed West Virginia on a course of gradual emancipation, which no other state had attempted since the war started. [10]

The new constitution was then submitted to the voters of the new state. Encouraging passage of the constitution, Willey pointed out that this referendum would be one of the most important days in the history of West Virginia. He predicted that "the very hour that [West Virginia] is admitted as a free state, there will be a great influx of capital, and instead of having four or five mills rolling up smoke, you [Wheeling] will have a dozen of them and millions and millions of capital will come here." He concluded, "The face of the country

---

8 "Address of Hon. Waitman T. Willey," *Debates and Proceedings of the First Constitutional Convention of West Virginia*, February 12, 1863, http://www.wvculture.org/history/statehood/cc021263.html.

9 Ambler, *Waitman Thomas Willey*, 99. On February 23, Willey presented a resolution to the U. S. Senate calling for the Congress to appropriate $2,000,000 to compensate loyal slave owners for the loss of their slaves. This proposal was not well received, but Carlile nevertheless insisted that it be brought to a vote, perhaps to embarrass Willey. The bill lost by a vote of 28-12 against. *Congressional Globe*, 37th Congress, 3rd Session, 1121 and 1178.

10 *Debates and Proceedings*, February 18, 1863.

will be changed. Industry, wealth, population, power, education, and moral influence will concentrate in your hills, and we will flourish."[11]

The voters approved the Willey Amendment on April 3, 1863 by the overwhelming count of 28,321 to 542, although ten counties did not participate in the election.[12] A triumphant Arch Campbell gloated in the *Wheeling Intelligencer*, "Congressional dictation, abolition, and all sorts of 'orgies and Gorgons dire' are rather popular than otherwise in West Virginia."[13]

The results of the election were certified to President Lincoln, who issued the following proclamation:

A PROCLAMATION

WHEREAS, By the act of Congress approved the 31st day of December last, the State of West Virginia was declared to be one of the United States of America, and was admitted into the Union on an equal footing with the original States in all respects whatsoever, upon the condition that certain changes should be made in the proposed constitution for that State; and

WHEREAS, proof of a compliance with that condition, as required by the second section of the act aforesaid has been submitted to me:

Now, therefore, be it known that I, Abraham Lincoln, President of the United States, do hereby, in pursuance of the act of Congress aforesaid, declare and proclaim that the said act shall take effect and be in force from and after sixty days from the date hereof.

In witness whereof, I have hereunto set my hand and caused the seal of the United States to be affixed.

Done at the city of Washington, this 20th day of April, A.D. 1863, and of the Independence of the United States the eighty-seventh.

ABRAHAM LINCOLN

By the President:

WILLIAM H. SEWARD, Secretary of State[14]

---

11 "The Working Men's Mass Meeting," *Wheeling Intelligencer*, March 23, 1863.

12 "The Last Formality Gone Through With," *Wheeling Intelligencer*, April 17, 1863.

13 "Note This," *Wheeling Intelligencer*, April 8, 1863.

14 Basler, *Collected Works of Abraham Lincoln*, 6:181.

Brig. Gen. William E. "Grumble" Jones, commander of the 1863 Jones-Imboden Raid.

(Library of Congress)

Sixty days later, West Virginia, at last, became the 35th State.

The birth of the new state did not go smoothly. In the spring of 1863, Gen. Robert E. Lee, moved to break up the critical supply line of the Baltimore & Ohio Railroad and to re-establish Confederate authority west of the Allegheny Mountains. Cavalry brigades under Brig. Gen. William E. "Grumble" Jones and Brig. Gen. John D. Imboden moved to destroy important bridges of the B & O at certain critical points. Lee also aimed to gather supplies and recruit new manpower for the Confederate armies. Jones attacked the B&O between Grafton, Virginia and Oakland, Maryland while Imboden's troopers attacked Union garrisons at Philippi, Beverly and Buckhannon. The Confederates even hoped to capture Governor Pierpont.

The month-long raid penetrated deep into West Virginia but failed to prevent the birth of the new state. Pierpont eluded Confederate forces, which burned his library at Fairmont. Senator Willey escaped to safety across the Ohio River. Jones reported that

Brig. Gen. John D. Imboden, who also helped to lead the Jones-Imboden Raid. (*USAHEC*)

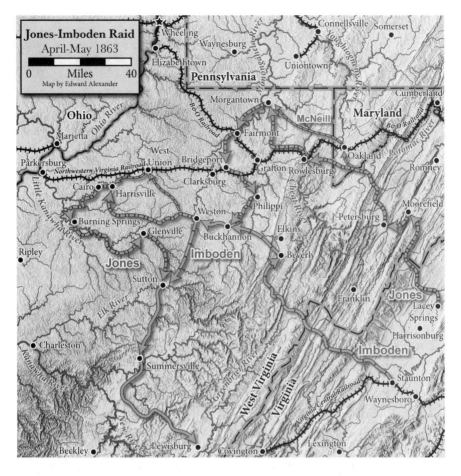

approximately 30 of the enemy were killed and 700 prisoners were taken. He claimed to have added some 400 new recruits, and that he captured a piece of artillery, 1,000 head of cattle, and some 1,200 horses. The raiders destroyed sixteen bridges, an oil field, many boats and some of the rolling rail stock of the B&O.[15] Despite the damage to its bridges and rolling stock, the B&O was back in business by May 4, 1863.[16]

15 Obviously, the details of the Jones-Imboden Raid stray far beyond the scope of this discussion. For a detailed discussion of the Raid, the only monograph devoted to it is Darrell Collins, *The Jones-Imboden Raid: The Confederate Attempt to Destroy the Baltimore & Ohio Railroad and Retake West Virginia* (Jefferson, N.C.: McFarland & Co., 2007).

16 Summers, *The Baltimore and Ohio in the Civil War*, 139.

Arthur I. Boreman, first governor of West Virginia. *(Library of Congress)*

Not long after the end of the Jones-Imboden Raid in May, Lee persuaded Confederate President Jefferson Davis and his cabinet to permit him to invade the North. Lee's advance began on June 10, and by June 15, elements of Lee's army commanded by Lt. Gen. Richard S. Ewell had captured Winchester and were advancing toward the Potomac River crossings at Williamsburg, Maryland. Only days before the official admission of West Virginia to the Union, twenty thousand Confederate troops marched through the new state on their ultimate journey to Gettysburg. While West Virginia faced existential danger at its birth, the Confederate invasion did not deter the launching of the new state.

Despite this mortal threat, Parkersburg attorney Arthur I. Boreman became the first governor of the new state on June 20, 1863.[17] In his inaugural address, Boreman referred to the new state of West Virginia as "the child of the rebellion." He declared, "to-day after many long and weary years of insult and

17 Born in Waynesburg, Pennsylvania on June 24, 1823, Arthur Ingram Boreman was the son of a town merchant. At the age of four, he and his family moved to Middlebourne, Tyler County in what is today West Virginia. In 1845, Boreman was admitted to the bar of Virginia and established a law practice at Parkersburg the following year. He represented Wood County as a Whig delegate in the Virginia General Assembly from 1855 to 1861. He served as a circuit judge under the Reorganized Government of Virginia and was elected West Virginia's first governor in 1863. He played a major role in establishing an infrastructure for the new state. In 1869, he resigned as governor to accept an appointment to the United States Senate six days before the end of his term. After one six-year term as Senator, he returned to Parkersburg to resume the practice of law. In 1888, he was elected as circuit judge once more, serving until his death in 1896. "Biography of Arthur Ingram Boreman," http://www.wvculture.org/history/government/governors/boreman.html.

The Linsly Institute, first capitol of West Virginia. *(Jon-Erik Gilot)*

injustice, culminating on the part of the East, in an attempt to destroy the Government, we have the proud satisfaction of proclaiming to those around us that we are a separate state in the Union."[18] After electing a full slate of statewide officials, West Virginia formally became the Union's thirty-fifth state on June 20, 1863, removing from Commonwealth of Virginia one-third of its population and one half of its territory.[19]

The following celebratory editorial ran in the *Wheeling Intelligencer* that day:

This day ushers into being the new State of West Virginia, and adds the thirty fifth star to the constellation of the American Union. To-day is the beginning of a new order of things with us here. The old Government goes out and the new one comes in. Today

18 "The Inauguration of the New State of West Virginia. Valedictory of Governor Pierpont. Inaugural of Governor Boreman. Speech of Ex-Senator Willey," *Wheeling Intelligencer,* June 21, 1863.

19 McGregor, *The Disruption of Virginia,* 320.

Governor Boreman inaugurating the State of West Virginia.

(Diss DeBar Collection, West Virginia State Archives)

Gov. Pierpont goes out and the new comes in. Today Governor Pierpont bids us a formal farewell, as our chief magistrate, and Gov. Boreman will be inaugurated as his successor. With the one the parting cannot be but sad. With the other the greeting cannot but be joyful. Gov. Pierpont goes to his new field of usefulness and labor, followed by the good wishes and benedictions of a grateful people. Governor Boreman comes to uses a worthy successor, the unanimously chosen and honored Chief Magistrate of the new State. While we gratefully remember the one, let us honor and support the other.

The new Commonwealth starts upon its career in the midst of turbulence and danger. Its officers have great difficulties and embarrassments to encounter. They will need the moral support of the whole people, and they are worthy of it. Let us give it to them in unstinted measure.

To-day the Legislature of the new State meets for organization. With the beginning of the week it commences the important labor assigned it, of putting the machinery of the new Government into smooth and successful operation. It has an arduous task before it, but, we believe the task will be creditably done.

The occasion is a peculiarly suggestive one, but we do not propose to indulge a retrospect now. To-day we enter into the reward of the long and toilsome struggle. Two years ago, this day, the people of Western Virginia, in Convention assembled signed the Declaration against the despotic usurpation and conspiracy at Richmond. That declaration embodied the spirit of all this Western Virginia movement, which on this, the second anniversary of that act, stands completed and consummated.- Never may we depart from either the spirit or letter of that Declaration, which declared that "the true purpose of all government is to promote the welfare and provide for the protection and security of the covered," and that the rebellion at Richmond seeks "to subvert the Union founded by Washington and his co-patriots, in the purer days of the Republic, which has conferred unexampled prosperity upon every class of citizens and upon every section of the country."

Let us not forget that our New State, which we inaugurate to-day amid happy auspices, will be destroyed, the liberty it protects overthrown, and the hopes it inspires, will be destroyed, the liberty it protects overthrown, and the hopes it inspires blasted, if the federal government is not able to sustain itself and enforce its authority. Our fate and the fate of our national Union must be the same. We go on together to prosperity, or we go down together to ruin. Even now the enemies of the country threaten to invade our homes, and the citizens soldiery is under arms for their defense. Let us each and all vow to-day, in turning this new leaf of our history, undying hostility to this atrocious rebellion which seeks the destruction of the rights of men, and realty to the government and Union, in and under which alone life, liberty and property are secure. As citizens we are of the State, but as patriots we belong to the whole country.[20]

Publisher Archibald W. Campbell, who played such a large and important role in bringing about the creation of the new state, triumphantly declared, "A grateful people will ever say 'God bless Abraham Lincoln.'"[21]

The process of creating a new state had only just begun. West Virginia lacked any infrastructure and, based on the Commonwealth of Virginia's institutions and laws, created its own executive branch and cabinet offices, a bicameral legislature, and its own judicial system, much of which had to be created from scratch.[22]

"On the 20th of June, 1863, is the natal day of this last born of the ever glorious galaxy of States, constituting the American Union," wrote the editor of the *Point Pleasant Register*, published at the confluence of the Kanawha and Ohio Rivers. "West Virginia on that day, ever memorable in her future history, proudly took her place among the sisterhood of States. Born amid the convulsions of revolution, she is destined to be cradled in the midst of contention, carnage and blood. Because of the darkness and gloom attendant

---

20 "The Day We Celebrate," Wheeling Intelligencer, June 20, 1863.

21 Ibid.

22 The new state had no established judicial system. The county circuit courts provided a good start, but the West Virginia needed its own Supreme Court. For two months per year, the Supreme Court of Virginia met in Lewisburg, the county seat of Greenbrier County. As a result, the Supreme Court maintained a full law library in Lewisburg. In August 1863, Union Brig. Gen. William W. Averell was ordered to take his brigade to Lewisburg to seize that law library for use by the new state Supreme Court. Confederate infantry commanded by Col. George S. Patton got across Averell's line of march at White Sulphur Springs, not far from the famous Greenbrier Hotel, and defeated the Union raiders in a harsh two-day battle. Averell was forced to withdraw, and the Confederates immediately evacuated the law library to Richmond, meaning that the Supreme Court of West Virginia would have to assemble its own law library. For a detailed tactical study of the Battle of White Sulphur Springs, which is sometimes known as the Battle of the Law Books, see Eric J. Wittenberg, *The Battle of White Sulphur Springs: Averell Fails to Secure West Virginia* (Charleston, SC: The History Press, 2011).

upon her entrance into political life, she is more cordially welcomed and elicits more fraternal solitude, than the old states are wont to bestow."[23]

As the new government of West Virginia settled in, the Civil War ground on in Virginia, finally ending on April 9, 1865, when Lee's Army of Northern Virginia surrendered to Union forces at Appomattox Court House. "After the war, Virginia invited the new State to reunite with it, but a polite reply was sent that West Virginia preferred to retain its statehood," observed a West Virginia historian.[24] As the Civil War ended and Virginia returned to the Union, the question of West Virginia statehood faced a new challenge.

23 "West Virginia," *The Weekly Register*, June 25, 1863.

24 W. B. Cutright, *The History of Upshur County, West Virginia From Its Earliest Exploration and Settlement to the Present Time* (Buckhannon, WV: privately published, 1907), 108.

CHAPTER NINE

Post-Civil War Virginia

THE Civil War devastated Virginia.[1] Following a nine-month siege by the Union Army of the Potomac, Richmond and Petersburg were in ruins. The farms and towns of the Shenandoah Valley lay in waste after Union troops burned farms in order to deprive the Confederacy of the bounty of the Valley's fertile soil. Northern Virginia had not recovered from the destruction wrought by four years of battling between the two largest armies fielded by either side. As the war ended, more than 100,000 Union troops occupied the state.

Who would govern Virginia became an urgent matter. One of the first office holders to hold forth on the matter was Salmon P. Chase. Lincoln finally accepted Chase's third offer of resignation as Secretary of the Treasury on June 30, 1864. Then, following the death of Chief Justice Roger B. Taney in October 1864, Lincoln appointed Chase as Chief Justice of the Supreme Court on December 6.[2] He was confirmed the same day and was sworn in on December 15. Chase wrote to Lincoln on April 11, 1865, just two days after the surrender at Appomattox and four days before his assassination. Despite his service on

---

1 J.T. Trowbridge, *The South: A Tour of its Battle-Fields and Ruined Cities*, (Hartford: L. Stebbins, 1866), 73.

2 Charles Fairman, "Reconstruction and Reunion, 1864-88," *History of the Supreme Court of the United States*, 9 vols. (New York: Macmillan, 1971), 6:2.

Andrew Johnson, seventeenth President of the United States. (*Library of Congress*)

the Supreme Court, Chase openly voiced his initial views on Reconstruction, at least in Virginia:

> And first as to Virginia. By the action of every branch of the government, we are committed to the recognition and maintenance of the state organization of which Governor Pierpont is the head. You know all the facts and recapitulation would be

useless. There will be pressure for the recognition of the rebel organization on the condition of the profession of loyalty. It would be easier and wiser, in my judgment, to stand by the loyal organization already recognized.[3]

Although his letter made no reference to West Virginia, the legitimacy of the new state depended upon the legitimacy of the state government headed by Pierpont. The letter foreshadowed the legal battle that later bedeviled the Supreme Court, with Chase as its Chief Justice.

Not long after Lincoln's assassination, President Andrew Johnson appointed Francis H. Pierpont the provisional governor of all of Virginia. Pierpont, as head of the Restored Government of Virginia located in Alexandria, had spent the Civil War in charge of only those lands of Virginia secured by the Union Army. On May 9, 1865, he became the leader of an entire state that only a month before housed the capital of the Confederacy.

Several weeks later, with Congress out of session for the next six months, President Johnson announced his plan for reconstruction of the former Confederate states. Each state was to hold a constitutional convention.[4] Johnson's plan required that the new state constitutions ban slavery. Most former Confederate soldiers and officeholders could vote and run for office, once they swore an oath to support and defend the Constitution of the United States.[5] A limited group of high-level Confederate officials and citizens of wealth would only have their civil rights restored after a pardon from the president, which he liberally granted.[6] Critically, Johnson devised his reconstruction plan with no concern for the views of Congress, which soon challenged his policies towards the Southern states.[7]

Pierpont, Virginia Attorney General Thomas R. Bowden, and the legislators of the Restored Government relocated to Richmond in June of 1865. Seeking support for his governorship, Pierpont quickly met with many

---

3 Chase to Lincoln, April 11, 1865, Lincoln Papers.

4 Eric Foner, *Reconstruction; America's Unfinished Business* (New York: Harper, 1988),183.

5 Ibid.

6 Ibid. Johnson's reconstruction plan required persons owning taxable property in excess of $20,000 to seek a presidential pardon before voting rights could be restored. By 1866, he had pardoned over 7,000 Southerners who had sought pardons. Ibid., 191.

7 Allen C. Guelzo, *Reconstruction, A Concise History:* (New York and London: Oxford University Press, 2018), 21.

members of the Virginia General Assembly elected in May of 1864.[8] Pierpont then encouraged the legislators to meet, resulting in a five-day session ending on June 23, 1865.[9] With Pierpont's approval, the legislature addressed one of the most contentious issues: who could vote or hold public office. The Restored Government of Virginia had previously imposed a requirement that each voter and office-holder swear that they had never given aide or support to the rebellion, as a condition of voting and holding office.[10] This ironclad oath prevented former Confederates from voting and presumably seizing control of state governments.[11] In Virginia, the ironclad oath disenfranchised three-fourths of voting age males, the percentage of white males who had served in the Confederate forces.[12] In his first month as Governor of all Virginia, Pierpont sided with conservatives on the critical issue of voting rights for ex-Confederates.[13]

Pierpont quickly drew fire for convening the General Assembly elected in 1864. Lewis McKenzie, a member of the U.S. House of Representatives under the Restored Government of Virginia, was highly critical. He declared, "When the legislature went to Richmond (June 20-25, 1865), they altered the constitutional provision in such a manner that I found the loyal men of the State were to be totally sacrificed and turned over to the power of the secessionists."[14]

---

8 Ambler, *Francis H. Pierpont*, 272.

9 Ibid., 274.

10 Ibid., 273.

11 The iron-clad oath was originally required for federal employees during the Civil War, as a method of detecting spies or saboteurs. During the Civil War Congress sought to apply the oath in Southern states during reconstruction in the Wade Davis Bill, passed on July 2, 1864, Lincoln pocket vetoed the measure. Harold Hyman, *A More Perfect Union; the Impact of the Civil War and Reconstruction on the Constitution* (A. Knopf; New York, 1973), 277-78.

12 Ibid., 273. See also Foner, *Reconstruction*, 185. He estimated that 70% of Southern white males served in the armed forces of the Confederacy.

13 *Journal of the House of Delegates, State of Virginia*, 1865-66, Dec. 5, 1865, 31.

14 Hamilton Eckenrode, *The Political History of Virginia During Reconstruction* (Baltimore; Johns Hopkins University Press, 1904), 52. McKenzie was prophetic. In October of 1865, he was soundly defeated in a race for the House. Ibid., 67.

On June 26, 1865, the day after the Virginia Assembly adjourned, Secretary of State William H. Seward urgently wrote Pierpont via telegram.[15] Seward demanded to know why Pierpont had convened a legislature elected during the Confederacy. Pierpont artfully claimed that the assembly was not in session and that he alone had made the decision regarding voting rights.[16] If Pierpont hoped that extending an olive branch to former Confederates would build support for his administration, those hopes soon shattered.

With ex-Confederates able to vote, elections for the Virginia Assembly were conducted on October 12, 1865.[17] While virtually no candidates ran under the former secessionist Democratic banner, few Republicans who supported Pierpont were elected.[18] Moreover, a significant number of former-Confederates returned to office, although none who had led the movement to leave the Union.[19] In the same election, Virginians voted overwhelmingly in favor of amending the state constitution, outlawing the requirement of an ironclad oath.[20] No blacks were permitted to vote under Virginia law.[21] Virginia officials made plans to hold state elections in Jefferson and Berkeley counties in advance of the October, 1865 balloting, even though both of these counties were now officially part of West Virginia.[22] Only the intervention of the U.S. Army prevented the government of Virginia from organizing elections in the soon to be disputed counties.[23]

Virginians also elected members of the House of Representatives. But on March 6, 1866, both the House of Representatives and United State Senate refused to seat any member from a former Confederate state until such state was readmitted to the Union.[24] Virginia remained unrepresented.

15 Ambler, *Francis H. Pierpont*, footnote 21, Chpt. XXI.

16 Eckenrode, *The Political History of Virginia During Reconstruction*, 30.

17 Ibid., 67.

18 Ibid.

19 Ibid.

20 Ambler, *Francis H. Pierpont*, 285.

21 Ibid., 273.

22 Charles H. Ambler, *History of West Virginia* (New York: Prentiss Hall, 1933), 397.

23 Ibid.

24 *Cong. Globe*, 39th Cong. 1rst Sess., 1146-47.

As the new Virginia General Assembly convened on December 5, 1865, Pierpont communicated to the body a lengthy statement as to his views on the Commonwealth. His message struck a conciliatory tone.

> I have made every exertion to restore to each man in the state the rights of a citizen. I have done this under a high sense of duty to my country . . . . I am satisfied that no state can be governed under a republican form of government where three-fourths of the people, embracing the largest tax-payers, are disenfranchised and denied a vote in making or executing the laws of the state . . . Protection and loyalty are reciprocal obligations. The man who acts in bad faith to the government under the laws he lives is not entitled to its protection, or to participate in the management of its affairs; but as long as he is faithful the government is bound to exert all its power to vindicate his rights. In this spirit I recommended to the last legislature. . . to remove the restrictions imposed by the constitution upon voting and eligibility to office.[25]

In the same message, and for the first time, he addressed the question of West Virginia statehood in his new role as Governor of the entire Commonwealth of Virginia. The division of the state, and the means employed, infuriated many Virginians. Given his role in the dismemberment, he could not seriously challenge the creation of the new state, which was probably his greatest liability as Governor of Virginia. Instead, Pierpont focused upon Berkeley and Jefferson Counties. On behalf of Virginia, he made a claim to two of the fifty-five counties in West Virginia. He noted:

> A question has arisen in regard to the status of the counties of Jefferson and Berkeley. By the action taken, these counties became organized by persons and officers who claim them as part of West Virginia. Upon the general reorganization of the state I found that I could not organize these counties under the laws and ordinances of Virginia without producing strife and collision; and as I do nothing to settle the question definitively, I considered it proper to let the whole subject be referred to the congress of the United States, where authoritative action could be taken, in which all parties will have to acquiesce. The general assembly may adopt such measures as may be deemed proper for bringing the question to an issue. I think it may be done by a petition of either party asking congress to pass a joint resolution expressive of its opinion in regard to the legislative and constitutional action heretofore had in the case.[26]

---

25 *Journal of the House of Delegates, of the State of Virginia*, 1865-1866 (Alexandria, VA: D. Turner, 1865), 32.

26 Ibid., 27.

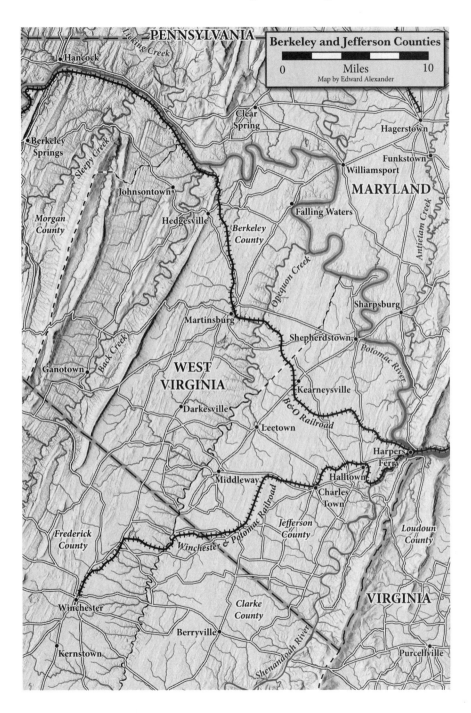

PENNSYLVANIA

Licking Creek

Hancock

Clear
Spring

Hagerstown

Berkeley
Springs

Sleepy Creek

Funkstown

Williamsport

Johnsontown

MARYLAND

Falling Waters

Morgan
County

Hedgesville

Berkeley
County

Opequon Creek

Antietam Creek

Sharpsburg

Martinsburg

Back Creek

Shepherdstown

Potomac River

Ganotown

WEST
VIRGINIA

Kearneysville

B&O Railroad

Darkesville

Leetown

Harpers
Ferry

Middleway

Halltown

Charles
Town

Winchester & Potomac Railroad

Jefferson
County

Loudoun
County

Frederick
County

VIRGINIA

Winchester

Clarke
County

Berryville

Shenandoah River

Kernstown

Purcellville

Pierpont may have hoped that a claim to the return of two of the fifty-five lost counties would limit the political damage resulting from his consenting to the formation of West Virginia. Wary former Confederates, suspicious of a Unionist governor, were not ready to concede that West Virginia was really lost. As the *Richmond Dispatch* bitterly noted, West Virginia claimed almost fifty percent of what had been the lands of Virginia and one-third of the white population.[27] The paper complained that pre-war Virginia contained 472,000 slaves, all now freed and no longer assets of the former owners, costing the state $236 million. In contrast, West Virginia had only 18,381 slaves, resulting in a loss of only $9 million.

In December 1865, the newly elected general assembly included many former Confederates disinclined to follow Pierpont's leadership.[28] The new Speaker of the House of Delegates, John Baldwin, had served as an officer in the Confederate Army, prompting Pierpont to refer to him as "the worst man in the state."[29] According to Pierpont, Baldwin and others "are determined no man shall ever hold office in Virginia who favored the Union."[30]

On December 6, 1865, the day after receiving Pierpont's message, the Virginia General Assembly voted to rescind its consent to the creation of West Virginia.[31] The legislation condemned both Pierpont and the Restored Government for the role they played in establishing West Virginia. Not a single member of the House or Senate voted against the legislation.[32] At the same time, the General Assembly also withdrew its consent to transfer Berkeley and Jefferson Counties to West Virginia.[33] Congress and Virginia had agreed to hold future elections in these two counties after West Virginia gained statehood. Following the county voting in 1863, and the validation of the electoral results by Governor Pierpont, neither Congress nor Virginia had passed additional

---

27 "The State Debt—West Virginia," *Richmond Dispatch*, December 20, 1866.

28 Ambler, *Francis Pierpont*, 279-80.

29 Letter from Pierpont to Willey, Feb. 6, 1866, Pierpont Papers.

30 Ibid.

31 *Journal of the House of Delegates, State of Virginia*, 1865-1866, Dec. 6, 865, 33.

32 Ibid.

33 Ibid.

legislation consenting to the transfer of Berkeley and Jefferson Counties to West Virginia.[34]

In December 1865, the legislature passed a great number of bills, most of which Pierpont opposed. The assembly first passed a vagrancy law directing authorities to arrest anyone without employment and then to hire such person out to a landowner for three-month contracts. Pierpont publicly denounced the proposal as tantamount to a return to slavery. Maj. Gen. Alfred H. Terry, military governor of Virginia, banned any official from acting on these vagrancy laws for those reasons.[35]

But the same legislature officially banned slavery within the state and, for the first time, directed the courts of Virginia to admit into evidence the testimony of black witnesses.[36] The General Assembly also forwarded a joint resolution to President Johnson declaring the state's allegiance to the United States. Yet, in the same resolution, the legislature asked Johnson to release the ex-president of the Confederacy, Jefferson Davis, from imprisonment.[37]

Only days after the session began, a number of prominent Virginia officials spoke openly in favor of choosing General Robert E. Lee to serve as governor. Speaker of the House of Delegates, John Baldwin, was the first, followed by Judge Robert M. Ould, editor of the *Richmond Whig*.[38] As support grew, Lee

---

34 *Acts of the General Assembly of the State of Virginia: Passed in 1865-1866*, 194-195.

35 Ambler, *Francis H. Pierpont*, 282-284. Recently, the Supreme Court described vagrancy laws passed by southern states in the aftermath of the Civil War as designed to "subjugate newly freed slaves and maintain the prewar racial hierarchy." *Timbs v. Indiana*, Case No, 17-1091, 2019 WL 691578, ---S.Ct.--- (February 20, 2019).

36 *Journal of the House of Delegates, State of Virginia*, 1865-1866, Dec. 20, 1865, 107-108.

37 Ibid.

38 Ibid. In 1861, Ould was the United States Attorney for the District of Columbia, appointed by President Buchanan. After the war broke out, Ould moved his family to Richmond and was appointed Assistant Secretary of War in the Confederate government. In July 1862, he was appointed to serve as the Confederate commissioner negotiating for the exchange of prisoners of war and the treatment of prisoners of war with the rank of colonel. He held this position until April 1865. He also served as judge advocate in Richmond and seems to have been heavily involved in the Confederate Secret Service. He was briefly held at Libby Prison after the war, but received a pardon from President Johnson on October 30, 1865. He subsequently defended former Confederate President Jefferson Davis from treason charges, and eventually became editor of the *Richmond Whig*. He served one term in the Virginia Senate and then in the Virginia House of Delegates from 1874-1875. In 1876, he was elected president of the Richmond, Fredericksburg & Potomac Railroad. He died on January 15, 1882 and was buried in

wisely declined, writing later that he would be "objectionable to the General Government . . . and increase the evils under which the state at present labors."[39]

Into this crucible came the bitter question of Virginia's sundering. As described many years ago by West Virginia historian Charles H. Ambler:

> A divided allegiance between West Virginia and Virginia also contributed to Pierpont's unpopularity in the mother state after 1866. In the last analysis Virginia's greatest and most permanent Civil War loss was the alienation of West Virginia and what is involved in prestige and natural resources. When Virginians seriously addressed themselves to their rehabilitation, this fact was driven home to them, and was especially reflected in their efforts to fund the state debt [and] recover Jefferson and Berkeley Counties.[40]

Approximately 32,000 West Virginians had served in the Union Army.[41] Eight thousand joined Confederate forces. Rebel armies that included 155,000 Virginians were responsible for killing more than 4,000 Union soldiers from the new state.[42] While Virginia and West Virginia shared a common history, four years of bitter civil war found the two states locked in mortal combat.

When the House of Delegates first met in session on December 4, 1865, the Speaker of the House appointed a five member Select Committee on the Restoration of Virginia.[43] Muscoe Garnett and two other members of the five-person committee submitted a majority report to the assembly just days after the legislative session began:

> That whatever mortifications and regret the people of Virginia may experience at the dismemberment of the still proud old commonwealth, they have the high and lofty consolation of knowing that it was by no act of theirs that this ungrateful deed was accomplished; that West Virginia has no cause to complain of her who has been the mother of so many states, which have not been slow to evince any other than a grateful

---

Richmond's Hollywood Cemetery near his former client, Davis. Bruce S. Allardice, *Confederate Colonels: A Biographical Register* (Columbia: University of Missouri Press, 2008), 296.

39 Robert E. Lee to David S. G. Cabell, Feb 25, 1867, Custis-Lee Family Papers, Manuscripts Division, Library of Congress, Washington, D.C.

40 Ambler, *Francis H. Pierpont*, 307.

41 Ambler, *History of West Virginia*, 336.

42 "*Soldiers and Camplife*," lva.virginia.gov/public/ guides/Civil-War/Soldiers.htm

43 *Journal of the Virginia House of Delegates, of the State of Virginia*, 1864-1865, 32.

remembrance of the fostering care and self-sacrificing spirit which she has manifested for their prosperity and general welfare . . . .

But West Virginia, forgetful of the past, and all the ties which should have bound her, as hooks of steel, to her who had given her life and being, in an evil hour elected for a separate state organization, with certainly no very friendly feelings towards those with whom she had been connected by such internal if not sacred relations. West Virginia is now a free and independent state, in the full and successful exercise of all functions . . . . If the position and condition of the two states were reversed, then might Virginia, without any loss of self-respect, or descent from the dignified position she has always sustained, and in accordance with that noble philanthropy, disinterested friendship and generosity which has always been characteristics of her people, invite back, and with outstretched arms receive her wayward daughter. But, poor and humiliated as the good mother of us all may be, she is not yet so poor but that there are some (and the undersigned claim to be of that number) 'who will still do her reverence;' and they earnestly protest against her further humiliation by inviting back those who, without just cause, have become a separate, independent, prosperous, and perhaps an alienated people, until they shall manifest, in some formal manner, a disposition for reunion.

The undersigned have not deemed it advisable to discuss the advantages or disadvantages which might result from a reunion, being of the opinion that it will be quite time enough for this when a reunion is at all probable...

Resolved by the general assembly of Virginia, That it is inexpedient at this time to legislate upon the subject of a reunion between West Virginia and Virginia; but whenever the people of the former state shall, through their constituted authorities, manifest a disposition therefore, then will Virginia be prepared to consider any overtures which may be so made.[44]

The committee report expressed a wide range of emotions regarding the dismemberment of the commonwealth. The statement was replete with pride, of the sort that prevented a defeated, but not humbled Virginia, from seeking a reconciliation with West Virginia. No, West Virginia must ask first. And that would never happen.

On January 19, 1866, dissenting members of the Select Committee on the Restoration of the State of Virginia submitted a minority report. The minority claimed, "If, in the past, any real conflict of interest existed between the eastern and western portions of the State, the same has been obliterated by the events of war, and there is no good reason why the people of both states should not be

44 Ibid., 187-188.

reunited, and live together under the flag of the Old Dominion as children of the same illustrious ancestry and heirs of a common State renown."[45] The minority on the Select Committee noted that the two states were jointly liable for bonds issued by Virginia before the states separated. Both states agreed to appoint commissioners to meet to adjust the debt. The minority went a step further and authorized the commissioners to "treat on the subject of restoration of the state . . . to its ancient boundaries."[46]

The Virginia General Assembly ultimately sided with the recommendation of the minority report. On February 28, 1866, the assembly adopted a resolution that declared:

> [T]he people of Virginia deeply lament the dismemberment of the old state, and are sincerely desirous to establish and perpetuate the re-union of the states of Virginia and West Virginia; and that they do confidently appeal to their brethren of West Virginia to concur with them in the adoption of suitable measures of co-operation in the restoration of the ancient commonwealth of Virginia, with all her people, and up to her former boundaries.[47]

Three commissioners were appointed to begin negotiations with West Virginia.[48] Not long after, however, the General Assembly recognized the futility of this mission. "Feelings had been engendered by the conflict, and interests created, which could not be reconciled."[49] In early 1866, the Governor of West Virginia, Arthur I. Boreman, put to rest a visible, symbolic affront to Virginian tradition and history. In June of 1864, the Union Army captured Lexington, Virginia, and the Virginia Military Institute (VMI). General David Hunter ordered his troops to remove the revered bronze statue of George Washington copied from the original cast by the famed French sculptor Jean-Antonie Houdon.[50] Hunter sent the statue to Wheeling, where it was placed on the grounds of the West Virginia State Capital. Boreman notified

---

45 Ibid., 182.

46 Ibid.

47 *Acts of the General Assembly of the State of Virginia*, 453.

48 George W. Munford, comp., *Third Edition of the Code of Virginia: Including Legislation to January 1, 1874* (Richmond: J. Goode, 1873), 19.

49 Ibid.

50 *OR* 37, 1:97.

Virginia's Governor Francis Pierpont in March of 1866 that the statue would be returned to VMI, thereby eliminating an obvious source of friction between the two states.[51]

Virginia then took a different tack. On March 1, 1866, the assembly passed a resolution finding that West Virginia was urging Congress to give formal consent to the transfer of Jefferson and Berkeley Counties to the new state. The legislation authorized and directed the governor and attorney general to initiate legal action against West Virginia if Congress consented to the transfer of Jefferson and Berkeley Counties to West Virginia. The legislation also authorized the governor to retain U.S. Senator Reverdy Johnson to serve as co-counsel with the attorney general.[52]

---

51 Jon-Erik Gilot, "A Monumental Controversy." Web blog post, *Emerging Civil War*, 5 Sept. 2017, https://emergingcivilwar.com/2017/09/05/a-monumental-controversy/.

52 This is the text of the resolution:

CHAP. 85.—AN ACT TO PROVIDE FOR THE ASSERTION OF THE RIGHTS OF THIS COMMONWEALTH TO JURISDICTION OVER THE COUNTIES OF JEFFERSON AND BERKELEY. PASSED MARCH 1, 1866

Whereas, notwithstanding the passage, during the present session of the general assembly, of an act repealing all laws giving consent to the annexation of the counties of Jefferson and Berkeley to the state of West Virginia, it appears that said state is making an effort to obtain the consent of the congress of the United States to said annexation: and whereas, in the judgment of the general assembly, such action on the part of congress would be wholly nugatory now that the consent of Virginia has been withdrawn: and whereas the state of West Virginia is exercising jurisdiction over said counties; and whereas it may be the congress of the United States will, after the adjournment of this legislature, give its consent to their annexation to West Virginia, thereby making it necessary, before the legislature shall again convene, for this commonwealth to have its rights to jurisdiction over said counties determined by the proper legal tribunals:

1. Be it therefore enacted, That it shall be the duty of the attorney general of this commonwealth, under the direction of the governor, in case the consent of congress should be given to such annexation, at once to institute such legal proceedings as may be proper, either at law or in equity, and to adopt and carry out all other measures as may be necessary on the part of this commonwealth, to secure as soon as possible, a decision by the appropriate legal tribunals, of any and all questions arising out of the attempt to annex said counties of Jefferson and Berkeley, or either of them, to the state of West Virginia, or of said state to exercise jurisdiction over them. And the governor is hereby authorized and directed to employ, and associate with the attorney general, in conducting said proceedings, Reverdy Johnson, and such other counsel as he may deem proper, and to pay them such just compensation as may be agreed upon, together with all other necessary expenses attending the same, out of the appropriation herein after made.

In 1862, Congress debated the methods used to create the State of West Virginia at length. Lincoln himself entertained serious doubts about the constitutionality of dividing Virginia into two states. His own cabinet split evenly on the question. Yet, as the matter headed to the Supreme Court, only two of West Virginia's fifty-five counties were at stake, and not the question of the constitutionality of the process employed to create the new state.

In the end, Muscoe Garnett was right. This was not the time to seek a reunion with West Virginia. The two states had recently opposed each other in the bloodiest war in American history. Moreover, the Radical Republicans firmly controlled Congress and the Union Army occupied the state. And the United States Supreme Court, Virginia's last hope in the federal government, had a Chief Justice, a former member of Lincoln's cabinet, who faced an increasingly hostile Republican Congress, ready to limit the Court's authority. The war had its consequences, and the dismemberment of Virginia was one of them.

On March 6, 1866, Congress responded by passing House Joint Resolution No. 17, consenting to the transfer of the two counties to West Virginia.[53] Senator Reverdy Johnson of Maryland was the only Democrat who voted for the transfer. Later that year, Virginia sued West Virginia in the Supreme Court. Reverdy Johnson indeed acted as counsel in the lawsuit, but for West Virginia.

Meanwhile, the Republican Congress rebelled against the post-war policies of President Johnson. Upon returning to session on December 4, 1865, both the House and Senate refused to seat Congressmen or Senators elected under

---

2. And be it further enacted, That the governor be and he is hereby authorized and requested, at the earliest day practicable after the refusal of congress to give such consent, or after a decision by the appropriate legal tribunal, in favor of this commonwealth, to proceed to have said counties fully organized in respect to all their functions, both judicial and political.

3. And be it further enacted, That to defray the expenses incurred under the first section of this act, the sum of ten thousand dollars is hereby appropriated, out of any money in the treasury not otherwise appropriated, to be paid from time to time, as required, under the direction of the governor, upon the warrant of the auditor of public accounts.

4. This act shall be in force from and after the passage thereof.
Acts of the General Assembly of the State of Virginia, 195-196.

53 Edward McPherson, Clerk of the House of Representatives, *A Political Manual for 1866 and 1867* {Washington, DC; 1867), 116.

Johnson's Reconstruction policies.[54] The President and Congress clashed as to the steps required before Southern states could return to the Union. For the next three years, with the exception of Tennessee, the Southern states had no representatives in the House or Senate.[55] Republicans controlled Congress by more than the two-thirds margin required to override a presidential veto.[56] Events in the South soon encouraged Congress to challenge the Democratic president. In May 1866, rioting killed forty-eight newly-freed African Americans in Memphis Tennessee and scores more in Norfolk, Virginia and New Orleans, Louisiana.[57] In response, Congress passed a proposed Fourteenth Amendment to the Constitution that was then sent to the states for ratification.[58]

By its terms, the Fourteenth Amendment repealed the *Dred Scott* case, as the amendment declared that all persons born within the United States are citizens of both the nation and the state wherein the person resides.[59] The same amendment prohibited the states from denying to any of its citizens equal protection or the due process of law.[60] While not addressing whether freed slaves could vote, Section 2 of the proposed amendment provided that, if a state excluded certain male inhabitants from voting, that state would have its share of House members reduced proportionally. This clause voided the provision of the original Article I, Section 2 of the United States Constitution that counted slaves as three-fifths of a person in apportioning the number of house seats per

---

54 Guelzo, *Reconstruction*, 24. A number of prominent former Confederate officeholders were elected to the United States Congress in the fall of 1865, including Alexander Stephens, former Vice President of the Confederacy, who was elected by the Georgia legislature as a U.S. Senator. Ibid.

55 Ibid.

56 Art. I, Sect. 7, U.S. Constitution. Guelzo, *Reconstruction*, 29.

57 Guelzo, *Reconstruction*, 36.

58 Hon. Bernice Bouie Donald, *When the Rule of Law Breaks Down: Implications of the 1866 Memphis Massacre for the Passage of the Fourteenth Amendment*, 98 B.U. L. Rev. 1607, 1643 (2018) ("The Republican Party relied upon their momentum in the 1866 midterm elections to continue advocating for state ratification of the Fourteenth Amendment. . . . Only a few months after the Memphis Massacre, the New Orleans Massacre extended federal interest in the atrocities against freedmen in the South.")

59 *Dred Scott v. Sanford*, 60 U.S. 393, 406 (1857); 14th Amend., Sect. 1. The majority of the Supreme Court held that slaves and descendants of slaves could never be citizens.

60 Ibid.

state. Section 3 provided that no person who had previously held civilian or military office and joined in the rebellion could again hold office, unless Congress eliminated such person's legal disability by a two-thirds vote. Section 4 also invalidated any debts incurred by the Confederacy and any state supporting the rebellion.

The Virginia Assembly took up the Fourteenth Amendment on January 9, 1867. Pierpont urged the legislature to ratify the measure, describing its terms as "not nearly as hard as they might be." The disabilities imposed upon former Confederates were temporary. The vote that followed demonstrated Pierpont's utter lack of public support. The Virginia Senate rejected the measure by a 27 to 0 vote. In the House, one member voted to ratify the amendment, and 74 rejected it.[61]

Only weeks later, Congress jettisoned the earlier terms offered the Southern States by Johnson as conditions of reunification. In February and March 1867, Congress passed three Reconstruction Acts that dramatically changed the terms for readmission of the former Confederate states.[62] Johnson vetoed all three enactments, but Congress overrode each of Johnson's vetoes.[63]

The first of the acts imposed a military governor on each of the former Confederate states, excepting only Tennessee, which had already been readmitted to the Union.[64] By appointing a military governor of Virginia, Congress set aside the fiction it created by recognizing the Restored Government of Virginia as the lawful elected officers of the state. If the Restored Government was not legitimate, as implied by the first Reconstruction Act, how could the same government have given lawful consent on behalf of Virginia in 1862 to the creation of West Virginia?

Nonetheless, on March 13, 1867, Maj. Gen. John M. Schofield became the military governor of Virginia.[65] All elections were suspended until a new state constitutional convention was held. The Reconstruction Acts required each state to revise its constitution by selecting delegates chosen by all citizens,

---

61 *Journal of the House of Delegates, State of Virginia*, 1866-1867, 108-109 and 508-509.

62 14 Stat. 428, 15 Stat. 2, 15 Stat. 14, 41 (1867).

63 Guelzo, *Reconstruction*, 49.

64 14 Stat. 428-430, March 2, 1867.

65 Foner, *Reconstruction*, 308.

including African Americans.[66] Elections for the delegates to the Constitutional Convention were held in October of 1867. Pierpont ran for delegate, but was defeated by a James Morrissey, who had just moved to Virginia.[67] Of the 105 delegates elected, 25 were African American.[68] Enthusiastic black voters nearly outnumbered whites.[69]

Pierpont continued to serve as governor, albeit with little authority. His term, established by the old Restored Government, extended through January 1, 1868. Because no elections were permitted, he held over as governor until April 4, 1868, when General Schofield finally removed him from office.[70] Henry H. Wells, a former Union general who had only recently moved to Virginia, replaced him.[71]

In April 1868, following the elections, the delegates proposed a new constitution that guaranteed black suffrage and universal education. The delegates also adopted the earlier ironclad oath for officeholders, requiring them to swear that they had not supported the Confederacy. The latter provision once again proved to be highly controversial, affecting seventy percent of white voters. In turn, General Schofield refused to authorize a statewide vote on the constitution.[72] Consequently, Virginia remained unreconstructed and unable to participate in the presidential election of 1868.[73]

Once in office, newly inaugurated President Ulysses S. Grant ordered Schofield to conduct an election on the proposed constitution. He also ordered that a separate vote be taken on the ironclad oath.[74] For the first time since the end of the war, Virginians also elected new state officeholders. The recently appointed Governor Henry H. Wells was the Republican candidate for the office. The Democrats nominated Gilbert C. Walker, who had no association

66 Reconstruction Act, March 2, 1867, 14 Stat. 428-70.

67 Ibid.

68 Ibid.

69 Ibid.

70 *Richmond Enquirer*, April 6, 1868.

71 Ambler, *Francis H. Pierpont*, 307.

72 Foner, *Reconstruction*, 412.

73 Guelzo, *Reconstruction*, 57.

74 Ibid., 413.

with secession.[75] Walker presented himself to voters as a moderate, not opposed to blacks voting, but opposed to ironclad oaths.[76] Both Wells and Walker were Northerners, competing to govern the state that included the capital of the former Confederacy. Walker also campaigned on a plan for the development of a railroad to rival the B & O. He formed a coalition of white moderates and conservatives joining with a significant number of black voters and handily defeated Wells. The voters also approved the new constitution on July 6, 1869, although they defeated the loyalty oath by a lopsided margin.[77]

On October 8, 1869, the new Virginia General Assembly, including twenty-nine black senators and delegates, ratified the Fourteenth Amendment, thereby fulfilling one of the conditions pursuant to the Reconstruction Acts. On the same day, the legislature also approved the Fifteenth Amendment, which prohibited states from denying a citizen the right to vote on the basis of race.[78] On January 26, 1870, President Grant signed legislation readmitting Virginia to the Union.[79]

Virginia's reconstruction was over, but the fate of Berkeley and Jefferson Counties remained in the hands of Salmon P. Chase and the United States Supreme Court.

---

75 Ibid.

76 Ibid.

77 Peter Wallenstein, *Cradle of America; A History of Virginia*, (Lawrence: University of Kansas Press, 2007). 223.

78 Ronald Heinman, *Old Dominion, New Commonwealth: a History of Virginia, 1607-2007* (Charlottesville: University of Virginia Press, 2008), 250.

79 41 Cong. Second Sess., 720 and 759.

CHAPTER TEN

Virginia Files Suit

A. The Complaint

On December 11, 1866, Thomas R. Bowden, acting in his capacity as the duly elected and authorized Attorney General of the Commonwealth of Virginia, filed a lawsuit in the United States Supreme Court against the State of West Virginia. The Complaint, a formal legal document initiating a lawsuit, set forth the legal claims, and described the relief sought by Virginia. The full text of the Complaint is included as Appendix B to this book.

In the first sentence, the Complaint set forth that the basis for filing the case as an original action in the Supreme Court, rather than in a trial or appellate court. Bowden claimed that Virginia, "one of the United States of America," brought the action against the "State of West Virginia, one of the United States of America."[1] Article III, Section 2, of the Constitution vests the Supreme Court with very little original jurisdiction, meaning the authority to initially hear and decide a case. The Constitution grants to the Supreme Court original jurisdiction only to cases "affecting Ambassadors, other public Ministers and Consuls, and those in which a State shall be a party."[2] In all other cases, the

---

1 Complaint, Par. 1.

2 Almost all cases heard by the Supreme Court involve appeals from lower courts. Not so in the small number of cases within the original jurisdiction of the Supreme Court. From 1789

Constitution provides that the Supreme Court shall have only "appellate jurisdiction," meaning authority to review trials and decisions first occurring in trial or other lower courts.

The claim by Virginia that its lawsuit was an action by one state against another might seem unremarkable. The claim, if true, vested the Supreme Court with original jurisdiction. If not true, the Supreme Court lacked jurisdiction to hear the case, which would have required dismissal of the action.[3] In December of 1866, the status of Virginia, and the other former Confederate states, was anything but settled in the aftermath of the Civil War. On March 2, 1867, only weeks after the Complaint was filed, Virginia was placed under military administration following passage of the first Reconstruction Act.[4] The Reconstruction Acts, which Congress passed over the veto of President Johnson, declared that the former Confederate States (other than Tennessee) had "no legal government." The simple recitation in the Complaint that the lawsuit was a claim by one state against another raised a fundamental legal question that deeply divided the other two branches of the federal government.

By modern standards, the Complaint was remarkably short. For reasons explored below, Virginia recited, without objection, that in 1862 "the general assembly of said Commonwealth passed an act giving consent of the said Commonwealth to the formation and erection of a new state, called West Virginia."[5] That general assembly sat in Wheeling (then part of Virginia and, later, the new capital of West Virginia) and claimed to be the legislative government for all of Virginia.

The Complaint did not question whether Virginia and Congress had both lawfully consented to the creation of a new state from Virginia's territory. Article IV, Section 3 of the Constitution expressly provides that "no new State shall be formed or erected within the jurisdiction of any other State . . . without

---

through 1959, the Supreme Court decided only 123 original jurisdiction cases, or fewer that one per year. Federal Judicial Center, *Jurisdiction: Original, Supreme Court.*

3 Original jurisdiction is distinct from exclusive jurisdiction, the latter of which requires the Supreme Court to hear a case. Since the Judiciary Act of 1789, the Supreme Court has original and exclusive jurisdiction to hear cases filed by one state against another. W.J. Wagner, *Original Jurisdiction of National Supreme Courts*, St. Johns Law Review, Vol. XXXII, No. 2 (May 1959), 217. See also, Judiciary Act of 1789, par.13, I Stat. 73.

4 14 Stat. 428-430.

5 Complaint, Par. 2.

the consent of the of the legislatures of the States concerned as well as of the Congress."

Instead, the Complaint focused upon just two of the so-called railroad counties, Berkeley and Jefferson, both situated to the east of the Allegheny Mountains and through both of which the all-important main line of the B & O Railroad passed. Jefferson County included the town of Harpers Ferry, a militarily important site, located at the confluence of the Potomac and Shenandoah Rivers. Martinsburg, the seat of Berkeley County, occupied equally important territory at the lower end of the Shenandoah Valley.

Virginia claimed that the General Assembly only conditionally consented to including these two counties in the new state. The same language was in the legislation adopted by Congress giving only conditional consent to inclusion of the two counties into the new State of West Virginia. According to the Complaint:

> [I]t was further provided that the consent of the legislation of the said Commonwealth was thereby given that the Counties of Berkeley, Jefferson and Frederick[6] . . . should be included in and form part of the State of West Virginia whenever the voters of said counties should ratify and assent to said constitution, at such time and regulations as commissioners named in said schedule annexed to the proposed constitution might prescribe.[7]

Thereafter, on January 21, 1863, the Complaint claims, the Virginia legislature enacted a law providing for an election on the question of whether Berkeley County should join West Virginia. The same legislation established the fourth Tuesday in May 1863 as the date of the election. Finally, the act also provided that "the governor of this State, if of the opinion that said vote has been opened and held, and the result ascertained and certified pursuant to law, shall certify the result."[8] Similar legislation also passed regarding Jefferson County.

---

6 A third county, Frederick, was involved in the legislation creating the special elections disputed in the lawsuit, but not in the case itself. The county seat, Winchester, was the scene of seven major military engagements of the Civil War, and Winchester changed hands 72 times during the course of the war. The county voted against the proposed new West Virginia Constitution and consequently remained part of Virginia.

7 Complaint, Par. 2.

8 Complaint, Par. 3.

The Complaint omitted reference to the reason special elections were required in the two challenged counties. A year earlier, most of other counties constituting the new State of West Virginia voted on a new constitution that also approved statehood, no elections were held at that time in Berkeley and Jefferson Counties. Both counties provided significant numbers of troops to the Confederacy and were closely aligned with the interests of eastern Virginia. The Union Army occupied those two counties on the date of the elections and did not trust the voters to support secession from Virginia. Consequently, their citizens were denied the right to vote in the special elections.[9]

On many occasions Union and Confederate forces battled in the two counties. The Shenandoah Valley provided Confederate forces with a physical roadway to Washington, D.C. and was the site of almost constant fighting. On May 23, 1861, Berkeley County voted in favor of secession by a count of 813 in favor and 365 opposed.[10] Jefferson County had voted against secession by a vote of 508 in favor and 1303 opposed.[11] In contrast, most of the counties in the new State of West Virginia voted against secession in large margins in 1861. Before the boundaries of the new state were established, Berkeley and Jefferson counties were required by Congress to vote upon joining West Virginia. By the early summer of 1863, the Union Army controlled both counties and remained in control of them for the balance of the war. Under the direction of the governor, the Army conducted the May 23, 1863 elections.[12]

The Complaint picks up the story: "[A]t the time fixed by said acts for opening the said polls, the State of the country in the aforesaid counties of Berkeley and Jefferson rendered it impracticable to open the polls at all the places, or any considerable part of the places, of voting…in either of them."[13]

Further, according to the attorneys for Virginia, voters

did not and could not attend the same by reason of the civil war then and there being waged and actively carried on; and by reason thereof could not be, and in point of fact was not, a full and free expression or any expression…of either of them, concerning

---

9 Lewis, *History of West Virginia*, 186.

10 "The Vote for Secession in Virginia."

11 Ibid.

12 Senate Misc. Doc. No. 98, 37th Congress, 2nd Session, 2-3.

13 Complaint, Par. 6.

such proposed annexation; and in point of fact, a great majority of the voters of the said counties then were and now annexation.[14]

Instead, Virginia claimed that the elections were fraudulent. According to the Complaint:

> [I]t having been falsely and fraudulently suggested, and falsely and untruly made to appear to the governor of said Commonwealth that the polls in said counties had been opened, and that a large majority of the votes were in favor of their annexation to said State of West Virginia, the said governor, acting under such false suggestion, and being wholly ignorant of the truth in the premises, did certify the same on or about the fourteenth of September in the year of Our Lord one thousand eight hundred and sixty three.[15]

The Complaint omitted the fact that the same Governor of Virginia who certified the allegedly false election results was also the current holder of the office when the lawsuit was filed. Instead, Virginia attacked the integrity of the elections held in the disputed counties, but artfully avoided any criticism of its own governor, who vouched for the results. According to the Complaint, the governor was "wholly ignorant" of the fraud and falsity that permeated the voting.[16]

In addition to these claims, Virginia charged that the consent required of Congress in Article IV, Section 3 of the Constitution never occurred before Virginia withdrew its own constitutionally required consent.[17] Virginia admitted to giving conditional consent in 1862, permitting the two counties to leave, if after an election, a majority of voters wished to join West Virginia. Yet, the state withdrew its consent by an act of its legislature on December 5, 1865. Since Congress had not yet consented and acted to transfer the counties to West Virginia, Virginia claimed the right to withdraw the state's consent, thereby effectively nullifying the earlier conditional approval.[18]

---

14 Ibid. In 1866, and well into the Twentieth Century, the United States Government referred to the conflict as the War of the Rebellion, not the Civil War.

15 Ibid., par. 5.

16 Ibid.

17 Ibid., par. 6.

18 Ibid.

According to Virginia, "the consent of Congress, as required by the Constitution of the United States, not having been obtained in order to give effect to the transfer, so that the proceedings heretofore had on this subject are simply inchoate, and said consent may be properly withdrawn."[19]

The somewhat obscure word "inchoate" encapsulated Virginia's argument. An inchoate right is one not vested or completed.[20] For example, when a living person makes a bequest to a friend in a Last Will and Testament, any right to that property is inchoate. The living person may at any time change her will or terminate the earlier bequest, thereby divesting the beneficiary of any right to the property. Virginia made a similar claim. No territory of a first state can be made the territory of a new state unless the first state and Congress consent. While Virginia may have first given consent, until Congress also gave its required consent, "the proceedings . . . are simply inchoate."[21] As a person could make a new will as long as life continues, so too could Virginia withdraw her consent, at least until Congress gave its express consent to the transfer of the two counties to West Virginia.

Responding to the attempted withdrawal of consent by the Virginia legislature, Congress swiftly passed legislation on March 10, 1866, formally consenting to the transfer of Berkeley and Jefferson Counties to West Virginia.[22] The Complaint concluded with a request for relief, describing the remedy Virginia sought from the Supreme Court: "The Commonwealth of Virginia prays that it may be ascertained . . . by the decree of this honorable court, that the aforesaid Counties of Berkeley and Jefferson now lawfully are, and ought to be, deemed part of the territory of the Commonwealth of Virginia."[23]

B. The Attorneys for the Commonwealth of Virginia

Two lawyers signed Virginia's Complaint, each coming from a very different background. The better known of the two, Benjamin Robbins Curtis,

19 Ibid.

20 *Black's Law Dictionary* (10th ed. 2014).

21 Ibid.

22 House Joint Resolution 17, 39th Congress, 2nd Session.

23 Ibid., par. 8.

[April 18, 1868.

BENJAMIN R. CURTIS, OF MASS.—[Phot. by Whipple.]

Justice Benjamin R. Curtis, former associate justice of the Supreme Court, who represented Virginia in *Virginia v. West Virginia (Library of Congress)*

had served on the United States Supreme Court from 1851 to 1857. Curtis, a Massachusetts native and graduate of the Harvard Law School, was the first Supreme Court justice to attend law school.[24] Known more as a lawyer than as an ideologue, Curtis nonetheless found himself in the midst of the slavery question when, during his tenure on the bench, the Supreme Court decided the case of *Dred Scott v. Sandford.*[25]

The majority opinion, authored by Chief Justice Roger Brooke Taney, held in part that Dred Scott could never become a citizen of the United States because his ancestors were slaves. Dissenting, Curtis penned a vigorous response:

> It has often been asserted that the Constitution was made exclusively by and for the white race. It has already been shown that, in five of the original states, colored persons then possessed the elective franchise, and were among those by whom the Constitution was ordained and established. If so, it is not true, in the point of fact, that

24 Benjamin Robbins Curtis was born on November 4, 1809 in Watertown, Massachusetts, as the son of a captain of a merchant ship. After attending local schools, Curtis enrolled at Harvard, graduating Phi Beta Kappa in 1829. He graduated from Harvard Law School in 1832 and was admitted to the bar the following year. He became a prominent attorney in Massachusetts. At the behest of Massachusetts Sen. Daniel Webster, President Millard Fillmore made a recess appointment of Curtis to be an associate justice of the U.S. Supreme Court on September 22, 1851, filling the vacancy caused by the death of Associate Justice Levi Woodbury. Fillmore formally nominated him on December 11, and Curtis was confirmed nine days later. Curtis served as an Associate Justice for six years. He resigned his position in protest of the *Dred Scott* decision, which exasperated him. For a detailed biography, see Benjamin R. Curtis, *A Memoir of Benjamin Robbins Curtis, L.L.D., with Some of His Professional and Miscellaneous Writings*, 2 vols. (Boston: Little, Brown & Co., 1879).

25 60 U.S. 393. (1857).

the Constitution was made exclusively by the white race. And that it was made exclusively for the white race is, in my opinion, not only an assumption not warranted by anything in the Constitution, but contradicted by its opening declaration that it was ordained and established by the people of the United States.[26]

Following the *Dred Scott* decision, Curtis resigned from the bench in disgust and resumed the private practice of law. Recognized as a leading trial lawyer of his era, President Andrew Johnson hired Curtis to defend him in his 1868 impeachment trial before the United States Senate while Virginia's case against West Virginia wended its way through the Supreme Court. As provided in Article I, Section 3 of the Constitution, Chief Justice Chase presided at the Senate trial. The Senate voted 35 to 19 to remove Johnson from office, one vote short of the two-thirds majority required by the Constitution. A grateful Johnson offered to nominate Curtis to be Attorney General, which he declined.[27]

Thomas R. Bowden, Attorney General of Virginia, came from a pro-Union family in Williamsburg, Virginia. Openly opposed to secession in a strongly pro-Confederate county, Bowden and his family fled to Alexandria. In 1863, at the precocious age of twenty-two, he ran for Attorney General in the few Virginia counties under control of the Union Army and Pierpont's Restored Government of Virginia. For most of the war, Bowden supported the Union war effort in a state leading the rebellion. Though not as conflicted as Virginia's chief executive, Bowden was Attorney General when Governor Pierpont certified the regularity and propriety of the elections held in Berkeley and Jefferson Counties on September 14, 1863.[28]

---

26 Ibid., 582.

27 For a detailed account of the Andrew Johnson impeachment case, see David O. Stewart, *Impeached: The Trial of President Andrew Johnson and the Fight for Lincoln's Legacy* (New York: Simon & Schuster, 2009).

28 Thomas R. Bowden was born in Williamsburg, Virginia on May 20, 1841, and grew up on his father's farm. He enrolled in the Collage of William and Mary in 1859, studying Latin, Green, French, history, and economics for two years. He also studied law in his father's law office in Williamsburg. The family was staunchly pro-Union, and his father represented Virginia in the U. S. Senate before his death in 1864. Only 22 years of age at the time, Bowden was elected attorney general of the Restored Government of Virginia on May 28, 1863, becoming Virginia's youngest-ever attorney general. Bowden served as attorney general until losing a bid for reelection in 1869, at which time he went into private practice in Richmond. He

Sen. Reverdy Johnson of Maryland, who represented West Virginia before the Supreme Court. *(Library of Congress)*

Both Pierpont and Bowden now served with a hostile Virginia legislature elected in the fall of 1865 and full of former Confederates. Radical Republicans remained firmly in control of both house of Congress, setting the stage for further conflict.

C. The Attorneys For West Virginia

West Virginia hired both a sitting United States Senator and a former colonel of the Confederate Army to defend its claim to Berkeley and Jefferson Counties. Senator Reverdy Johnson of Maryland was as distinguished a lawyer as Benjamin Curtis. He served as Attorney General under President Zachary Taylor, and also served in the United States Senate for many years. As a private attorney, Johnson was involved in a great number of high-profile cases, and represented the slaveholder, John Sandford, in the *Dred Scott* case.[29] During the Civil War, Johnson defended Maj. Gen. Fitz John Porter in a politically charged, controversial court martial.[30] While Porter was convicted, years later the judgment was overturned and Porter was reinstated to his prior rank of colonel

---

died in Washington, D.C. on July 6, 1893. See Donald W. Gunter, "Bowden, Thomas Russell, *Dictionary of Virginia Biography*, 2:132-133.

29 Bernard C. Steiner, *The Life of Reverdy Johnson* (Baltimore: The Norman Remington Co., 1914), 37.

30 Ibid., 55.

in the United States Army. In 1865, Johnson defended Mary Surratt, convicted of conspiring with John Wilkes Booth to murder Abraham Lincoln.[31]

Though a Democrat, Johnson supported Lincoln. In turn, Lincoln entrusted him with sensitive war matters. Maj. Gen. Benjamin F. Butler, an influential Democratic politician and lawyer from Massachusetts and one of many political generals, proved difficult for Lincoln to control. While in charge of the 1862 military occupation of New Orleans, Butler assumed nearly complete control of the city and soon caused an international controversy when he ordered the seizure of assets held by foreign governments in local consulates. Lincoln enlisted Johnson to review Butler's orders.[32] Johnson rescinded Butler's foreign seizures, an action Lincoln supported.[33] Johnson complained to Lincoln that Butler's conduct was hurting the Union case. Lincoln couched his response in flattery, allowing him to bare his teeth:

> You remember telling me . . . that it would crush all union feeling in Maryland for me to attempt bringing troops over Maryland soil to Washington. I brought the troops notwithstanding, and yet there was union feeling enough to elect a legislature the next

---

31 Reverdy Johnson was born in Annapolis, Maryland on May 21, 1796. He was the son of distinguished Maryland lawyer John Johnson, who served as attorney general of Maryland and as chancellor of Maryland. Reverdy Johnson graduated from St. John's College in 1812 and then studied law. He was admitted to the bar in 1815. He practiced law in Baltimore, and became involved in first Democratic Party local politics and then in national politics, twice serving as U.S. Senator from Maryland and as Attorney General of the United States during the administration of President Zachary Taylor. During his second stint in the Senate, from 1863-1868, he advocated for a softer Reconstruction policy than that supported by the Radical Republicans. He also defended Mary Surratt during the trial of the Lincoln assassination conspirators. He briefly served as ambassador to Great Britain before returning home to represent West Virginia before the Supreme Court. Johnson died on February 10, 1876 after slipping, falling, and striking his head on a sharp masonry corner. He loomed large over Maryland politics for much of the Nineteenth Century. For a full-length biography of Johnson, see Steiner, *Life of Reverdy Johnson.*

32 Steiner, *Life of Reverdy Johnson,* 58.

33 While acting as military governor of New Orleans, Butler ordered the seizure of $800,000 that had been deposited in the office of the Dutch consul, imprisoned a French champagne magnate, and refused to cooperate with a British citizen whom Butler accused of aiding the Confederate cause. Secretary of State Seward dispatched Reverdy Johnson to New Orleans to investigate the complaints of foreign consuls against Butler's policies. Butler countermanded a direct order by Lincoln to restore a sugar shipment claimed by Europeans. Butler also imposed a strict quarantine to protect against yellow fever, which inhibited foreign commerce and triggered complaint by most foreign consuls. See John D. Winters, *The Civil War in Louisiana* (Baton Rouge: Louisiana State University Press, 1963), 128-129.

autumn, which in turn elected a very excellent Union United States Senator. I am a patient man, always willing to forgive on the Christian terms of repentance . . . still I must save this government, if possible. What I cannot do, of course, I will not do, but it may as well be understood, once and for all, that I will not surrender this game, leaving any card unplayed.[34]

While the case brought by Virginia remained pending in the Supreme Court, Johnson was the only Democratic member of Congress to support the Reconstruction Acts of 1867. During the pendency of the Virginia's lawsuit, the House of Representatives impeached President Johnson. While the narrowly drawn charges concerned Johnson's firing of the Secretary of War, Edwin M. Stanton, the larger struggle between Congress and the President involved the question of whether the Congress or the President would control Reconstruction policy. As a senator, Reverdy Johnson sat in judgment of President Johnson while Chief Justice Chase presided at the impeachment trial and Benjamin Curtis defended the President. Despite his support of the Reconstruction Acts, Reverdy Johnson was one of 19 senators who did not vote to remove President Johnson from office.

Johnson saw no conflict between his service as U.S. Senator from Maryland and his work as a nationally recognized lawyer. Only a year after the war ended, Johnson wrote to G.A. Chairs, a confidant of Jefferson Davis, indirectly, but plainly offering his legal services to the former President of the Confederacy, who was imprisoned and soon to be charged with treason.[35] On May 15, 1866, Johnson wrote: "I shall write you and our Southern friends in solicitation of sympathy for Mr. Davis, and would rejoice to see him released. I am not however one of his counsel, not having been applied to by him, or under his authority, to do so." He concluded, "If I had been, and his trial was to be had, when my duties in the Senate (at this time, as, I suppose you know, all important), were at an end, I would serve him faithfully. He has, however, I hear, a counsel who I doubt not will do all that can be done in his defence."[36] In holding and expressing such sentiments, it seems obvious that Johnson strongly

---

34 Steiner, *The Life of Reverdy Johnson*, 59-60.

35 Direct solicitation of a client by a lawyer is generally prohibited. See Rule 7.3, Model Rules of Professional Conduct. Johnson obliquely stated that he "would serve him [Davis] faithfully," rather than expressly offering his legal services.

36 Dunbar Rowland, ed., *Jefferson Davis, Constitutionalist, His Letters, Papers, and Speeches*, 9 vols. (Jackson: Mississippi Dept. of Archives and History, 1923), 9:415.

sympathized with the plight of the former Confederate president, suggesting that he might also sympathize with the plight of Virginia.

By 1866, Reverdy Johnson's worth as a pro-Union, Democratic Senator from Maryland, had lost much of its value in a post-war government dominated by Republicans bent on remaking the South. The same year, he argued the case of *Cummings v. Missouri* in the Supreme Court.[37] In the aftermath of the state's internecine war, Missouri enacted a constitutional provision banning anyone who served in, aided, or expressed support for the Confederacy from holding any office or position of trust, including one in a religious organization.[38] Cummings, a Catholic priest, refused to take the oath. He was charged, convicted, ordered to pay a $500 fine and jailed for lack of payment.[39] Johnson argued that the law criminalized conduct long after the acts occurred, in violation of the prohibition against ex post facto laws set forth in the Constitution.[40]

The case drew national attention. Whether ex-Confederates could vote or hold public office remained a contentious issue which sharply divided President Johnson from the Republican Congress.[41] The Supreme Court adjourned at the end of the 1866 session without deciding the polarizing case.[42] While campaigning for Democratic candidates in Missouri, Reverdy Johnson audaciously claimed that he had heard from a Supreme Court justice that the body was about to declare the loyalty oath unconstitutional.[43] If true, such a breach of confidentiality as to discussions of a pending case was highly inappropriate. In private correspondence, two justices criticized Johnson.

---

37 71 U.S. 277 (1867).

38 Ibid., 280.

39 Ibid., 282.

40 Ibid., 318. The ex post facto clause is found in Article I, Sect. 9, clause 3 of the Constitution, and provides, "No bill of attainder or ex post facto law shall be passed." This clause prohibits the enactment of laws that retroactively change the legal consequences (or status) of actions that were committed, or relationships that existed, before the enactment of the law.

41 Michael A. Ross, *Justice of Shattered Dreams: Samuel Freeman Miller and the Supreme Court During the Civil War Era* (Baton Rouge, LA: Louisiana State University Press, 2003), 132.

42 Ibid., 133.

43 Ibid.,133-134.

Justice Stephen J. Field called Reverdy Johnson's claim "indefensible."[44] Justice Samuel Freeman Miller was even more critical, calling Johnson "an old political prostitute" who was "hated by all loyal men worse than a thousand times than they hate many honest rebels."[45] On January 14th, in a five to four decision, the Supreme Court struck down Missouri's loyalty oath as an unconstitutional ex post facto enactment.[46]

By the time Virginia brought suit against West Virginia, Reverdy Johnson had angered Republican leaders and editors. Horace Greeley, editor of the *New York Tribune* and a prominent Republican, wrote:

> Mr. Reverdy Johnson, of Maryland, has lately achieved some notoriety by appearing, not for the first time, as counsel on the side of the Rebellion. His previous performances in that line were of considerable service to the rebel cause while it still had some chance of success. The cause being dead, Mr. Johnson exerts himself with the same zeal in behalf of its still surviving leaders. His chosen arena is the Supreme Court of the United States. . .but he is really the advocate of the host of unpardoned traitors in whose pathway to fortune, fame, and political success the test-oath is a stumbling block. . . . We suppose Mr. Johnson considers it his professional privilege to argue on any side for which he gets a retainer . . . . Yet Mr. Johnson allows himself to be quoted on that side where his pecuniary interest lies, and not on that side where his vote in the Senate stands recorded.[47]

Only weeks after this editorial ran in one of the most influential newspapers in America, the Virginia General Assembly authorized state officials to hire Reverdy Johnson as counsel in the suit to be filed against West Virginia. The Virginia legislature undoubtedly knew of Johnson and his long, pro-Union war record. The same legislature also knew of his opposition to most of the Republican reconstruction policies.

Johnson declined to represent Virginia, instead choosing to represent West Virginia. If Johnson had simply been a practicing lawyer, his retention by West Virginia would be of little import. But as a sitting Senator from a former slave state that remained in the Union, his choice of clients is more telling. Dominant Republican members of Congress no longer saw Reverdy Johnson as an ally in a

---

44 Ibid., 134.

45 Miller to William Pitt Ballinger, Feb. 6, 1867, Samuel Freeman Miller Papers, Manuscripts Division, Library of Congress, Washington, D.C.

46 71 U.S. 277(1867).

47 "Reverdy Johnson on Test Oaths," *New York Daily Tribune*, December 29, 1865.

Rep. Charles J. Faulkner of Berkeley County, who represented West Virginia in *Virginia v. West Virginia. (Library of Congress)*

war that had ended. Johnson, a political survivor, chose to represent West Virginia, understanding the animosity he faced if he represented Virginia, the largest of the Confederate states.

West Virginia also retained Charles J. Faulkner, a lifelong resident of the disputed Berkeley County, as Johnson's co-counsel. Faulkner served several terms in the Virginia House of Delegates and later as a member of Congress from 1851 through 1859.[48] President Buchanan appointed him Ambassador to France in 1860, but a year later Lincoln recalled him. Upon his return in 1861, he was arrested and charged with purchasing munitions for the Confederate Army and was imprisoned for several months. Faulkner was eventually released in an exchange of prisoners of war.

Once freed, he promptly joined the Confederate Army, serving as assistant adjutant general under Stonewall Jackson. When the war ended, Faulkner returned to Berkeley County and resumed his practice of law. For many years, he refused to take an oath of allegiance to the United States, which prevented him from voting or holding public office. Only in 1872, after a special bill in Congress restored his civil rights, did Faulkner take the oath. In 1863, during the Civil War, West Virginia also enacted ironclad oaths.[49] Because he had served in the Confederate army, Faulkner was denied the right to practice law

48 For a biographical sketch of Faulkner, see his obituary from the *Martinsburg Independent*, November 8, 1884.

49 Kenneth R. Bailey "Test Oaths, Belligerent Rights and Confederate Money: Civil War Lawsuits before the West Virginia Supreme Court of Appeals," *West Virginia History*, Vol. 7, No. 1 (Spring 2013), 7.

after the end of the war because he refused to take that ironclad oath. Faulkner brought suit in the West Virginia Supreme Court, which vindicated him, holding that he was not a public official covered by the oath and thus, his civil liberties were restored. Faulkner then resumed his legal career.[50]

Thus, at the time suit was filed in the United States Supreme Court, one of the two attorneys representing West Virginia was a former Confederate officer who was then barred from holding public office, but not from the practice of law. The same attorney was a resident of Berkeley County during the Civil War. It is fair to assume that he did not vote in the May 23, 1863 election conducted by the Union Army. It is also fair to conclude that, as a serving Confederate officer, had he voted, he would have elected to keep his county in Virginia.

When Virginia claimed that residents of Berkeley County wished to remain in Virginia, West Virginia's own lawyer proved that claim.

D. West Virginia's Response to the Complaint

On April 24, 1867, Reverdy Johnson filed a demurrer to the complaint, which stated, "The defendant . . . not confessing or acknowledging all or any of the matters and things in the said complaint's bill to be true doth demur thereto, because the complaint hath not . . . made or stated such a case . . . to entitle her to any such relief."

In language more familiar to modern day legal proceedings, West Virginia responded that, even if all the factual allegations of Virginia were true, Virginia had presented no legal claim for which it could receive legal relief.[51] According to West Virginia, the facts alleged did not entitle Virginia to a return of the two counties.

Such a response obviated the need for witness testimony in a trial, which must have been some relief for members of a Supreme Court that rarely conducted trials. Instead, the demurrer turned the case into a battle of law, not one of disputed facts.

---

50 *Ex Parte Faulkner*, 1 W.Va. 269 (1866).

51 The Federal Rules of Civil Procedure, adopted in 1937 upon the recommendation of the Supreme Court, eliminated demurrers. See Note 3 to Rule 7 of the Advisory Committee Notes. Today, such a motion would be filed pursuant to the provisions of Rule 12(b)(6).

E. Argument Before the Supreme Court

On May 7 and 8, 1867, two of the best-known lawyers in America argued for hours before the Supreme Court. Former Justice Curtis, arguing for Virginia, explained in detail Virginia's claim that the votes in the two counties were invalid and fraudulent. Curtis also claimed that Congress did not follow the certification of the Governor of Virginia with the affirmative consent required before such transfer of counties could become final. Virginia withdrew its consent on December 5, 1865, thereby preventing a later action of Congress purporting to join in Virginia's earlier, but now withdrawn, consent.

Curtis urged the Supreme Court to consider that the Reconstruction Acts, which imposed a military government on Virginia only weeks before the oral arguments, ignored the fact that Virginia had a loyal, Restored Government throughout the recent war.[52] A rebel state government set upon the Restored Government he readily conceded but also argued that the federal government itself failed to protect its loyal citizens in Virginia. Congress, he argued, had no power "to destroy the State of Virginia; and if it be found that such recent legislation of Congress has that extent, I respectfully insist and submit to this court that Congress exceeded its power."[53]

Johnson launched a spirited defense on behalf of West Virginia. Like Curtis, Johnson ignored the irony baked into the dispute. Sitting Virginia Governor Pierpont certified the two now disputed elections held in Berkeley and Jefferson Counties. Several years later, Pierpont, still the authorized governor, now claimed that he had, albeit in ignorance, certified a fraudulent election and wrongfully transferred the two counties to West Virginia.

Johnson dismissed each of the arguments made by Virginia. As to Congressional consent, nothing could be clearer. On December 31, 1862, Congress consented to the admission of West Virginia as a state of the Union. The legislation adopted the identical language of the West Virginia Constitution, which stated that the disputed counties could become part of West Virginia, upon the certification by the Governor of Virginia that, after a proper election, the citizens of the counties affirmed their desire to join West Virginia. According to Johnson, Congress gave express consent to the transfer,

---

52 Transcript of oral arguments in *Virginia v. West Virginia*, U.S. Supreme Court Archives, Special Collections, Columbia University, New York, New York, at 32 ("Transcript").

53 Ibid.

subject to a later vote. From this, he concluded that the requirement of Congressional consent under Article IV, Section 3 of the Constitution had been fully satisfied.

Johnson next addressed whether the Virginia general assembly could withdraw the state's consent by post-war action taken on December 5, 1865. Johnson asserted that once the Governor of Virginia certified the election, West Virginia could "extend her laws over them and its inhabitants."[54] Since 1863, the agreement "was as between the parties fully executed . . . nothing further was to be done to give it validity . . . as binding on both sides as a treaty is upon ratification."[55] Rather than an inchoate arrangement, all three governments—the United States, Virginia and West Virginia—recognized the transfer of the two counties to West Virginia.

Johnson also attacked Virginia's argument that the agreement violated Article I, Section 10 of the Constitution, which provides, "No state shall, without the consent of Congress...enter into any Agreement or Compact with another State." Johnson first contended that Congress approved this agreement between two states, which is all the Constitution required.[56] Second, Virginia claimed that its own conduct was unconstitutional. If so, then the entire State of West Virginia was created in an unconstitutional manner, a claim heretofore not made by Virginia.[57]

Johnson's final arguments brought to the fore bitter memories of the recent war. Virginia claimed that many citizens of the two counties were prohibited from voting in 1863 by reason of the war. According to Virginia, the majority of voters in the two disputed counties wanted to remain part of Virginia. Echoing Lincoln's views on West Virginia statehood, Johnson responded:

> When the acts in question were passed, in January and February, 1863, the war was being waged. . . . It is said that most of the voters in the two counties, particularly those of Jefferson, were in the Confederate military or civil service. Their object was to separate Virginia from the Union . . . . The legislature of the State which passed the laws was, however, loyal. It never, therefore, have been their purpose to make the

54 Ibid., 18.

55 Ibid.

56 Ibid., 11.

57 Ibid.

consent to the secession depend upon the votes of their people who were seeking to destroy their government.[58]

Governor Pierpont (whose name was never uttered by either side on either day of the hearing) certified that in the two elections held in 1863 a majority of voters wished to join the State of West Virginia. According to Johnson, those not voting because of their active involvement in Confederate service were of no consequence in the balloting.

Johnson's final point drew the Court into the most contentious issue of the post-Civil War debates. What was the status of the former Confederate states at the end of the war? If statehood had been lost through rebellion, how and when would it be recovered? The determination of the issues that splintered the other two branches of government also determined whether the Supreme Court possessed original jurisdiction to even entertain Virginia's claims. Was Virginia a state in 1867, asked Johnson? If not, then the Supreme Court lacked original and exclusive jurisdiction to hear a case that did not involve a dispute between two states.[59] Johnson first raised this issue in his summation. Whether a court has subject matter jurisdiction, meaning the legal authority to adjudicate a case, is the first issue a court must address. Absent jurisdiction, a court is without authority to address any other issue presented. Johnson knew this, of course. And as a sitting Senator, he knew the explosiveness of the issue.

President Johnson invited the former Confederate states to hold new elections only months after the war ended. Without consulting Congress, he encouraged the defeated states to send representatives to the U.S. House and Senate in early 1866. When many ex-Confederates, including the former Vice President, were elected to the House and Senate, the Radical Republicans reacted. As Reverdy Johnson argued, the Constitution provides that "Each House shall be the judges of the elections, returns and qualifications of its own members."[60] Using such authority, Congress refused to seat the members elected from the former Confederate states and, through the Reconstruction Acts, imposed military governments throughout the South.

---

58 Ibid., 10.

59 If Virginia was not a state, ipso facto, an entity claiming erroneously to be the state could not maintain a lawsuit.

60 U.S. Constitution, Art. 1, Sect. 5.

Johnson set forth his conclusion:

> But whatever be the opinion of the Court . . . I submit it is clear that each House of
> Congress has the exclusive power to decide whether a state is entitled to representation
> or not, or, to state it more correctly, whether a community is a State for that meaning
> within the Constitution. They may decide wrong; but it is a decision conclusive upon
> the other departments. The Constitution authorizes no appeal, and there is no way to
> bring it before this Court.[61]

In refusing to seat the members sent to Congress, he argued, the House and
Senate declared that the former Confederate jurisdictions were no longer states
entitled to representation. Given this conclusive determination of Congress,
unreviewable by a Court by virtue of the language of the Constitution, he urged,
"the complainant is not a state competent to sue in this Court. For such a
purpose, she must be a State for every other under the Constitution, and
therefore, if the Congressional decision settles the question . . . she has no right
to sue." The issue of Virginia's status as a state of the Union was now squarely
before the Supreme Court.

Johnson ended his long exposition with reference to a bitter past and the
hope for a better future:

> [I]t is absolutely that the powers delegated to the Government should be paramount to
> State powers . . . . The South forgot or denied this. They acted upon a different theory.
> They maintained that the allegiance of the citizen was due first to his state, and the late
> war was the consequence. The result of that war I hope has convinced them that their
> theory is unsound . . . secession, therefore, as a state right, is at an end—lost, never to
> be retrieved. And Virginia and her erring sisters will, I believe, soon attain even more
> than their former prosperity, and share with renewed and equal pride in the great
> future of wealth and power and fame which awaits out common country.[62]

With that, Johnson concluded. The case was now in the hands of the Supreme
Court.

61 Transcript, 17.

62 Ibid., 18.

The Justices of the Supreme Court of the United States in 1868. From left to right: D. W. Middleton, Clerk of the Court, Justice David Davis, Justice Noah H. Swayne, Justice Robert C. Grier, Justice James M. Wayne, Chief Justice Salmon P. Chase, Justice Samuel Nelson, Justice Nathan Clifford, Justice Samuel F. Miller, Justice Stephen J. Field.

(Archives and Special Collections, Dickinson College, Carlisle, PA)

CHAPTER ELEVEN

The Supreme Court Settles the Issue

A. The Supreme Court Deadlocks

ONE week after oral arguments in the case, the Supreme Court adjourned for the summer. On July 5, 1867, Justice James Moore Wayne died, leaving the court with eight members. During the following Supreme Court term, Chief Justice Chase made the following entry on January 21, 1868 in the official record: the Court "is equally divided on the demurrer, and equally divided also upon the order which should be made in consequence of that division."[1]

The votes taken in a case by members of the Supreme Court are held in confidence prior to the issuance of a decision. No record was made of the votes or of the issues that caused the deadlock. In theory, the members could have disagreed on the question of whether, during Reconstruction, Virginia was a State of the United States, able to invoke the original jurisdiction of the Supreme Court. Alternatively, the justices may have split on the question of whether a majority of voters in Berkeley and Jefferson Counties wished to join West Virginia. Finally, the justices could have disagreed on whether Congress had approved the transfer of the two counties before the Virginia legislature

---

1 Minutes of the Supreme Court, *Virginia v. West Virginia*, (January 21, 1868); Fairman, *History of the Supreme Court*, 6:625.

withdrew consent. The formal record in the case offers no answers to these questions.

Tie votes in the Supreme Court are not common, but have happened occasionally. From 1925 through 1982, the Supreme Court deadlocked 123 times, or roughly two times per year.[2] Most such splits occur when the Court is staffed by an even number of justices, as in the case of a vacancy or a recusal from a conflict of interest by a single justice.

Cases subject to a deadlock may be scheduled for a rehearing in the next term of the Supreme Court.[3] Often, a delay of a year means that a new justice might join the Court and presumably break the deadlock. In many cases involving a tie vote, the Supreme Court reveals the tie and the decision below, from a federal court of appeals or a state supreme or appellate court, is upheld.[4] An even thornier question arises when the case is first filed in the Supreme Court as a matter of original jurisdiction, which means no other court has initially considered the matter. Cases involving the Supreme Court's original jurisdiction are rare, with ties even rarer.[5] In such cases, there is no decision from a lower court for the simple reason that the case started in the Supreme Court.[6] Consequently, tie votes leave a case undecided, which is simply not a suitable ultimate option.

The Supreme Court held the case over for the next three tumultuous years.

2 William L. Reynolds and Gordon G. Young, "Equal Division in the Supreme Court: History, Problems, and Proposals," *North Carolina Law Review*, Vol. 62 (1983), 29-30.

3 Ibid., 36.

4 For examples, see *Durant v Essex Co.*, 74 U.S. 107(1868) and *Neil v. Biggers*, 409 U.S. 188 (1972).

5 As noted, infra at footnote 335, the Supreme issued decisions in only 123 original jurisdiction cases from 1789 through 1959.

6 In *Ohio v. Wyandotte Chemicals*, 401 U.S. 493 (1971), the Supreme Court held that its grant of original jurisdiction did not divest other courts from exercising proper jurisdiction. Instead, the Supreme Court today decides whether other courts are better suited to handle a dispute between a state and a private party or whether the case implicates important federal interests. Id at 500.

B. The Republican Congress Threatens the Independence of the Supreme Court

As the Civil War ended, supporters of the Union war effort viewed the Supreme Court with deep distrust. Three of the nine sitting justices sided with slaveholding interests in the pre-war *Dred Scott v. Sanford* decision, a significant incitement to the bloody conflict.[7] According to noted Supreme Court historian Charles Fairman, the post war years were "a dark period" for the institution: "Those who lost in battle early sought sanctuary in appeals to the Court; the portents it gave out were such as to bring upon it the menaces of Congress. For a season, judicial authority was openly defied."[8] By 1866, President Johnson and the Republican Congress battled over vastly different views on Reconstruction. The struggle that embroiled the two elected branches of government soon drew in the third, as the federal judiciary became the locus of challenges to the reordering of the South.

The framers of the Constitution designed the federal courts "as separated from the legislative and executive powers."[9] Alexander Hamilton wrote, "The complete independence of the courts of justice is peculiarly essential in a limited Constitution." Without such independence from the elected branches of government, the constitutional guarantees of civil liberties and limitations on government itself would be subject to "whatever a momentary inclination happens to lay hold of a majority."[10]

To effectuate judicial independence, the framers established Article III, Section 1 of the Constitution, which requires that all federal judges "shall hold their offices during good behavior and shall, at stated times, receive for their services, a compensation, which shall not be diminished during their continuance in office." Hamilton described these safeguards of independence as "one of the most valuable of the modern improvements in the practice of government. In a monarchy, it is an excellent barrier to the despotism of the

---

7 *Dred Scott v. Sanford*, 60 U.S. 393 (1857). The three included Justices John Catron, Samuel Nelson and Robert Cooper Grier. Catron died on May 30th, 1865. Fairman, *History of the Supreme Court*, 6:3.

8 Fairman, *History of the Supreme Court*, 6:89.

9 *The Federalist Papers*, 78, Alexander Hamilton.

10 Ibid.

prince; in a republic, it is no less an excellent barrier to the encroachments and oppressions of the representative body."[11]

Yet, the drafters of the Constitution understood that "the judiciary is beyond comparison the weakest of the three departments of power."[12] In the midst of the turmoil following the Civil War, the Republican Congress found two mechanisms capable of controlling an independent court—the method of appointment of justices and the power to regulate the Supreme Court's jurisdiction.

The Constitution does not establish the number of justices on the Supreme Court. Following the ratification of the Constitution, Congress enacted the Judiciary Act of 1789, which established a Supreme Court consisting of seven justices.[13] As new states joined the Union, by 1837, Congress expanded the Supreme Court to nine justices.[14] In 1863, Congress raised the number of justices to ten, one for each Court of Appeals circuits, which grew to the same number.[15] When Justice John Catron died on May 30, 1865, the number of Justices was reduced to nine, which has never again been exceeded.[16]

On April 16, 1866, President Johnson nominated Henry Stanbery to fill Catron's seat on the Supreme Court.[17] With Catron's death, the majority of the Justices on the Court had been appointed by Abraham Lincoln.[18] The Republican-controlled Congress viewed Stanbery with distrust. Only weeks earlier, the nominee had drafted Johnson's veto message of the Civil Rights Act of 1866, which granted citizenship to all persona, including slaves born in the United States.[19] Seven days before Johnson nominated Stanbery, Congress

---

11 Ibid.

12 Ibid.

13 1 Stat. 73.

14 The Eight and Ninth Circuits Act of 1837, 5 Stat. 176.

15 Then Circuit Act of 1863, 12 Stat. 794.

16 Judicial Act of 1866, 14 Stat. 209; Judiciary Act of 1869, 16 Stat. 44.

17 Fairman, *History of the Supreme Court*, 6:162.

18 Philip S. Bonforte, "Pushing Boundaries: The Role of Politics in Districting the Federal Circuit System, Seton Hall Circuit Review", Vol. 6;29, p. 39 (2009).

19 Fairman, *History of the Supreme Court*, 6:162. Similar language was later enshrined in the Constitution via the Fourteenth Amendment, Section 1.

overrode the veto by a two-thirds margin.[20] For the next three months, Stanbery's nomination languished in the Senate.

With the support of a majority of justices, both houses debated the creation of a new intermediate appeals court, separate and apart from the district or trial court and an overburdened Supreme Court.[21] As the controversial nomination of Henry Stanbery stalled, an angry Congress abruptly enacted the Judicial Circuits Act.[22] The statute provided in part: "That no vacancy in the office of associate justice of the supreme court shall be filled by appointment until the number of associate justices shall be reduced to six; and thereafter said supreme court shall consist of a chief justice of the United States and six associate justices."[23]

The Judicial Circuits Act precluded President Johnson from filling the next two vacancies on the Supreme Court. Since the position no longer existed, Stanbery's nomination was effectively killed. For the next three years, no new justice replaced the deceased Justice Wayne. By the end of Johnson's term, only seven justices remained on the Court. In his authoritative work on the Supreme Court, Charles Fairbanks does not describe the Judiciary Act of 1866 as partisan court packing. See History of the Supreme Court, 170–172. He notes that the genesis of the final legislation was the plan to create new courts of appeal. He also describes in detail the machinations of Chief Justice Chase. Ibid. According to Fairbanks, Chase urged a reduction in the size of the Court from ten to seven members as a way to increase the salaries of the remaining justices. Ibid. Yet, the salaries of the justices were neither increased nor were courts of appeal created, as is seen in the legislation itself. Instead, the Republican Congress effectively negated the Stanbery nomination to the Court and prevented any new-term future appointments by a Democratic President. For a seasoned official as Chase, this result could hardly have been coincidental. The fact that Johnson did not veto the legislation say more about his relative weakness than the motives of Congress.

The Constitution also provides that "the Supreme Court shall have appellate jurisdiction, both as to law and fact, with such exceptions, and under

---

20 14 Stat. 30, Sess. I., 1866.

21 Fairman, *History of the Supreme Court*, 6:160–174. The courts of appeal were not created until 1891. 26 Stat. 826.

22 14 Stat. 209. 1866 Sess. I.

23 Ibid.

such regulations as the Congress shall make."[24] Scholars have long debated whether this provision permits Congress to "control substantive judicial outcomes" by stripping the Supreme Court of jurisdiction to hear a particular case or type of appeal.[25] Prior to 1866, no act of Congress ever attempted to strip the Supreme Court of jurisdiction to hear a pending case. An expansive reading of Congress' power to regulate or make exceptions to the Supreme Court's jurisdiction could eviscerate the very judicial independence the framers crafted into the Constitution.

The federal courts soon confronted the difficult questions surrounding the respective roles of the U.S. Army and the local courts in the Southern states during Reconstruction. Both during and immediately after the war, the army utilized military commissions in the South to try civilians on criminal charges.[26] On May 1, 1866, President Johnson issued General Order 58, directing the army to refer criminal charges against civilians to local courts.[27] Congress did not trust the local courts to protect newly freed slaves and pro-Union citizens. In the Reconstruction Act of March 2, 1867, Congress found that, "no legal State governments or adequate protection for life or property now exists in the rebel States." Congress expressly provided, "That it shall be the duty of each officer assigned as aforesaid to protect all persons in their rights of persons and property, to suppress insurrection, disorder and violence, and to punish or cause to be punished, all disturbers of the public peace and criminals . . . he may allow local civilian tribunals to take jurisdiction . . . or, when in his judgment it may be necessary for the trial of offenders, he shall have power to organize military commissions or tribunals for that purpose."[28]

---

24 Art. III, Sec. 2, U.S. Constitution. This authority given to Congress applies only to the Supreme Court's appellate jurisdiction and not to its original jurisdiction, which is expressly stated in the same paragraph of the Constitution.

25 Michael J. Gerhardt, *The Constitutional Limits to Court Stripping*, Lewis and Clark Law Review, 2004, Vol 9:2, 347, 355. Tara Leigh Grove, *The Exceptions Clause as a Structural Safeguard*, Columbia Law Review, 2013, Vol. 113.

26 In *Ex Parte Milligan*, 71 U.S.2 (1866), the Supreme Court held that, where civilian courts were operating, military commissions were unconstitutional. Milligan lived in Indiana and was charged in a military court with conspiracy against the federal government during the Civil War. All of the charged conduct occurred in Indiana.

27 James D. Richardson, ed., *A Compilation of the Messages and Papers of the Presidents, 1789-1897*, 10 vols. (Washington, DC: U. S. Government Printing Office, 1896-1899), 6:440-442 (1897).

28 Reconstruction Act, March 2, 1867, 14 Stat. 428.

The Constitution makes no provision for military commissions. During the Civil War, military commissions tried more than 2000 cases.[29] While the Supreme Court never addressed the propriety of such commissions, lower courts upheld military tribunals established by the president to be consistent with the powers bestowed upon the President as Commander in Chief in Article II of the Constitution.[30]

After the war ended, the federal government faced a difficult choice. Southern state courts functioning during the Confederacy were ill-suited to enforce the legal rights and safety of newly freed slaves. The federal district courts, also functioning in the same states, lacked jurisdiction to try basic cases involving violence against persons or property.[31] Yet, military commissions withheld from civilian defendants many basic rights enshrined in the U.S. and most state constitutions, such as the right to indictment by a grand jury and to trial by jury.[32] The conundrum soon engulfed the Supreme Court.

On November 8, 1867, General E.O.C. Ord ordered the arrest of William H. McCardle, editor of the *Vicksburg Times*.[33] McCardle was charged with inciting insurrection, disorder and violence after writing about the upcoming elections in Mississippi that "We again urge every decent white man, every honorable gentleman of the Caucasian race, to avoid General Ord's election as he would avoid pestilence and prison."[34] In the same edition of the newspaper, as a way to sabotage elections in which freed slaves could participate, McCardle offered a dollar for the name of each person who voted, which he intended to print.[35] McCardle called General Ord and other prominent Union generals

---

29 William Winthrop, *Military Law and Precedents*, 2nd ed. (Washington, DC: U.S. Government Printing Office, 1920), 1896.

30 See *Ex Parte Mudd*, 17 F. Cas. 954 (Dist. Ct. Fla. 1868). Article II of the Constitution provides that the President "shall be the Commander in Chief of the Army and Navy of the United States."

31 Article III of the Constitution creates and limits the jurisdiction of the federal courts. Such jurisdiction is limited to matters "arising under this Constitution {and}, Laws of the United States". The Constitution provided no basis for federal courts to try, for example, local murder cases. Likewise, the Constitution did not authorize Congress to criminalize local offenses.

32 See 5th and 6th Amend., U.S. Const.

33 Fairman, *History of the Supreme Court*, 6:437.

34 November 6, 1867, *Vicksburg Times*.

35 Ibid.

"cowardly" and that they "should have their heads shaved, their ears cropped, their foreheads branded, and their precious persons lodged in a penitentiary."[36]

McCardle quickly challenged his incarceration and sought a writ of habeas corpus from the U.S. District Court for the Southern District of Mississippi.[37] In a habeas corpus proceeding, a petitioner in custody may challenge the constitutionality of his detention before an appropriate court.[38] McCardle asserted that the creation of military commissions long after the end of the war was unconstitutional. District Judge Robert A. Hill, nominated by President Johnson and confirmed by the Senate only a year before, held that the military commissions authorized by Congress were essential "to protect the citizens in their rights of person and property."[39] On November 25, 1867, Judge Hill denied McCardle a writ of habeas, finding his confinement lawful.[40] McCardle then appealed to the Supreme Court.[41]

The Supreme Court promptly scheduled arguments in McCardle's appeal for March 9, 1868.[42] The press widely reported the arguments before a packed Supreme Court, and an anxious Congress watched them carefully. According to the *Richmond Examiner*, "the public mind is becoming intensely excited in its desire for a speedy decision on the Constitutionality of the Reconstruction Acts."[43] The Supreme Court scheduled the case for six full hours of argument, three times the standard period permitted.[44] After the long arguments, the Supreme Court took the case under advisement, with a decision to follow.

Congress refused to entrust to the Supreme Court such a keystone of its Reconstruction plan. Both Houses acted in great haste. Only three days after

---

36 *Vicksburg Times*, November 2, 1867.

37 Fairman, *History of the Supreme Court*, 6:437. Article I, Sect. 9 states in part "The Privilege of the Writ of Habeas Corpus shall not be suspended, unless in times of rebellion or invasion the public safety may require it."

38 *Black's Law Dictionary*, "Habeas Corpus."

39 The decision is not reported or published. Judge Hill's oral rendering was recorded in the *Jackson Clarion*, November 26, 1867.

40 *Jackson Clarion*, November 26, 1867.

41 Ibid

42 *Ex Parte McCardle*, 74 U.S. 506 (1868).

43 *Richmond Examiner*, March 8, 1868.

44 Fairman, *History of the Supreme Court*, 6:451.

oral argument in the Supreme Court, Congress removed the Supreme Court's jurisdiction to consider an appeal in a habeas corpus case. On March 12, 1868, Congress exercised its powers to make "regulations" of the Supreme Court's appellate jurisdiction to hear habeas corpus cases.[45] If the legislation applied to McCardle's case, the appeal was over and Judge Hill's denial of relief would stand as the final order in the case.

President Johnson vetoed the bill on March 25, 1868, writing that the enactment "establishes a precedent which, if followed, may eventually sweep away every check on arbitrary and unconstitutional legislation. Thus far during the existence of the Government and the Supreme Court of the United States has been viewed by the people as the true expounder of their Constitution . . . any act which may be construed...for an attempt to prevent or evade its decisions on a question which affects the liberty of the citizens...cannot fail to be attended with unpropitious consequences."[46] Two days later, both houses of Congress overrode the presidential veto, thereby enacting the only legislation that stripped from the Supreme Court the jurisdiction to decide a pending case.

On April 12, 1868, a unanimous Supreme Court dismissed the appeal and concluded that it lacked jurisdiction in light of the recent legislation. Chief Justice Chase wrote that "It is quite clear, therefore, that this court cannot proceed to pronounce judgment in this case, for it no has longer jurisdiction of this appeal."[47] Chase duly noted that the Supreme Court's appellate jurisdiction is conferred "with such exceptions and under such regulations as Congress shall make."[48]

Shortly after the decision, Chief Justice Chase wrote a remarkable letter to U.S. District Judge Robert A. Hill, who had denied relief to McCardle. Chase wrote in a postscript, "P.S. I may say to you that had the merits of the McCardle case been decided the court would doubtless have held that his imprisonment for trial before a military commission was illegal."[49] On many levels, the letter from Chase was highly unusual. First, Chase told the trial court judge that he

---

45 See Art III, Sect. 2, U.S. Constitution. Congressional Act of March 27, 1868, 15 Stat. 44.

46 144 Con. Globe, 40-2, 2094.

47 *Ex Parte McCardle*, 74 U.S. 506 and 515 (1869).

48 Ibid, at 513, citing Art. III, Section 2, U.S. Constitution.

49 John Nivan, *The Salmon P. Chase Papers*, 5 vols. (Kent, OH: Kent State University Press, 1998), 5:302.

had wrongly decided the case and the Supreme Court would have told him so, but for Congressional interference. Second, Chase disclosed the highly confidential inner workings of the Supreme Court. The Court's decisions are publicly announced in written form. In all of the Court's history, pre-decisional and non-decisional matters discussed in conference have always been "as secret as any in government."[50]

Chase himself added to the turmoil. He often wrote in opposition to Congress' Reconstruction policies and openly sought the 1868 Democratic nomination for president, which he did not obtain. Despite his service in Lincoln's Cabinet, Congressional Republicans viewed Chase with deep suspicion. In addition to his obvious political ambitions, Chase, ironically, had a long history of advocating for states' rights prior to the Civil War.[51] As a lawyer and Governor of Ohio, Chase claimed that Ohio law freed fugitive slaves notwithstanding any federal law to the contrary.[52] Both Northern and Southern press reminded the public of Chase's antebellum views on states' rights, which were now at odds with Congressional Reconstruction policies.[53]

Yet, with the election of General Ulysses S. Grant as president in 1868, the raging national debate cooled. With Reconstruction proceeding upon the course set by Congress, the Supreme Court no longer faced existential threats to its independence. Grant took office as a strong Republican president elected with large Republican majorities in both houses. Congress quickly increased the number of Supreme Court Justices from seven to nine, enabling Grant to nominate two new members of the Court. The plan to pack the Court with Republican justices had worked.[54]

Not long after, a new challenge to military commissions began when Edward M. Yerger was accused of stabbing to death Major Joseph G. Crane.[55] Yerger was charged with murder before a military commission in Jackson,

---

50 "The Supreme Court Historical Society, How the Court Works," March 15, 2019, www. supremecourthistory.org/htcw_justiceconference.html.

51 Cynthia Nicoletti, *Secession on Trial* (Cambridge: Cambridge Univ. Press, 2017), 202.

52 Paul Finkelman, *An Imperfect Union: Slavery Federalism, and Comity* (Chapel Hill: University of North Carolina Press, 1981), 169.

53 See *Cincinnati Commercial*, May 10, 1866; *New Orleans Crescent*, Oct. 8, 1866; *New York Herald*, Oct. 15, 1866.

54 Cong. Globe, 40-3, 1489, 1895.

55 *Jackson Clarion*, June 19, 1869.

Mississippi. During a lengthy trial, Yerger sought habeas corpus relief before a federal district court, which denied relief.[56] Yeager subsequently appealed to the Supreme Court. The same jurisdictional bar that caused the dismissal of *McCardle* stood in the way for Yerger. Yet, a unanimous Supreme Court ignored *McCardle* and held that the March 25, 1868 law could limit appeals from authority given by Congress,[57] but could in no way limit authority given the Court by the Constitution, which expressly provides for habeas corpus relief from the federal courts.[58] According to Chase, the 1868 legislation stripping the Supreme Court of jurisdiction could not "touch the appellate jurisdiction the appellate jurisdiction conferred by the constitution."[59] As Chase described the importance of habeas corpus, he claimed that such right included "a necessary consequence that if the appellate jurisdiction extends to any case, it extends to this."[60] Thus, the Court rejected its own decision in *McCardle* from a year earlier. But the *Yerger* decision only addressed the jurisdiction of the Supreme Court. The question of whether military commissions were constitutional remained unresolved and was scheduled for additional briefing and oral argument.[61]

The aftermath of *Yerger* gives a fuller picture. Before the 1868 elections, Reconstruction issues riveted the country and threatened the Supreme Court. When Congress passed the 1868 legislation to strip the Supreme Court of jurisdiction approved in *McCardle*, the same Republican Congress came within one Senate vote of convicting President Johnson and removing him from office in his impeachment trial. Leaders in Congress spoke openly of handcuffing the Supreme Court by requiring a two-third's vote of the Supreme Court to find legislation unconstitutional and to remove all Reconstruction measures from the appellate jurisdiction of the Supreme Court.[62]

After the *Yerger* decision, the Supreme Court minutes reflect the following:

---

56 Fairman, *History of the Supreme Court*, 6:565.

57 On February 5, 1867, the Judiciary Act of 1867 expanded the jurisdiction of the federal courts in habeas corpus cases. The same act authorized appeals in such cases to the Supreme Court. 14 Stat. 385.

58 *Ex Parte Yerger*, 75 U.S. 85, 105 (1868).

59 Ibid.

60 Ibid. 102.

61 Fairman, *History of the Supreme Court*, 6:584.

62 Ibid. 6:461-2.

Mr. Phillips [counsel for Yerger] stated to the Court that on account of an arraignment in progress between the Attorney General and the counsel for the petitioner [Yerger], no motion will be made this morning for further proceedings but if there be no objection on the part of the Court, counsel will postpone moving until a subsequent day of the term.

The Chief Justice said, It is undoubtedly a matter of discretion with the counsel for the petitioner to move for the writ of habeas corpus. The point of jurisdiction having been determined, the Court will hear a motion for the writ whenever counsel shall see fit to make it.[63]

The minutes memorialized an agreement between Yerger's attorney and Ebenezer Hoar, the Attorney General of the United States. While the Supreme Court reasserted its jurisdiction, neither side was confident that military commissions would be struck down as unconstitutional, so the parties agreed to a delay of unlimited duration. On February 23, 1870, the State of Mississippi was re-admitted to the Union.[64] Days later, Yerger was transferred from military custody to the Hinds County, Mississippi Court, now operating as a state court within the United States, which once again possessed the proper jurisdiction to prosecute murder charges.[65]

By the end of formal Reconstruction, the Supreme Court had reasserted its authority as the highest court in the land. Yet, the Court, threatened by an empowered Congress, dodged one of the greatest constitutional questions of the Reconstruction Era. As the Court survived the greatest existential threat to its independence, the case brought by Virginia against West Virginia was ready for re-argument before a hobbled Supreme Court.

More recently, in *Hamdan v. Rumsfeld*, the Supreme Court cited *Ex Parte Yerger* and *Ex Parte McCardle*, in a modern case involving military tribunals for trial of alleged terrorists.[66] The Court noted that the cases stood in conflict, while observing the denial of the right to appeal in a habeas corpus case "would greatly weaken the efficacy of the writ."[67] In *Hamdan*, decided a century and a half after *McCardle* and *Yerger*, the Court again avoided the question of the

63 Minutes of the Supreme Court, October 26, 1869.

64 Forty-First Cong. Session II, Cp. 19, 20, p, 67-68 (1870).

65 Yerger escaped from state custody, turned himself in, made bail, moved to Baltimore and was never prosecuted for murder. *Baltimore Sun*, April 24, 1875.

66 548 U.S. 557, 575 (2006).

67 Ibid. at 575 (citing *Ex Parte Yerger*, 8 Wall. at 102-103).

constitutionality of military commissions, finding it "unnecessary to reach either of these arguments."[68]

C. The Court Expands Again

Only five weeks after Grant took office, the Republican Congress restored the number of justices on the Supreme Court to nine.[69] Several months later, Justice Robert Cooper Grier resigned due to poor health. The new president now had two vacancies to fill.

Grant first nominated Edwin M. Stanton, the former Attorney General and Secretary of War who had been so instrumental to the Union victory in the Civil War. Stanton's dismissal as Secretary of War was the pivotal issue in triggering President Johnson's impeachment trial. By nominating Stanton, Grant openly sided with the Republican Congress. The Senate quickly confirmed Stanton, but he died four days later.[70]

On February 18, 1870, Grant nominated William Strong, a former associate justice of the Pennsylvania Supreme Court. Prior to the Civil War, Strong served in Congress as a Democrat openly opposed to slavery. Like Curtis, he was a law school graduate, having attended Yale Law School. Four weeks later, Grant selected Joseph Bradley for the second vacancy. Bradley had a long career as a highly successful commercial litigator. Prior to his appointment to the Supreme Court, Bradley held no other public office. The Senate quickly confirmed both Strong and Bradley. By March of 1870, two new justices had joined the court. Nine justices would now rehear the case of *Virginia v. West Virginia*.

D. The Supreme Court Rehears the Case

For three eventful years of American history, the case brought by Virginia against West Virginia languished in the Supreme Court. As if the passage of

---

68 Ibid.

69 16 Stat. 44.

70 Stanton was also at the center of President Johnson's impeachment trial, and when Johnson moved to fire Stanton, Congress responded with a law requiring Congressional approval before Stanton could be removed. Johnson claimed the restriction was an unconstitutional restraint on executive power.

time caused the heat of the case to cool, the most divisive issue initially raised was now eliminated. Virginia had been re-admitted to the Union, thereby settling the question of its ability to bring its claims in the first place. With its status as a state now conclusively determined, Virginia could now successfully invoke the original jurisdiction of the Supreme Court under Article III of the Constitution.[71]

The parties reargued the case over several days, from February 13 through 16. On behalf of West Virginia, Benjamin Stanton, a former Member of Congress from Ohio, joined Reverdy Johnson and Charles J. Faulkner. After the war, Stanton moved to Martinsburg, the county seat of Berkeley County, where he practiced law.[72] Stanton filed a supplemental brief on behalf of West Virginia arguing that the setting of state boundaries was a political question, a legal term of art described in the case of *Rhode Island v. Massachusetts*.[73] In *Rhode Island v. Massachusetts*, which involved a boundary dispute between two states, the Supreme Court held: "There is neither the authority of law or reason for the position that the boundary between nations or states is, in its nature, any more a political question than any other subject on which they may contend."[74] This doctrine took center stage in Benjamin Stanton's supplemental arguments.

The two states continued to dispute the regularity or fairness of the elections in the two counties. While conceding that Virginia was once again a member of the Union, West Virginia claimed that the legislature of Virginia lacked any authority to act when it passed the December 5, 1865 revoking consent to transfer the two counties to West Virginia. In essence, the West Virginia statehood issues that had so vexed Lincoln, his cabinet and the Congress, and which so angered the Virginia Commonwealth, were now reduced to narrow issues of law and fact.

E. The Supreme Court Decides

---

71 Even before Virginia was re-admitted to the Union, in 1869, the Supreme Court held that a former Confederate state not formally readmitted to the Union could still bring suit pursuant to the Supreme Court's Article III original jurisdiction. *Texas v. White*, 74 U.S. 700 (1869).

72 Benjamin Stanton does not appear to have been related to former Secretary of War Edwin M. Stanton.

73 37 U.S. 657 (1838).

74 Ibid., 659.

On March 6, 1871, the Supreme Court issued a final decision in the case. Justice Samuel Freeman Miller wrote for a six-member majority, which included Chief Justice Salmon Chase, Samuel Nelson, Noah Swayne, William Strong and Joseph Bradley.[75]

Chief Justice Chase served as Lincoln's Secretary of the Treasury during most of the Civil War. In 1862, Chase participated in Lincoln's decision to admit West Virginia to the Union, which Chase strongly supported. Despite his active involvement in the political matter pending before the Supreme Court, Chase took no steps to recuse himself from a case involving contested matters in which he played an earlier role in the Lincoln Administration. Chase probably should have recused himself in order to avoid any appearance of impropriety, but he declined to do so. Given the secrecy of the pre-decisional discussions among the justices, the record is silent as to the role played by the conflicted Chief Justice.

Miller's majority opinion first summarily addressed Stanton's argument that the issues presented were political questions, beyond the subject matter jurisdiction of the Supreme Court. Miller concluded that the Court had jurisdiction to determine the boundary between two states, even if the case

---

75 Samuel Freeman Miller was born in Richmond, Kentucky on April 5, 1816, the son of a local farmer. He earned a medical degree from Transylvania University in Lexington, Kentucky in 1838, and practiced medicine Barbourville, Kentucky for a decade. For most of that time, he studied law on his own, and was admitted to the bar in 1847. He was a member of the Whig Party who supported the abolition of slavery. In 1850, he moved to Iowa, which was a free state. He became a member of the new Republican Party in the mid-1850's, and supported the election of Lincoln in 1860. On July 16, 1862, Lincoln nominated him to the Supreme Court, and due to his sterling reputation, the Senate confirmed the nomination within half an hour of learning of it. Miller wrote more opinions than any other Justice in the history of the Supreme Court, including the opinions in some of the most important civil rights cases of the era, prompting Chief Justice William Rehnquist to call Miller "very likely the dominant figure on the Court at that time." When Chase died in 1873, some called for Miller to be named his replacement as Chief Justice, but President Ulysses S. Grant was determined to nominate an outsider to the position, so he passed Miller over in favor of Morrison Waite. In 1876, Miller served on the electoral commission that awarded the disputed election to Rutherford B. Hayes over Samuel Tilden. He died while still serving on the Court on October 13, 1890 and was buried in Oakland Cemetery in Keokuk, Iowa. For a full-length biography, see Ross, *Justice of Shattered Dreams*.

implicated the validity of an agreement between the states and the consent of Congress.[76]

Miller then addressed the three specific questions raised by Virginia in the litigation. The first question was: "Did the State of Virginia ever give consent to this proposition that became obligatory on her?" The second question was: "Did the Congress give such consent as rendered the agreement valid?" Finally, the third question was: "If both these are answered affirmatively . . . whether the circumstances…authorized Virginia to withdraw her consent and restor[e] the two counties to that State."[77]

In answering the first question, Miller briefly reviewed the history of Pierpont's Restored Government of Virginia. The President and Congress had both recognized the Restored Government as the lawful government of Virginia, which enacted legislation consenting to the formation of West Virginia. Regarding the second question, Miller noted that Congress consented to the dismemberment of Virginia and to the admission of the new state of West Virginia on December 31, 1862, noting that both conditions had subsequently been satisfied.[78]

Miller devoted most of his analysis to the third question. Both Virginia and the federal government understood that the two counties in question had yet to vote as of December 31, 1862. The legislation enacted by Congress and the Virginia legislature contained but one condition: the affirmative vote of Berkeley and Jefferson Counties to join West Virginia.[79] According to the legislation passed by the Restored Government, the governor—Pierpont—was to determine the means and manner of the elections, at a time deemed suitable for balloting.[80] As Miller put it, "The legislature might have required the vote to have been reported to it, and assumed the duty of ascertaining and making

---

76 *Virginia v. West Virginia*, 11 Wall. 39, 55. (1871). The majority distinguished *Rhode Island v. Maryland* by citing more recent cases: *Missouri v. Iowa*, 48 U.S. 660 (1849), *Florida v. Georgia*, 58 U.S. 478 (1854) and *Alabama v Georgia*, 64 U.S. 505 (1860).

77 Ibid., 56.

78 Ibid., 57.

79 Ibid., 59.

80 Ibid.

known the result to West Virginia; but it delegated that power to the governor."[81]

Miller then posed a series of rhetorical questions: "Do the allegations authorize us to go behind all this and inquire as to what took place at this voting? To inquire how many votes were actually caste? How many men were then in the rebel army?"[82] He then answered his own rhetorical questions. The allegations of Virginia were "indefinite and vague . . . no act of unfairness is alleged . . . . No particular act of fraud is stated . . . . No charge of any kind of moral or legal wrong is made against the defendant, the State of West Virginia." In summary, the act of the Governor of Virginia in certifying the election results was conclusive and binding on the parties.[83]

Miller dismissed the revocation of consent as to the two counties passed by the Virginia General Assembly on December 5, 1865. He wrote that "She [Virginia] can have no right, years after all this has been settled, to come into a court of chancery to charge that her own conduct has been a wrong and a fraud."[84] With that, even though it never explicitly said so, the Supreme Court's majority held that the creation of West Virginia had been conducted constitutionally and that Berkeley and Jefferson Counties would remain a part of West Virginia.

Three justices dissented. Justice David Davis, joined by Justices Nathan Clifford and Stephen Field, wrote a narrow opinion focused exclusively upon what he viewed as the need for Virginia and the Congress to give further consent to a transfer of the counties after the elections held in 1863. The majority viewed consent as given, with a condition that the two counties subsequently demonstrate majority support for joining West Virginia. The dissenting justices took the view that both Virginia and the Congress had to ratify the elections in the two counties before consent was fully given.

In the view of the dissenting justices, Congress only gave the required consent on March 10, 1866, in a bill passed in reaction to the Virginia Assembly's attempt to withdraw consent on December 5, 1865. To Justice Davis, Congress's consent came too late. Virginia had already withdrawn the

81 Ibid., 62.

82 Ibid.

83 Ibid., 63.

84 Ibid.

state's consent. Since Article IV, Section 3 of the Constitution required the consents of both the government of Virginia and Congress the two counties could not be transferred to a new state.

And so, the Supreme Court laid to rest the dismemberment of Virginia. The constitutional issues that so troubled Lincoln's mind were nowhere to be found in the majority or dissenting opinions of the Supreme Court, perhaps as a result of the behind the scenes machinations of Salmon P. Chase. The dissent reduced its disagreement to a mere question of timing: when acceptance or consent became final, much like a quotidian contract dispute, rather than a significant matter of Constitutional interpretation.

Virginia's case began while the nation still burned red-hot in the aftermath of its bloodiest war. Four and a half years later, as the Supreme Court legitimized West Virginia, the country's mood had changed, and the fever had broken. By the time the Court decided the case, all eleven states of the former Confederacy had been readmitted to the Union. The Supreme Court laid to rest, in a dry and conclusory fashion, one of the great constitutional issues of the Civil War.

Conclusion

F OR more than a century and a half, citizens living in the lands of West Virginia shared what Lincoln called "the mystic chords of memory" with the Commonwealth of Virginia.[1] By 1865, the Revolutionary War memories of Bunker Hill and Yorktown were displaced by the horrors of Antietam and Gettysburg. To be sure, the decades of struggle between the planter class of the East and the yeomen farmers of the West bitterly divided the two lands before the Civil War. But the split over secession and the four bloody years that followed made the rendering of Virginia a wound that would not heal.

West Virginia was the "child of the storm," according to Maj. Theodore F. Lang of the 6th West Virginia Cavalry, an early chronicler of the history of the Mountain State.[2] The presence of large bodies of Union troops made the new state possible once the North seized the B & O Railroad at the start of the war. Many of the same troops conducted the elections in the 50 counties, raising serious questions as to the legitimacy of these elections and acts that followed. A government claiming to represent all of Virginia, though elected by a small portion of the state, gave purported consent to the creation of a new state within the territory of the Commonwealth.

---

1 Lincoln's First Inaugural Address, March 4, 1861, in Basler, *Collected Works of Abraham Lincoln*, 4:271.

2 Lang, *Loyal West Virginia*, 133.

In 1862, the question of emancipation of the slaves came to the forefront of social and political issues facing the Lincoln Administration. The Senate debated whether emancipation should be gradual or immediate. Abolitionists like Ben Wade of Ohio and William Fessenden of Maine preferred gradual emancipation to no emancipation at all. West Virginia's constitution established gradual emancipation as the law in the new state. Thus, when Congress permitted the admission of West Virginia to the Union, it became the first slave state to join the Union with a gradual emancipation clause in its constitution, meaning that the Willey Amendment took on a significance that Waitman Willey probably never contemplated. Earlier that year, Lincoln recommended, and Congress accepted, "tending our aid and support to those States that will inaugurate a system of gradual emancipation." West Virginia tested that policy, which provided Congress with another reason to approve the admission of the new state.[3]

The movement to create a new state in this manner deeply troubled Lincoln and many members of Congress. Thaddeus Stevens contentedly relied upon a euphemistic claim of war powers, claiming that, in the midst of the rebellion, the North had the troops and the power to make a new state possible. In contrast, Lincoln struggled to preserve both the Union and the Constitution. The Framers of the Constitution had not conceived of the sectional split that opened large numbers of unanswered legal and political questions during the Civil War. In the end, Lincoln's sympathy and concern for the Unionists of West Virginia prevailed, and he overcame his hesitations about the constitutionality of signing the statehood bill.[4] Without Abraham Lincoln, there would be no West Virginia.

At the same time, Lincoln was determined to do whatever it took to preserve the Union. In August 1862, responding to an editorial that ran in the *New York Tribune*, Lincoln responded in a letter to the publisher, Horace Greeley. Lincoln's response, which was published in the *Tribune* on August 22, 1862, foreshadowed his approach to the West Virginia question. "I would save the Union. I would save it the shortest way under the Constitution. The sooner the national authority can be restored; the nearer the Union will be 'the Union as

---

3 See the Senate debate at *Congressional Globe*, 37th Cong., 2nd Sess., 3034-3035 and "The Proceedings of Congress," New York Times, July 2, 1862.

4 Michael Burlingame, *Abraham Lincoln: A Life*, 2 vols. (Baltimore: Johns Hopkins University Press, 2007), 2:460.

it was,'" wrote Lincoln. "If there be those who would not save the Union, unless they could at the same time *save* slavery, I do not agree with them. If there be those who would not save the Union unless they could at the same time *destroy* slavery, I do not agree with them. My paramount object in this struggle *is* to save the Union, and is *not* either to save or to destroy slavery. If I could save the Union without freeing *any* slave I would do it, and if I could save it by freeing *all* the slaves I would do it; and if I could save it by freeing some and leaving others alone I would also do that." The President concluded, "What I do about slavery, and the colored race, I do because I believe it helps to save the Union; and what I forbear, I forbear because I do *not* believe it would help to save the Union. I shall do *less* whenever I shall believe what I am doing hurts the cause, and I shall do *more* whenever I shall believe doing more will help the cause." Lincoln very plainly stated his pragmatic approach just a few months before the West Virginia question came to his attention. The outcome of the West Virginia question should, therefore, have been predictable.[5]

Confederate President Jefferson Davis addressed these events at great length in his memoir, penned late in life. He attacked the dismemberment of Virginia:

> Will any intelligent person assert that the consent of the State of Virginia was given to the formation of this new State, or that the government of Francis H. Pierpont held the true and lawful jurisdiction of the State of Virginia? Yet the Congress of the United States asserted in the act above quoted that "the Legislature of Virginia did give its consent to the formation of a new State within the jurisdiction of the State of Virginia." This was not true, but was an attempt, by an act of Congress, to aid a fraud and perpetuate a monstrous usurpation. For there is no grant of power to Congress in the Constitution nor in the American theory of government to justify it. If it is said that the government of Francis H. Pierpont was the only one recognized by Congress as the government of the State of Virginia, that does not alter the fact. The recognition of Congress can not make a State of an organization which is not a State. There is no grant of power to Congress in the Constitution for that purpose. If it is said that the government of Francis H. Pierpont was established by the only qualified voters in the State of Virginia, that is as equally unfounded as the other assertions. Neither the Congress of the United States nor the Government of the United States can determine the qualifications of voters at an election for delegates to a State Constitutional Convention, or for the choice of State officers. There was no grant of power either to the President or to Congress for that purpose. All these efforts were usurpations, by which it was sought, through groundless fabrications, to reach certain ends, and they

5 Basler, *Collected Works*, 5:388-389.

add to the multitude of deeds which constitute the crime committed against States and the liberties of the people.[6]

Davis claimed, "The perversion of true republican principles was greater in Virginia than in any other State, through the cooperation of the Government of the United States."[7]

To a point, the entire premise upon which the admission of West Virginia to the Union was based was a legal fiction. Article IV, Section 3 of the Constitution is specific in its requirements. Was the new state lawfully conceived? On one hand, the application for the admission of the new state was made by the Restored Government, which purported to speak for the entire Commonwealth of Virginia even though it actually represented only a small portion of the state's population. On the other hand, the Restored Government, claiming to speak for the entire population of Virginia, approved the dismemberment of the state. The same legislative body performed both tasks in spite of the obvious conflict of interest. This legal fiction then provided the mechanism for West Virginia to be admitted to the Union.[8]

Many scholars have written of Lincoln's keen understanding of public opinion through his extensive correspondence and almost daily personal encounters with large numbers of people.[9] Lincoln met with scores of people from the proposed new state in the months before he signed the legislation creating West Virginia. His judgment was born out by contemporary events and those that followed, that the vast majority of people in all but a few counties of the new state favored a permanent schism with Virginia. Four years of deadly war only reinforced what Lincoln sensed.

Muscoe Garnett, chair of the post-war Virginia legislative Committee on the Restoration of the State of Virginia, believed that West Virginia, would

---

6   Davis, *The Rise and Fall of the Confederate Government*, 2:306.

7   Ibid., 304.

8   A recent, lengthy legal analysis of the constitutionality of the admission of West Virginia to the Union concluded this way, reflecting the ambiguity that continues to haunt this question to this day: "West Virginians may rest secure in the knowledge that their State is not unconstitutional. Probably." See Kesevan and Paulsen, "Is West Virginia Unconstitutional," 400.

9   James Oakes, *The Radical and the Republican; Frederick Douglass, Abraham Lincoln, and the Triumph of Antislavery Politics* (New York: W.W. Norton, 2008), 93; Allen C. Guelzo, *Abraham Lincoln: Redeemer President* (Grand Rapids, MI: Eerdmans, 2003), 276-277.

The monument to Francis H. Pierpont outside West Virginia Independence Hall in Wheeling.

(Authors' photo)

someday remember "the past, and all the ties which should have bound her", and seek reunion with the Commonwealth.[10] He was wrong. By the end of the war, the two states had gone their separate ways. Reunion never came.

The 1871 decision by the Supreme Court implicitly validated Virginia's rendering.[11] Forty years later, in 1911, Justice Oliver Wendell Holmes, Jr. wrote more explicitly for a now unanimous court in a case involving the apportionment of pre-Civil War debt between the two states. With the certainty gained from the passage of time, the Civil War veteran wrote of the creation of West Virginia:

> The grounds are…matters of public history. After the Virginia ordinance of secession, citizens of the state who dissented from that ordinance organized a government that was recognized as the state of Virginia by the government of the Unites States. Forthwith a convention of the restored state, as it was called, held at Wheeling, proceeded to carry out a long-entertained wish of many West Virginians by adopting an ordinance for the formation of a new state out of the western portion of the old commonwealth.[12]

10 *Acts of the General Assembly of the state of Virginia; Passed in 1865-66, in the Eighty-Ninth Year of the Commonwealth* (Richmond: Allegre & Good, 1866), 187-88.

11 *Virginia v. West Virginia*, 78 U.S. 39 (1871).

12 *Commonwealth of Virginia v. State of West Virginia*, 220 U.S. 1, 25. (1911).

This historical description by Holmes was "constituting an agreement between the old state and the new.[13]" These matters were "practically to have been decided" in the 1871 decision of the Supreme Court.[14] The Supreme Court decisively decided the dilemma that confounded Lincoln.

West Virginia's tortured road to statehood took twists and turns, and only ended successfully because the determined leaders of the new state persevered and overcame opposition from both within and from outside its borders, all while a brutal civil war raged. However, as historian George E. Moore put it, "the loyal men of West Virginia took comfort from the fact that their devotion to a cause had placed in the American flag a new star—there to bear witness for the Constitution and the Union."[15]

As West Virginia took its place as a permanent state of the Union, Lincoln's words provide a final testament: "The division of a state is dreaded as precedent. But a measure made expedient by war is no precedent for times of peace. It is said that the admission of West Virginia is secession, and tolerated only because it is our secession. Well, if we call it by that name, there is difference enough between secession against the constitution and secession in favor of it."[16]

---

13 Ibid., 26.

14 Ibid.

15 George E. Moore, *A Banner In The Hills: West Virginia's Statehood* (New York: Appleton-Century-Crofts, 1963), 207.

16 Basler, *Collected Works of Abraham Lincoln*, 6:28.

The Letters to Abraham Lincoln From His Cabinet Regarding the Question of Whether to Admit West Virginia to the Union

F OLLOWING are the full text of the letters written by his six cabinet secretaries to President Abraham Lincoln in December 1862. Lincoln asked each of his cabinet secretaries to opine on whether the admission of West Virginia to the Union was constitutional, and whether it was expedient to do so. Each of these letters is found in the Abraham Lincoln Papers, which are in the collections of the Manuscripts Division of the Library Congress, Washington, D.C.

A. From Montgomery Blair to Abraham Lincoln, December 26, 1862

Sir:

On the questions submitted by you relating to the admission of West Virginia into the Union, I submit the following considerations.

1. As to the constitutional question.

The first clause of the Third section of the fourth article of the Constitution provides that "new states may be admitted by the Congress into this Union, but no new state shall be formed or erected within the Jurisdiction of any other State; nor any state be formed by the junction of two or more states or parts of States without the consent of the States concerned as well as of the Congress." The objection that this language in the present case requires the consent of both East and West Virginia because it requires the consent of both the States concerned, seems to me not to be well taken, because 'till West Virginia be admitted there are not two States concerned.

The question is only whether the State of Virginia has consented to the partition of her Territory and the formation of that part of it called Western Virginia into a separate State. In point of fact it will not be contended that this has been done, for it is well known that the elections by which the movement has been made did not take place in more than a third of the counties of the state, and the votes on the Constitution did not exceed twenty-thousand.

The argument for the fulfilment of the constitutional provisions applicable to this case rests altogether on the fact that the Government organized at Wheeling (in which a portion of the District in which it is proposed to create the new state is represented with a few of the Eastern counties) has been recognized as the Government of the State of Virginia for certain purposes by the Executive and Legislative branches of the Federal Government, and it is contended that by these acts the Federal Government is estopped from denying that the consent given by this Government of Virginia to the creation of the new State, is a sufficient consent within the meaning of the constitution. It seems to me to be a sufficient answer to this argument to say: First, that it is confessedly merely technical, and assumes unwarrantably, that the qualified recognition which has been given to the Government at Wheeling for certain temporary purposes, precludes the Federal Government from taking notice of the fact that the Wheeling Government represents much less than half the people of Virginia when it attempts to dismember the State permanently. Or, Second, That the present demand, of itself, proves the previous recognitions relied on to enforce it, to be erroneous. For, unquestionably, the 4th Article of the Constitution prohibits the formation of a new state within the jurisdiction of an old one without the actual consent of the old State, and if it be true that we have so dealt with a third part of the people of Virginia as that to be consistent we should now permit that minority to divide the State, it does not follow that we should persist, but on the contrary it demonstrates that we have heretofore been wrong, and if consistency is insisted on, and is deemed necessary, we should recede from the positions heretofore taken.

2. As to the Expediency of the measure

But I do not think it either necessary to recede from these positions or pro per to take the new step insisted on now. There is no positive prohibition in the constitution against the action taken by the Senate and House of Representatives in relation to the recognition of the Wheeling Government, or in relation to the action taken by the Executive, and all that can be said, if we reject the claim of the Wheeling Government to represent the people of Virginia for the purpose now under consideration will be that it admits our previous action to have been irregular. The answer to this is, that if not regular, it was substantially just, and the circumstances of the case excuse the irregularity. For it was proper that the loyal people and the State of Virginia should be represented in Congress, and the representation allowed was not greater than their numbers entitled them to. But whilst it was just to the people of Western Virginia, whose country was not over-run by the rebel armies, to allow this representation, and for this purpose, and for the purposes of local government to recognize the State Government instituted by them, it would be very unjust to the loyal people in the greater part of the State, who are now held in subjection by rebel armies, and who far exceed in number the twenty thousand who have voted on the constitution for

Western Virginia, to permit the dismemberment of their state without their consent. It is no fault of the loyal people of Virginia that they are not in condition to be heard on this question according to the forms of law. The State is held by armies which they could not resist, and which so far the Federal Government itself has not been able to eject from the State. If these armies were driven from the State, and the people still refused to recognize their obligations to the General Government, their wishes might be properly disregarded in the action of that government with respect to the question before us. But until that is done, I think a measure which affects them so greatly should be postponed. If hurried through now, it will probably be the source of lasting irritation between the people of the two sections of the State—and it will I am sure form the only obstacle, but a most serious one to an immediate restoration of the proper relations of the State to the General Government after the rebel armies are driven from it.

But there are yet more important considerations which would induce me to postpone this movement. It has been said with truth that Western Virginia has been a step-child to the Eastern portion of the State where hitherto all political power has resided—And it is the injustice and oppression—the disfranchisement—and unequal taxation which has been exercised by the ruling class in the commonwealth for many long years which has alienated the people of the West. These wrongs have been familiar to me from childhood for among the people of Kentucky they found warm sympathy. It is not therefore from want of sympathy with them that I oppose their wishes at this moment—But it is because in my view of the situation at present the days of their tyrants have passed away never to return and the hour is near when they have but to reach forth their hands & redress not only their own greivances but to restore the old commonwealth to honor & power in the sisterhood of States—Each county as we remove the armed rebel hordes now overrunning the state will affiliate with the free government of the west & of the Union—and the men of the west who have lead the vanguard of freedom in the State will naturally control the policy of the Regenerated State—what a glorious prospect thus opens to a state with one front on the Ocean with such a port as Hampton Roads, and another front on a great tributary of the Mississippi River—Give the people of the west time to consider this subject in the light of events which cannot be distant and which will open to their view the power they will possess to make the State of Virginia one of the greatest of the new world and they will thank the Statesman who refused his sanction to their wishes formed amidst the exasperations of civil war and a sense of wrongs which they will soon see can never be perpetrated again.

If ever there was a case of hasty legislation calling for the interposition of the Executive this bill is one of that kind—No measure of such importance to the interests of a great people was ever passed through Congress with so little discussion. The condition of the country when the bill was before the Senate & House of Representatives seems to have so occupied the attention of the able men in those bodies, that they seem with rare exceptions not to have appreciated the importance of the measure, and it lead to but little discussion in either house—The only consideration which seems to have invited favor or opposition was the fact that a free state was to be made of the part to be erected into a new State—This consideration would weigh with me if it believed the Union was to be divided and that the eastern portion of the State was to be left the Rebels & to Slavery—But I look for neither result—I do not believe disunion possible & I shrink from a measure which looks like preparing for it—But as the reestablishment of the Federal power in Eastern Virginia extinguishes Slavery there & thus removes the great cause of oppression upon the west & at the same time puts the power of the State in the hands of those who have been oppressed, every ground upon which the measure was advocated will be speedily removed.

The bugbear of the indebtedness created by the Rebel Legislature which is paraded by the friends of the measure, is easily disposed of—It will be repudiated of course by the true Legislature of the State—As respects the old & legal debts of the State the benefits of which it is alleged have not been fairly apportioned between the east & the west,—the new Regime will have the power to regulate the subject fairly & will doubtless do so—The Federal government might aid them greatly in this object & at the same time contribute greatly to the reconstitution of Society in the State upon a healthy basis by turning over to the State the forfeited Estates of traitors within it—The forfeitures will be more thoroughly enforced by such means and the property more rapidly passed into the hands of new men whose tenure will be fealty to the new order of things in the state and to the old flag of the Union—But without any pecuniary help from the Federal government the boon of Freedom which the Federal arms will ere long give to the State will soon bring wealth to it—which will make these old debts light, and all the more rapidly if the old boundaries are preserved so that the enlightened and enterprising men of the west who will rule in the councils of the great commonwealth are not shorne of their power by this measure—The idea that the mountains which divide the sections require the proposed political division has become obsolete by the use of Rail-Roads and Canals—What sane man would propose to divide the state of Pennsylvania which is divided physically by the same ranges of mountains? What irreparable mischief would have been done to that magnificent State if such a sacrifice had been made of her real & permanent interests on account of some temporary wrongs, as is now proposed with respect to the interests of Virginia for reasons not worth a thought to a Statesman—It may it this moment please the Western Virginians to favor a measure so cruel to the great interests of the State—But in my judgment the time is not far removed when no man among them would regard the measure otherwise than a Western Pennsylvania man would now regard a proposition to dismember that State—and I believe if the President refuses his sanction to the measure because it is pernicious to their best interests, the people of West Virginia will soon see in such refusal a thoughtfulness for their welfare which will endear his name to them forever.

I think the measure will be distasteful to the people generally—The legality of the act will be questioned and the reply we have to give is as I have said technical only—We cannot say truly that the measure has the sanction of the people of Virginia or, even to the majority of the loyal people of that State—We cannot plead necessity for the act as we have for other acts which have been questioned—It will serve therefore to fix upon the dominant party here the charge of disregarding the law & the constitution by which our adversaries have sought to destroy the confidence of the people in the administration.

The subject is one which will engage public attention hereafter if not immediately so that our action on it will characterize the administration in the annals of the country—It is with the rights of the States we are dealing—we have heard indeed something too much of such things lately and some persons may therefore be disposed at this moment to ignore them altogether—But this will be found to be a great error.

The people of all the States have always manifested a wise solicitude for the just rights of the States & have never tolerated the slightest invasion of them—This arises not from mere State pride or vanity so ostentatiously displayed by Coxcombs—It is founded on the knowledge possessed by the thinking & controlling minds that the excellence of our system of government depends on carefully guarding those rights.—In dismembering the State which has still a hold on the hearts of our people as the land of Washington, Jefferson, Madison, Monroe and other immortal names, there should therefore be no room for debate on the legality of the act.

Very respectfully

Your obt sevt

M Blair

P M Genl

P O Dept

Washington Decr. 26. 1862

B. From William H. Seward to Abraham Lincoln, December 26, 1862

Western Virginia is organized unquestionably with all the constitutional elements and faculties of a State, and with a republican form of government. It, therefore, has a title to be a candidate for admission into the Federal Union. Congress has power to admit new States, but it is a power restricted within certain limitations. One of these limitations is that no new State shall be formed or erected within the jurisdiction of any other State without the consent of that State as well as the consent of the new State and the consent of Congress. It is an undisputed fact that the new state of Western Virginia has been both formed and erected within the jurisdiction of the State of Virginia. Has the consent of the State of Virginia to the formation and erection of the State of West Virginia been given, or has it not been given? Upon this point the constitutionality of the Act of Congress now before me turns. The constituted and regular authorities of a State called the State of Virginia sitting at Wheeling, within the jurisdiction of that State, claiming to be the St ate of Virginia, and acting as such, have in a due and regular manner declared and given the consent of the State of Virginia to the formation and erection of the State of West Virginia within the jurisdiction of the State of Virginia. Thus far the case seems simple and clear. But it is just at this point that a complication begins. If we would unfold it successfully we must first state the existing facts in regard to the constitutional position of the State of Virginia, as well as those which belong to the formation and erection of the new state of West Virginia.

About the month of April, 1861, an insurrection against the Federal Union broke out within the State of Virginia. The constituted authorities, with the seeming consent of a majority of the People of the State, inaugurated a revolutionary war which they have carried to the extreme points of pronounced independence and the setting up of a pretended revolutionary and belligerent government. The organized political body which has committed this treason, having broken and trampled under its feet the Constitution, and even the Union, of the United States, is still standing in that treasonable attitude within the jurisdiction of the State of Virginia, but it has been dislodged from that portion of that jurisdiction which is contained within the new state of West Virginia. This organization has not given its consent to the formation and erection of the state of Western Virginia, and in its present attitude it is clear that it neither can nor will give that consent. The State of Virginia having thus fallen into revolution, the people living within that part of its jurisdiction which is embraced within the new state of West Virginia, adhering in their loyalty to the State of Virginia and also to the United States, availed themselves of the fortune of the civil war to discard the treasonable authorities of Virginia, reorganized the State, and with all needful forms and solemnities chose and constituted the public functionaries for the state as nearly in conformity with the constitution of Virginia as in the revolutionary condition of that State was practicable. The State of Virginia, thus reorganized, appeared in Congress by its representatives in both Houses, and was then deliberately acknowledged and recognized by the Executive, as well as by the Legislature of the United States, as the State of Virginia, one of the original members of the Federal Union. This State of Virginia, thus constituted and acknowledged, has given its consent to the formation and erection of the State of West Virginia, within the jurisdiction of the State of Virginia. Why is not this consent an adequate one?

We can object to it only on the ground that the political body which gave the consent is not in fact and in law really the State of Virginia. It is replied with great force that the United States are estopped from assuming that position. I do not think it necessary, however, to rely upon that ground. There is no nee d of the plea of estoppel when justice can be done without it, and, whatever may be the force of an estoppel in law when it works injustice, it ought not to be allowed in politics when it works in that way. It seems to me that the political body which has given consent in this case is really and incontestably the State of Virginia. So long as the United States do not recognize the secession, departure, or separation of one of the States, that State must be deemed as existing and having a Constitutional place within the Union, whatever may be at any moment exactly its revolutionary condition. A State thus situated cannot be deemed to be divided into two or more states merely by any revolutionary proceeding which may have occurred, because there cannot be constitutionally two or more States of Virginia. There must and can be, in the view of the Constitution, at all times only one State of Virginia. Here are two distinct political bodies, each asserting itself to be that one State of Virginia. Some constituted power must decide this dispute. The point in dispute necessarily affects the Federal Union. No matter whether the one or the other of these two bodies is the real State of Virginia, the Federal Union has authority to maintain within the State, which cannot and must not be left in abeyance, and the body which is truly the State of Virginia has rights and holds obligations upon the Federal Union which must be conceded and fulfilled. The United States must therefore decide for themselves, so far as their rights and responsibilities extend, which of the two political bodies asserting themselves respectively to be the State of Virginia is truly the State, and which is not. The United States are not shut up within a necessity for deciding it in favor of either body. They can say that, although the old organization is for the present moment disloyal, treasonable, and insurrectionary, yet it shall not be deprived of its powers and privileges. Or they may say, on the other hand, that this old organization has forfeited and lost its right to be regarded as a constitutional one, and it shall be suppressed, and a new and loyal one, constituted in its place, shall be acknowledged as the State of Virginia, and dealt with accordingly. It is a practical question, to be decided by the United States upon the grounds of public necessity or expediency, with a view to the best and permanent interests of the State of Virginia and of the United States. As I have already intimated, the question has been heretofore decided by the United States in favor of the new and against the old organization. The newly organized State of Virginia is therefore, at this moment, by the express consent of the United States, invested with all the rights of the State of Virginia, and charged with all the rights, powers, privileges and dignity of that State. If the United States allow to that organization any of these rights, powers and privileges, it must be allowed to possess and enjoy them all. If it be a state competent to be represented in Congress and bound to pay taxes, it is a state competent to give the required consent of the State to the formation and erection of the new State of West Virginia within the jurisdiction of Virginia.

But in reply to this it is said that the new State of West Virginia includes substantially all of the State of Virginia which is actually occupied by and submissive to the re-organized State of Virginia, so that this re-organized State of Virginia must cease to exist the moment that by its consent the State of West Virginia shall have come into the Federal Union. This argument seems to me unsatisfactory and inconclusive. Western Virginia will not then be the State of Virginia, nor will the State of Virginia cease to exist, although, through accidents of Civil war, there shall for the moment be no loyal and constitutional political organization of the state. Within that part of the jurisdiction of the original state of Virginia which will remain, there will still be a State of Virginia, the old State, wit h its constitutional functions wholly or in part suspended or in abeyance, but capable of complete reconstruction and reorganization by its people, just as the state was reorganized and reconstructed when the government now at Wheeling was organized. If it be said that his is unjust to the State of Virginia, I answer that the constitutional reservation of a right on the part of that State to object to the foundation and erection of a new state within her limits, was a reservation for her benefit. If, through perverseness and disloyalty, a majority of her people, in a revolutionary way, put themselves into a condition in which they cannot and will not assert that right, they cannot by that wrongful and injurious course deprive the loyal people of Western Virginia of their claim to be heard when, in a constitutional manner, they form and erect a new State, or deprive Congress of the power to decide the question as the interests and the Safety of the whole country require.

I am therefore of opinion that the Act for the admission of West Virginia is a constitutional one.

Upon the question of expediency I am determined by two considerations. First. The people of Western Virginia will be safer from molestation for their loyalty, because better able to protect and defend themselves as a new and separate State, than they would be if left to demoralizing uncertainty upon the question whether, in the progress of the war, they may not be again reabsorbed in the State of Virginia, and subjected to severities as a punishment for their present devotion to the Union. The first duty of the United States is protection to loyalty wherever it is found. Second. I am of opinion that the harmony and peace of the Union will be promoted by allowing the new State to be formed and erected, which will assume jurisdiction over that part of the valley of the Ohio which lies on the South side of the Ohio river, displacing, in a constitutional and lawful manner, the jurisdiction heretofore exercised there by a political power concentrated at the head of the James river.

Respectfully submitted:

William H. Seward.

Department of State.

Washington. December 26. 1862.

C. From Edwin M. Stanton to Abraham Lincoln, December 26, 1862

Washington City. D. C.

December 26th 1862

Sir,

In conformity with your request for my written opinion in respect to the constitutionality and expediency of the Act of Congress " for the admission of the State of West Virginia into the Union and for other purposes", I answer:

1st. That in my opinion the above mentioned Act of Congress is constitutional

2d It is, in my judgment, expedient.

Some of the reasons for the foregoing opinion may be briefly stated.

The Constitution expressly authorizes a new state to be formed or erected within the jurisdiction of another state. The Act of Congress is in pursuance of that authority. The measure is sanctioned by the Legislature of the State within whose jurisdiction the new state is formed. When the new state is formed, its consent can be given, and then all the requirements of the Constitution are complied with. I have been unable to perceive any point on which the Act of Congress conflicts with the Constitution.

By the erection of the new state, the Geographical boundary heretofore existing between the free and slave states will be broken, and the advantage of this upon every point of consideration surpasses all objections which have occurred to me on the question of expediency. Many prophetic dangers and evils might be specified, but it is safe to suppose that those who come after us will be as wise as ourselves and if what we deem evils be really such, they will be avoided. The present good is real and substantial, the future may safely be left in the care of those whose duty and interest may be involved in any possible future measures of legislation.

I have the honor to be

Very respectfully

Your obedient servant

Edwin M Stanton

Secretary of War

D. From Edward Bates to Abraham Lincoln, December 27, 1862

Attorney General's Office,

December 27, 1862.

The President having before him for his approval a bill passed by both houses of Congress, entitled an "Act for the admission of the State of 'West Virginia' into the Union, and for other purposes," has submitted to all the members of the Cabinet, separately, the following questions, for their opinion and advice thereon.

1. Is the said act constitutional?

2. Is the said act expedient?

I am of opinion that the bill is not warranted by the Constitution. And, in examining this proposition, I think it well be the more clearly apprehended, if viewed in two aspects: —1. In the letter of the particular provision, and 2. In the spirit, as gathered from the letter, from the whole context, and from the known object, and

First, the letter— Art 4. §3. "New States may be admitted by the Congress into this Union; but no State shall be formed or erected, within the jurisdiction of any other state, nor any state be formed by the junction of two or more States, or parts of States, without the consent of the Legislatures of the States concerned, as well as of the Congress". I observe, in the first place, that the Congress can admit new States into this Union, but cannot form States: Congress has no creative power, in that respect; and cannot admit into this Union, any territory, district or other political entity, less than a state. And such State must exist, as a separate independent body politic, before it can be admitted, under that clause of the Constitution—and there is no other clause. The new state which Congress may admit, by virtue of that clause, does not owe its existence to the fact of admission, and does not begin to exist, coëval with that fact. For, if that be so, the Congress makes the State; for no power but Congress can admit a State into the Union. And that result, (i. e. the making of the State by Congress) would falsify the universal and fundamental principle of this country, that a free American State can be made only by the people, its component members. Congress has no power to make a State.

It is not very important to my argument whether the last clause of the sentence quoted—"without the consent of the legislatures of the State concerned, as well as of the Congress", do or do not apply to the case of a new State "formed or erected within the jurisdiction of any other State", as well as to the case of a new State "formed by the junction of two or more States or parts of States". If it do not apply, then, there stands the naked unconditional prohibition of the formation of a new State, within the jurisdiction of any other State—direct, simple, and incapable of being misunderstood.

If, admitting that the clause does not apply, it be claimed that the prohibition is overruled and annulled by practice, in the cases of Maine, Kentucky, and Tennessee, which were, respectively, " formed and erected within the jurisdiction" of Massachusetts, Virginia and North Carolina, I have two, alternative answers—1. In the absence of proof to the contrary, I assume, that both Congress and the people did obey the constitution, and fulfil all its requirements, in form and substance. 2. If it be shown that, in those instances, the Constitution was disregarded and broken, still I insist that those abuses, do not absolve us from the duty to obey the plain letter and sense of the Constitution.

But if the clause do apply, still, in this case, its terms have not been complied with. It speaks in the plural—"the legislatures of the States concerned"—i. e. Virginia and West Virginia. The consent required by the Constitution is not the consent of the State, generally, nor of its Governor, nor its Judiciary, nor its Convention, but "the consent of the Legislatures of the States concerned". And that is not the only instance in which the Constitution vests very important powers in the Legislatures of the States—they choose the Senators absolutely, and they direct the manner in which electors of President and Vice President shall be chosen. And these are constitutional functions which cannot be exercised by substitute, nor usurped by any other functionary. The division and allotment of powers, as established by the Constitution is not mere form, but vital substance, dear to our fathers, who designed and used it as a guard against the unity of power—to prevent the concentration of power in a single hand or a few hands. Here the proposition is to make two States out of one.—Each one, of course, must have a legislature, and the Constitution requires the consent of both legislatures, before the thing can be done. Now, it is said that the legislature of Virginia (Old Virginia) has consented; but it is not pretended that the legislature of West Virginia has consented—nor that there is, in fact, any such legislature to give consent.

It is a very grave and important thing to cut up and dismember one of the original States of this nation—for a time, in our national youth, the greatest of all—and if we must do it, it behooves us to know that we are acting within the letter of the Constitution, and with a decent respect for the forms of law.

So much for the letter of the law. Let us now examine a little into the sense and spirit of it.

When the rebellion broke out, all the State authorities of Virginia joined it, and made organized and official, as well as individual, insurrection, against the national government, defying its power, and, in order the more effectually to resist it, inviting invasion from States further South. Still a remnant, chiefly in the northwestern counties, remained faithful; and the duty rested upon this government to protect that remnant; to repel that invasion and suppress that insurrection; and thereby to restore Virginia, as she was before the insurrection, to her proper place in the Union. That was and is the plain constitutional duty of this Government; and all that this government has yet done, by legislation, by executive action, or by actual war, has been done with that avowed and only object.

When all the governmental officers of the State of Virginia acting in organic form, had renounced their allegiance to the Constitution, and had risen, in armed revolt against the nation, carrying along with them, into flagrant war, a great majority of the people of the State, this government found itself in a strange and anomalous condition. It was charged with duties which could be neither denied nor evaded; and constrained to the use of powers, which undoubtedly exist in contemplation of law, and yet the modes of their action had not been prescribed, only because the necessity to put those powers into practical exercise had not been foreseen.

In this state of things, we took the only course which lay open before us—a course of prudence, of moderation, and of conformity to the principles and objects of the

Constitution. It was our sacred duty to suppress the insurrection, to repel the invasion, to put down the official treason in Virginia, which had perverted all the organic powers of the state, into active hostility against the nation. And in performing this duty, we could do no less than recognize all of Virginia which remained faithful to the Constitution, and which demanded the protection and support of the national government.

In this view, and only in this, we advised and consented to the organization of a new government for Virginia, seated, for the present, in the northwest, where alone it could act in safety. Those who organized that government were a small minority, but they were all that remained to us and to the Constitution. And we all knew (certainly I did) that such a government could not be organized by such a people, at such a time, and under such circumstances, in exact conformity to all the minute requirements and particulars of the Virginia Constitution. But, for that reason—for the crimes of a comparatively few individuals which render an exact compliance with forms impossible, shall a nation be allowed to perish, a State be blotted from the map of the world? No, God forbid. The substance must not be sacrificed to the forms. Our first great constitutional duty is to save the nation: and the States: and, if possible, we must save them according to law. But if the two duties conflict, still the greater must be performed, and the lesser must yield, even as a conflicting act of Congress must yield to the Constitution.

We all know—everybody knows—that the government of Virginia, recognized by Congress and the President, is a government of necessity, formed by that power which lies dormant in every people, which though known and recognized, is never regulated by la w, because its exact uses and the occasions for its use, cannot be foreknown, and it is called into exercise by the great emergency which, overturning the regular government, necessitates its action, without waiting for the details and forms which all regular governments have. It is intended only to counteract the treacherous perversion of the ordained powers of the State, and stands only as a political nucleus around which the shattered elements of the old Commonwealth may meet and combine, in all its original proportions, and be restored to its legitimate place in the Union. It is a provisional government, proper and necessary for the legitimate object for which it was made and recognized. That object was not to divide and destroy the State, but to rehabilitate and restore it.

That government of Virginia, so formed and so recognized, does not and never did, in fact, represent and govern, more than a small fraction of the State—perhaps a fourth part. And the legislature which pretends to give the consent of Virginia to her own dismemberment, is, (as I am credibly informed) composed chiefly if not entirely of men who represent those forty eight counties which constitute the new State of West Virginia. The act of consent is less in the nature of a law than of a contract. It is a grant of power, an agreement to be divided. And who made the agreement, and with whom? The representatives of the forty-eight counties, with themselves! Is that fair dealing? Is that honest legislation? Is that a legitimate exercise of a constitutional power, by the legislature of Virginia? It seems to me that it is a mere abuse, nothing less than attempted secession, hardly veiled under the flimsy forms of law.

Fortunately, however, even that flimsy veil does not cover the substantial wrong. I think I have already shown that under either construction of the clause of the Constitution above cited, the forms of the Constitution have not been fulfilled. The bill was introduced and has been thus far pushed forward towards its completion, under the erroneous idea that it was in verbal and technical conformity to the constitution, and therefore, and only therefore, that it could ever ripen into a binding law. That was its only foundation; for I think that no reflecting man will seriously affirm that "the legislature of Virginia" which, at Wheeling, on the 13th of May 1862, gave its consent (not the consent of Virginia) to the dismemberment of the Old Commonwealth, was, in truth and honesty, such legislature of Virginia as the Constitution speaks of—a legislature representing and governing the whole, and therefore honestly and lawfully speaking for the whole, in a matter which concerns the fundamental conditions of the State, and its organic law.

In proceeding to answer the second question—"Is the said act expedient?" it becomes necessary to look into the bill itself. It is a strange composition, bearing upon its face, unmistakable marks of haste and inconsideration.

The preamble, after various recitals, gives the consent of Congress, "that the forty-eight counties (which had been named above, without any general boundary) may be formed into a separate and independent state".

The first section declares "that the State of West Virginia be, and is hereby declared to be one of the United States of America, and admitted into the Union; on an equal footing with the original States, in all respects whatever", and allows three representatives, until the next general census. But this is immediately followed by a provision, "That this act shall not take effect until after the proclamation of the President of the United States hereinafter provided for". Which proclamation, very possibly, may never happen, for there is no after-provision in the bill, making it the duty of the President to issue it.

Then follows a paragraph (which seems to be only a preamble to §2) to the effect that "it being represented to Congress that, since the convention of the 26th of November 1861, which framed the proposed constitution for the said state of West Virginia, the people thereof have expressed a wish to change the seventh section of the eleventh article of said constitution, by striking out the same and inserting the following"—giving the exact form of what Congress chooses to have inserted in the State Constitution! The bill does not inform us when, how, or by whom it was "represented to Congress", that the People wished to change their constitution, so recently made by their convention, and ratified by their own votes, as stated with exact particularity, in the preamble. If the people of West Virginia had a right to call a convention and make a constitution for themselves, what is to hinder them from amending the one or making another by the same means, and without waiting for Congress to instruct them what to do and how to do it? It looks badly. However pure the real motive, it lays Congress open to the suspicion of assuming unconstitutional powers, by dictating to a State, in a matter so important and so enduring as its constitution.

And the second section brings no relief, but strengthens the suspicion and magnifies the evil. "Therefore, Sec. 2. Be it further enacted, That whenever the People of West Virginia shall, through their said convention, and by a vote", &c, "make and ratify the change aforesaid, and properly certify" &c. "it shall be lawful for the President of the United States to issue his proclamation stating the fact, and thereupon this act shall take effect and be in . . . force from and after sixty days from the date of said proclamation".

In view of this section, it is manifest that the very existence of the act, even after you have signed it, is made to depend upon the implicit obedience of the people of West Virginia. They must "make and ratify the change aforesaid", and in the precise manner prescribed. They cannot choose new agents to amend their own constitution. They must do it "through their said convention"—the same which sat at Wheeling on the 26th of November 1861. None other can be trusted! Perhaps that convention is no longer in existence. It was called for a particular purpose, and having done its work, and the people having ratified it—perhaps the Convention is functus officio, dead and gone. Surely it was not intended as a permanent institution, to last through all time. Yet that seems to be the idea of the bill, for it fixes no limit of time—whenever the people shall do it, through their said Convention.

Again, when all this is done, as ordered, still, the act may fail and the new State perish in the birth, for want of a proclamation. The bill declares that "it shall be lawful for the President to issue his proclamation;" but it is not made his duty to issue it. And surely it is not his duty to do whatever may be lawfully done. By express act of Congress, it is lawful for the President, by proclamation, as in this case, to close all the Southern ports, but he has not found it expedient to exercise the power.

I need not trouble you with many remarks upon the very awkward shape and inconvenient geographical relations, of the new State, and the still greater awkwardness and inconvenience in which the old state would be left, by the proposed division. Such a division, Such a division, if now made by force of untoward circumstances, could not long stand. Its evils would not be long endured.

I consider this proceeding revolutionary, all the more wrong, because it is needlessly begun at a moment when we are strained to the uttermost, in efforts to prevent a far greater revolution. If successful, it will be "at once an example and fit instrument" for tearing into pieces the regions further south, and making out of the fragments a multitude of feeble communities. And, for what good end? We may thereby stimulate the transient passions and prejudices of men in particular localities, and gratify the personal ambition and interest of a few leaders in those little sections. We may disjoint the fabric of our national government, and destroy the balance of power in Congress, by a flood of senators representing a new brood of fragmentary States.

And now, Sir, I give it as my opinion, that the bill in question is unconstitutional; and also, by its own intrinsic demerits, highly inexpedient.

And I persuade myself that Congress, upon maturer thought, will be glad to be relieved by a veto, from the evil consequences of such improvident legislation.

All which is, most respectfully submitted,

by your obedient servant,

Edwd. Bates

Attorney General.

E. From Salmon P. Chase to Abraham Lincoln, December 29, 1862

Treasury Department

Dec. 29, 1862.

Sir:

My most thoughtful attention has been given to the questions which you have proposed to me as the Head of one of the Departments, touching the Act of Congress admitting the State of West Virginia into the Union.

The questions proposed are two:—

1. Is the Act constitutional?

2. Is the Act expedient?

1. In my judgment the Act is constitutional.

In the Convention which framed the Constitution, the formation of new States was much considered. Some of the ablest men in the Convention, including all or nearly all the Delegates from Maryland, Delaware and New-Jersey, insisted that Congress should have power to form new States, within the limits of existing States, without the consent of the latter. All agreed that Congress should have the power, with that consent. The result of deliberation was the grant to Congress of a general power to admit new States; with a limit on its exercise in respect to States formed within the jurisdiction of old States, or by the junction of old States or parts of such, to cases of consent by the Legislatures of the States concerned.

The power of Congress to admit the State of West-Virginia, formed within the existing State of Virginia, is clear, if the consent of the Legislature of the State of Virginia has been given. That this consent has been given cannot be denied, unless the whole action of the Executive and Legislative branches of the Federal Government for the last eighteen months has been mistaken, and is now to be reversed.

In April, 1861, a Convention of citizens of Virginia assumed to pass an Ordinance of Secession; called in rebel troops; and made common cause with the insurrection which had broken out against the Government of the United States. Most of the persons exercising the functions of State Government in Virginia joined the rebels, and refused to perform their duties to the Union they had sworn to support. They thus abdicated their powers of government in respect to the United States. But a large portion of the people, a number of members of the Legislature, and some judicial officers, did not follow their treasonable example. Most of the members of the Legislature who remained faithful to their oaths, met at Wheeling and reconstituted the Government of Virginia, and elected Senators in Congress who now occupy their seats as such. Under this reconstituted Government, a Governor has been elected, who now exercises Executive authority through out the State, except so far as he is excluded by armed rebellion— By repeated and most significant acts, the Government of the United States has recognized this Government of Virginia as the only legal and constitutional Government of the whole State.

And, in my judgment, no other course than this was open to the National Government. In every case of insurrection involving the persons exercising the powers of State Government, when a large body of the people remain faithful that body, so far as the Un ion is concerned, must be taken to constitute the State. It would have been as absurd as it would have been impolitic to deny to the large loyal population of Virginia the powers of a State Government, because men whom they had clothed with Executive or Legislative or Judicial powers had betrayed their trusts and joined in rebellion against their country.

It does not admit of doubt, therefore, as it seems to me that the Legislature which gave its consent to the formation and erection of the State of West-Virginia was the true and only lawful Legislature of the State of Virginia. The Madison Papers clearly show that the consent of the Legislature of the original State was the only consent required to the erection and formation of a new State within its jurisdiction. That consent having been given, the consent of the new State, if required, is proved by her application for admission.

Nothing required by the Constitution to the formation and admission of West-Virginia into the United States is, therefore, wanting; and the Act of admission must necessarily be constitutional.

Nor is this conclusion technical as some may think. The Legislature of Virginia, it may be admitted, did not contain many members from the Eastern Counties. It contained, however, Representatives from all Counties whose inhabitants were not either rebels themselves, or dominated by greater numbers of rebels. It was the only Legislature of the State known to the Union. If its consent was not valid, no consent could be. If its consent was not valid, the Constitution as to the People of West Virginia has been so suspended by the rebellion that a most important right under it is utterly lost.

It is safer, in my opinion to follow plain principles to plain conclusions, than to turn aside from consequences clearly logical because not exactly agreeable to our views of expediency.

2. And this brings me to the second question: Is the Act of admission expedient?

The Act is almost universally regarded as of vital importance to their welfare by the loyal people most immediately interested, and it has received the sanction of large majorities in both Houses of Congress. These facts afford strong presumptions of expediency.

It is, moreover, well known that, for many years, the people of West-Virginia have desired separation on good and substantial grounds; nor do I perceive any good reason to believe that consent to such separation would now be withheld by a Legislature actually elected from all the Counties of the State and untouched by rebel sympathies.

However this may be, much—very much—is due to the desires and convictions of the loyal people of West-Virginia. To them, admission is an object of intense interest; and their conviction is strongly expressed that the Veto of the Act and its consequent failure would result in the profound discouragement of all loyal men and the proportionate elation and joy of every sympathizer with rebellion. Nor is it to be forgotten that such a Veto will be regarded by many as an abandonment of the views which have hitherto guided the action of the Government in relation to Virginia; will operate as a sort of disavowal of the loyal Government; and may be followed by its disorganization. No act not imperatively demanded by Constitutional duty should be performed by the Executive, if likely to be attended by consequences like these.

It may be said, indeed, that the admission of West-Virginia will draw after it the necessity of admitting other States under the consent of extemporized Legislatures assuming to act for whole States, though really representing no important part of their territory. I think this necessity imaginary. There is no such Legislature, nor is there likely to be. No such Legislature, if extemporized, is likely to receive the recognition of Congress or the Executive. The case of West-Virginia will form no evil precedent. Far otherwise. It will encourage the loyal by the assurance it will give of National recognition and support; but it will inspire no hopes that the National Government will countenance needless and unreasonable attempts to break up or impair the integrity of States. If a case parallel to that of West-Virginia shall present itself, it will, doubtless, be entitled to like consideration; but the contingency of such a case is surely too remote to countervail all the considerations of expediency which sustain the Act.

My answer to both questions, therefore, is affirmative.

S P Chase

F. From Gideon Welles to Abraham Lincoln, December 29, 1862

Navy Department,

December 29, 1862.

Sir:—

The bill entitled "an act for the admission of the State of West Virginia, and for other purposes," which has passed the two Houses of Congress, will, if it become a law, divide the commonwealth of Virginia, and erect a new State within its jurisdiction.

The Constitution declares that "new States may be admitted by the Congress into this Union, but no new State shall be formed or erected within the jurisdiction of any other State; nor any State be formed by the junction of two or more States without the consent of the Legislatures of the States concerned as well as of the Congress."

While permission is herein granted to Congress and the Legislatures of the States directly interested to create a new State, there is, at the same time, a guarantee that the integrity of the States respectively shall be maintained, and that no new States hall be erected within the limits of any one of them without its consent.

Has such consent of the Legislature and people of Virginia been obtained to the formation and erection within its limits of the proposed new State as to place it clearly and unequivocally, in honest good faith, within the letter and spirit of the constitutional guarantees and requirements?

If the consent of the Legislature of the State of Virginia has been obtained in accordance with the constitutional design and intent, there is not, that I am aware, any constitutional objection to the measure. The decision should not, however, be a forced and mere technical one, for the dismemberment of a State against its wishes and in violation of the spirit of the Constitution will be fraught with evil, now and in the future, to the State and to the Union.

An extraordinary condition of affairs exists at this time in Virginia and the country, and the period is not the most propitious opportunity for a calm and dispassionate consideration and decision of a measure of this gravity and importance. A deep and wide-spread insurrection, having for its object a division of the Union, and taking on the forms of a government, is convulsing the country. Virginia is involved in this conspiracy. A large proportion of its territory is overrun by the insurgents, and the loyal feeling of its inhabitants suppressed by invasion. The Federal Government has failed, thus far, to extinguish the insurrection, or to expel the invaders, or to abrogate the pretended form of Government which they have established; and in the mean time, the loyal citizens of a particular section of the State avail themselves of the occasion to forward a movement for the dismemberment of the commonwealth by proceedings which, having certainly their origin in a revolutionary state of facts, may be deemed in themselves somewhat revolutionary, and which, if carried into effect at this juncture, will be likely to aggravate our national troubles.

Under existing necessities, an organization of the loyal citizens, or of a portion of them, has been recognised, and its Senators and Representatives admitted to seats in Congress. Yet we cannot close our eyes to the fact, that the fragment of the St ate which, in the revolutionary tumult, has instituted the new organization, is not possessed of the records, archives, symbols, traditions, or capital of the commonwealth. Though calling itself the State of Virginia, it does not assume the debts and obligations contracted prior to the existing difficulties. Is this organization then, really and in point of fact, any thing else than a provisional government for the State? It is composed almost entirely of those loyal citizens who reside beyond the mountains, and within the prescribed limits of the proposed new State. In this revolutionary period, there being no contestants, we are compelled to recognise the organization as Virginia. Whether that would be the case, and how the question would be met and disposed of were the insurrection this day abandoned, need not now be discussed.

Were Virginia, or those parts of it not included in the proposed new State invaded and held in temporary subjection by a foreign enemy instead of the insurgents, the fragment of territory and population which should successfully repel the enemy and adhere to the Union would doubtless, during such temporary subjection, be recognised, and properly recognised, as Virginia. When, however, this loyal fragment goes farther, and not only declares itself to be Virginia, but proceeds, by its own act, to detach itself permanently and forever from the commonwealth, and to erect itself into a new State within the jurisdiction of the State of Virginia, the question arises whether this proceeding is regular, legal, right, and, in honest good faith, conformable to, and within the letter and spirit of, the Constitution.

I confess that from the brief examination I have been able to give the subject, it is not, to my mind, entirely divested of all constitutional doubt & objection.

If the act submitted for approval be unconstitutional, or if its constitutionality is susceptible of a doubt, it certainly cannot be expedient that it should be consummated. A dismemberment or division of one of the States is prima facie inexpedient, and it should not be done except with the clear, full, and explicit consent of the State which is to be severed.

To preserve the States in their integrity is an imperative duty of the government and country. It would be no trivial act to break up, even in the most regular and formal manner, and in time of peace, an ancient commonwealth; and unless the people themselves, in the mode prescribed by the Constitution, deliberately and voluntarily consent to the formation or erection of a new State within the jurisdiction of an old one, Congress should not, by any exercise of questionable authority, attempt to enforce a division or separation. An observance of the rights of the States is conducive to the union of the States, and a regard for both should prevent such hasty action as will seriously affect either. The Federal government is not authorized to divide or dismember a State; and yet there is no denying the fact that on the approval or rejection of this act, presented to the Executive at this unfortunate time for calm and deliberate action, depends the division or integrity of the State of Virginia. Can it be said to be the wish of the people of Virginia that a new State shall be erected within its jurisdiction, or that they have duly signified their consent to it?

Congress may admit new States into the Union; but any attempt to dismember or divide a State by any forced or unauthorized assumption would be an inexpedient exercise of doubtful power to the injury of such State. Were there no question of doubtful constitutionality in the movement, the time selected for the division of the State is most inopportune. It is a period of civil commotion, when unity and concerted action on the part of all loyal citizens and authorities should be directed to a restoration of the Union, and all tendency towards disintegration and demoralization avoided. Cannot the people of the forty-eight counties comprising the proposed new state of Western Virginia do more to effect this restoration, to secure peaceful relations, and to give Virginia her rightful position, by remaining with her, a part of her, one and indivisible, than by separation? If such be the case, it is assuredly inexpedient at this time to divide the old Commonwealth and erect Western Virginia, with its proposed objectionable boundaries, into a new State. It would, I fear, if consummated, tend to separation rather than to union, and make more difficult the great object which all loyal people aim to secure.

I do not perceive that injury will be inflicted by postponing for the present the erection of a new State within the limits of Virginia. Those who constitute the present organization and those who would compose the proposed new State are almost identical, so much so, that they can shape the laws and institutions of the community in which they reside. They have their full representation in the national Councils, and their full vote and influence on all national questions. Should this disturbing element of a desire for a division of Virginia remain after the insurrection shall have been suppressed, a peaceful, constitutional, and satisfactory arrangement may then be effected. The consummation of the measure at the present time will, I apprehend, farther complicate and embarrass the Government, and retard its efforts for an effective and speedy adjustment of our national affairs.

Believing as I firmly do in the restoration of the Union and the establishment of the Government on a basis more enduringly satisfactory and correct than ever heretofore, I also anticipate a state of things that will, in the progress of events, make north-western Virginia serviceable in promoting the great cause of State and national regeneration. The loyal spirit of West Virginia will, I trust and believe, infuse itself into the disloyal section, and render the whole united people of that great commonwealth, which has unsurpassed natural advantages, as conspicuous in the future as in the past in support of the Union, the Constitution, and the rights of man. It is undoubtedly the true policy of Virginia to preserve its territorial integrity; and the day cannot be distant when, under an improved dispensation, the people beyond the mountains, no less than those of the valley and of the tide-water section, will be converts to that policy, and satisfied that a division would be unwise and inexpedient.

I do not therefore deem it expedient that West Virginia should be erected into a State, nor advise that the bill be approved.

I have the honor to be,

Very respectfully,

Gideon Welles

Secretary of the Navy.

The Complaint in *State of Virginia vs. State of West Virginia*

BELOW is the lawsuit that was filed in the United States Supreme Court in *State of Virginia vs. State of West Virginia*, filed on December 11, 1866. The entire complaint, along with supporting documents, is included.

SUPREME COURT OF THE UNITED STATES
NO. 11—ORIGINAL

THE COMMONWEALTH OF VIRGINIA, COMPLAINANT,

VS.

THE STATE OF WEST VIRGINIA

To the honorable the Chief Justice and the associate justices of the Supreme Court of the United States:

The Commonwealth of Virginia, one of the United States of America, by Thomas R. Bowden, esquire, the attorney general of the said Commonwealth, brings this bill against the State of West Virginia, one of the United States of America.

And thereupon the said Commonwealth complains and says:

That on the thirteenth day of May, in the year of our Lord one thousand eight hundred and sixty-two, the general assembly of the said Commonwealth passed an act giving the consent of the said Commonwealth to the formation and erection of a new State, called West Virginia, within the jurisdiction of the said Commonwealth, to include the counties named in the said act, according to the boundaries and under the provisions set forth in the constitution for the said State of West Virginia and the schedule thereto annexed, proposed by the said convention which assembled at Wheeling on the twenty-sixth day of November, in the year of our Lord eighteen hundred and sixty-one. And in and by the second section of said act it was further provided that the consent of the legislature of the said Commonwealth was thereby given that the counties of Berkeley, Jefferson, and Frederick, which were not within the described boundaries of the proposed new State, and not of the counties enumerated and specified as constituting the territory of the proposed new State, should be included in and from part of the State of West Virginia whenever the voters of the said counties should ratify and assent to the said constitution, at an election held for that purpose, at such time and under such regulations as the commissioners named in the said schedule annexed to the said proposed constitution might prescribe; all of which will more fully and at large appear by reference to a copy of the said act, which is hereunto annexed, and marked as "Exhibit I."

And the Commonwealth of Virginia states that no action [illegible] was had or taken under or in accordance with the said section [illegible] of the said act, and that afterwards, when such proceedings [illegible] that on the twentieth day of April, in the year of our Lord one thousand eight hundred an sixty-two, it was proclaimed by the Congress of the United States, under the authority of an act of the Congress of the United States, that the State of West Virginia, in sixty days from the last-mentioned date, would be admitted into the Union of states thereof, neither of the said counties of Berkeley, Jefferson and Frederick was included in or then made part of the territory of the said new State, nor were the said counties or either of them part of the territory of the said new State at the expiration of the said sixty days mentioned in the said proclamation.

The Commonwealth of Virginia further states that, on the twenty-first day of January, in the year of our Lord one thousand eight hundred and sixty-three, an act of the general assembly of the said Commonwealth was passed, whereby, among other things, it was provided and enacted, that polls should be opened and held on the fourth Thursday of May then next, at the several places for holding elections in the county of Berkeley, for the purpose of taking the sense of the qualified voters of said county on the question of including said county in the State of West Virginia. And, in and by the said act it was further provided and enacted that the governor of the said Commonwealth of Virginia, if of the opinion that the said vote has been opened and held, and the result ascertained and certified according to law, should certify the result of the same, under the seal of the said Commonwealth, to the governor of the said State of West Virginia; and that if a majority of the votes given at the polls opened and held pursuant to that act should be in favor of the said county of Berkeley becoming part of the State of West Virginia, then the said county should become part of the said State of West Virginia when admitted into the same with the consent of the legislature thereof; all which will more fully and at large appear by reference to a copy of the last-mentioned act, which is hereto annexed, and marked "Exhibit II."

And the Commonwealth of Virginia further states that, by an act of its general assembly, passed on the fourth day of February, in the year of our Lord one thousand eight hundred and sixty-three, it was among the things provided and exacted, that at the general election on the fourth Thursday of May then next, it should be lawful for the voters in the district composed of the counties of Frederick and Jefferson, or either of them, to declare by their votes whether the counties of the last-named district should be annexed to, and become a part of, the said State of West Virginia; and for that purpose that there should be a poll opened at each place of voting in each of said districts; and the consent of the said Commonwealth was given for the annexation to the said State of West Virginia of such of the said districts as a majority of the votes so polled in each district might determine, provided said State of West Virginia should also consent and agree to the said annexation, after which all jurisdiction of the said Commonwealth over the districts so annexed should cease; and that the governor of the said Commonwealth should ascertain and certify the result as other elections are certified. All of which will more fully and at large appear in and by a copy of the last-mentioned act, which is hereto annexed, and marked "Exhibit III."

And the Commonwealth of Virginia further states that it appears in and by each of the said last-named acts, copies whereof are marked "Exhibit No. II" and "Exhibit No. III," and so the fact was, that consent of the Commonwealth of Virginia to the annexation of the said counties of Berkeley and Jefferson to the State of Virginia was not intended to be given, and in fact was not given except upon conditions therein prescribed among those were these: That there should in fact be a poll opened at each place of voting established by law in each of the said counties, and that the polling thereat should be safely, fairly, and lawfully conducted; and that on the day named in each of the said acts fro opening such polls, the state of the country should be such as to permit each and all the said polls to be safely and fairly held, so that full and free expression of opinion of the people could be had thereon.

And the Commonwealth of Virginia further states that, at the time fixed by the said acts for opening the said polls, the state of the country in the aforesaid counties of Berkeley and Jefferson rendered it impracticable to open the polls at all the places, or any considerable part of the places, of voting in the last-named counties, or in either of them, nor, in point of fact, were the same, or any considerable part thereof, opened or held, nor was it practicable for the voters of the said counties, or either of them, or any considerable part thereof, to have notice of such polling or to attend the same, and in point of fact, they did not have such notice, and did not and could not attend the same by reason of the civil war then and there being waged and actively carried on; and by reason thereof there could not be, and in point of fact was not a full and free expression, or any expression, or any opportunity for any expression of the opinion of the people of the last-mentioned counties, or other of them, concerning such proposed annexation; and, in point of fact, a very great majority of the voters of each of the said counties then were and now are opposed to such annexation. All which was well known to all persons concerned in procuring the certificate hereinafter mentioned.

And the Commonwealth of Virginia further states that, it having been falsely and fraudulently suggested, and falsely and untruly made to appear unto the governor of the said Commonwealth that the said polls in the said counties had been opened, and that a very large majority of the votes given were in favor of their annexation to the said State of West Virginia, the said governor, acting such false suggestion, and being wholly ignorant of the truth in the premises, did certify to the same on or about the fourteenth day of September in the year of our Lord one thousand eight hundred and sixty-three; and thereupon the said State of West Virginia, without any consent of Congress being had thereto, and before any lawful and binding compact with the consent of Congress had been made by and between the said Commonwealth and the said State, did proceed to extend its jurisdiction over the said counties of Berkeley and Jefferson, and over their inhabitants, as if the same had fully and lawfully become a part of its territory; and still maintains the same.

And the Commonwealth of Virginia further states that the premises having been made fully to appear unto the general assembly of the said Commonwealth, an act was passed, and approved by the governor on the fifth day of December, in the year of our Lord eighteen hundred and sixty-five, wherein it is recited: "Whereas it sufficiently appears that the conditions prescribed in the several acts of the general assembly of the restored government of Virginia, intended to give consent to the transfer, from this State to the State of West Virginia, or jurisdiction over the counties of Jefferson and Berkeley, and the several other counties mentioned in the act of February fourth, eighteen hundred and sixty-three, hereinafter recited, have not been complied with; and the consent of Congress as required by the Constitution of the United States, not having been obtained in order to give effect to the transfer, so that the proceeding heretofore had on this subject are simply inchoate, and said consent may properly be withdrawn; and this general assembly regarding the contemplated disintegration of the Commonwealth, even if within its constitutional competency, as liable to many objections of the gravest character, not only n respect to the counties of Jefferson and Berkeley, over which the State of West Virginia has prematurely attempted to exercise jurisdiction, but also as to the several other counties above referred to;" and thereupon the second section of the act of the said Commonwealth, hereinbefore referred, and marked Exhibit I, and the whole of the said acts hereinbefore referred, and marked Exhibits II and III, were repealed, and all consent theretofore given for the transfer of either of the said counties of Berkeley and Jefferson was withdrawn; all which will ore fully and at large appear by reference to a copy of the last mentioned act hereto annexed, and marked Exhibit IV.

And the Commonwealth of Virginia represents unto this honorable court that, by reason of the premises, a controversy has arisen and now exists between this Commonwealth and the State of West Virginia in regard to the boundary between the said States, and especially whether the said counties of Berkeley and Jefferson, or either of them, has been lawfully annexed to, and have lawfully become a part of the territory, and are within the jurisdiction and authority the State of West Virginia, or whether the same counties have lawfully remained, and are lawfully part of the territory, and within the jurisdiction and authority of the Commonwealth of Virginia.

And the Commonwealth of Virginia prays that it may be ascertained, declared, and established by the decree of the honorable court, that the aforesaid counties of Berkeley and Jefferson now lawfully are, and ought lawfully to be, deemed part of the territory of the Commonwealth of Virginia, and now lawfully should be within its jurisdiction and authority, and that the boundary line between the Commonwealth of Virginia and the State of West Virginia should be ascertained and so established and made certain by the decree of this honorable court as to include the said counties of Berkeley and Jefferson as s part of the territory and within the jurisdiction and authority of the Commonwealth of Virginia, and for all such further or other relief in the premises as justice and equity may require.

May it please this honorable court to grant unto the complainants a write of subpoena, directed to the State of West Virginia, therein requiring the said State at a certain day to appear before this honorable court and answer this bill, and to abide by and perform such decree therein as to this honorable court shall seem meet.

THOS. R. BOWDEN,
Attorney General of Virginia

B. R. CURTIS,
Of Counsel with the Complainants

EXHIBIT I—Acts of the General Assembly

CHAPTER 1—AN ACT GIVING THE CONSENT OF THE LEGISLATURE OF VIRGINIA TO THE FORMATION AND ERECTION OF A NEW STATE WITHIN THE JURISDICTON OF THE STATE. PASSED MAY 13, 1862.

§ 1. *Be it enacted by the General Assembly* that the consent of the Legislature of Virginia be, and the same is hereby, given to the formation and erection of the State of West Virginia, within the jurisdiction of this state, to include the Counties of Hancock &c. [forty-eight counties being named (being the forty-four first mentioned, with Pendleton, Hardy, Hampshire, and Morgan), but the Counties of Berkeley, Jefferson, or Frederick, not being included], *according to the boundaries and under the provisions set forth in the constitution for the said State of West Virginia and the schedule thereto annexed, proposed by the convention which assembled at Wheeling on the 26th day of November, 1861.*

§ 2. That the consent of the Legislature of Virginia be, and the same is hereby, given that the Counties of *Berkeley, Jefferson, and Frederick*, shall be included in and form part of the State of West Virginia WHENEVER the voters of said counties shall ratify and assent to the said constitution at an election held for the purpose, at such time and under such regulations as the commissioners named in the said schedule may prescribe.

§ 3. That this act shall be transmitted by the Executive to the senators and representatives of this Commonwealth in Congress, together with a certified original of the said constitution and schedule, and the said senators and representatives are hereby requested to use their endeavors to obtain the consent of Congress to the admission of the State of West Virginia into the Union.

§ 4. This act shall be in force from and after its passage.

EXHIBIT II

CHAP. 54.—AN ACT GIVING THE CONSENT FOR THE STATE OF VIRGINIA TO THE COUNTY OF BERKELEY BEING ADMITTED INTO, AND BECOMING PART OF, THE STATE OF WEST VIRGINIA. PASSED JANUARY 31, 1863.

Whereas, by the Constitution for the State of West Virginia, ratified by the people thereof, it is provided that additional territory may be admitted into and become part of said state with the consent of the legislature thereof, and it is represented to the General Assembly that the people of the County of Berkeley are desirous that said county should be admitted into and become part of the said State of West Virginia, now, therefore,

1. *Be it enacted by the General Assembly* that polls shall be opened and held on the fourth Thursday of May next, at the several places for holding elections in the County of Berkeley for the purpose of taking the sense of the qualified voters of said county on the question of including said county in the State of West Virginia.

2. The poll books shall be headed as follows, *viz*.: "Shall the County of Berkeley become a part of the State of West Virginia?" and shall contain two columns, one headed "Aye" and the other "No", and the names of those who vote in favor of said county becoming a part of the State of West Virginia shall be entered in the first column, and the names of those who vote against it shall be entered in the second column.

3. The said polls shall be superintended and conducted according to the laws regulating general elections, and the commissioners superintending the same at the courthouse of the said county shall, within six days from the commencement of the said vote, examine and compare the several polls taken in the county, strike therefrom any votes which are by law directed to be stricken from the same, and attach to the polls a list of the votes stricken therefrom, and the reasons for so doing. The result of the polls shall then be ascertained, declared, and certified as follows: the said commissioners shall make out two returns in the following form, or to the following effect:

"We, commissioners for taking the vote of the qualified voters of Berkeley County on the question of including the said county in the State of West Virginia, do hereby certify that polls for that purpose were opened and held the fourth Thursday of May, in the year 1863, within said county, pursuant to law, and that the following is a true statement of the result as exhibited by the poll books, *viz*., for the County of Berkeley becoming part of the State of West Virginia, _____ votes; and against it _____ votes. Given under our hands this ___ day of _____, 1863;"

which returns, written in words, not in figures, shall be signed by the commissioners; one of the said returns shall be filed in the clerk's office of the said county, and the other shall be sent, under the seal of the secretary of this commonwealth, within ten days from the commencement of the said vote, and the governor of this state, if of opinion that the said vote has been opened and held, and the result ascertained and certified pursuant to law, *shall certify the result of the same under the seal of this state, to the governor of the said State of West Virginia.*

4. If the governor of this state shall be of opinion that the said polls cannot be safely and properly opened and held in the said County of Berkeley, on the fourth Thursday of May next, he may by proclamation postpone the same, and appoint in the same proclamation, or by one to be hereafter issued, another day for opening and holding the same.

5. If a majority of the votes given at the polls opened and held pursuant to this act be in favor of the said County of Berkeley's becoming part of the State of West Virginia,

then shall the said county become part of the State of West Virginia when admitted into the same with the consent of the legislature thereof.

6. This act shall be in force from its passage.

EXHIBIT III

CHAP. 78—AN ACT GIVING CONSENT TO THE ADMISSION OF CERTAIN COUNTIES INTO THE NEW STATE OF WEST VIRGINIA UPON CERTAIN CONDITIONS. PASSED FEBRUARY 4, 1863.

1. *Be it enacted by the General Assembly of Virginia* that at the general election on the fourth Thursday of May, 1863, it shall be lawful for the voters of the district composed of the Counties of Tazewell, Bland Giles, and Craig to declare by their votes whether said counties shall be annexed to and become a part of the new State of West Virginia; also, at the same time, the district composed of the Counties of Buchanan, Wise, Russell, Scott, and Lee, to declare, by their votes, whether the counties of the said last-named district shall be annexed to and become a part of the State of West Virginia; also, at the same time, the district composed of the Counties of Alleghany, Bath, and Highland to declare by their votes whether the counties of such last-named district shall be annexed to and become a part of the State of West Virginia; also, at the same time, the district composed of the Counties of Frederick and *Jefferson,* or *either* of them, to declare by their votes whether the Counties of the said last-named district shall be annexed to and become a part of the State of West Virginia; also, at the same time, the district composed of the Counties of Clarke, Loudoun, Fairfax, Alexandria, and Prince William, to declare by their votes whether the Counties of the said last-named district shall be annexed to and become a part of the State of West Virginia; also, at the same time, the district composed of the Counties of Shenandoah, Warren, Page, and Rockingham to declare by their votes whether the Counties of the said last-named district shall be annexed to and become a part of the State of West Virginia; and for that purpose, there shall be a poll opened at each place of voting in each of said districts headed 'For *annexation*' and '*Against annexation.*' And the consent of this General Assembly is hereby given for the annexation to the said State of West Virginia of such of said districts, or of either of them, as a majority of the votes so polled in each district may determine, provided that the Legislature of the State of West Virginia shall also consent and agree to the said annexation, after which all jurisdiction of the State of Virginia over the districts so annexed shall cease.

2. It shall be the duty of the *governor of the Commonwealth to ascertain and certify the result as other elections are certified.*

3. In the event the state of the country will not permit or from any cause said election for annexation cannot be fairly held on the day aforesaid, it shall be the duty of the governor of this Commonwealth, as soon as such election can be safely and fairly held and a full and free expression of the opinion of the people had thereon, to issue his proclamation ordering such election for the purpose aforesaid, and certify the result as aforesaid.

4. This act shall be in force from its passage.

EXHIBIT IV

CHAP. 84—AN ACT TO REPEAL THE 2ND SECTION OF AN ACT PASSED ON THE 13TH DAY OF MAY, 1862, ENTITLED AN ACT GIVING THE CONSENT OF THE LEGISLATURE OF VIRGINIA TO THE FORMATION AND ERECTION OF A NEW STATE WITHIN THE JURISDICTION OF THIS STATE; ALSO, REPEALING THE ACT PASSED ON THE 31ST DAY OF JANUARY, 1863, ENTITLED AN ACT GIVING THE CONSENT OF THE STATE OF VIRGINIA TO THE COUNTY OF BERKELEY BEING ADMITTED INTO, AND BECOMING PART OF, THE STATE OF WEST VIRGINIA; ALSO, REPEALING THE ACT PASSED ON THE 4TH DAY OF FEBRUARY, 1863, ENTITLED AN ACT GIVING CONSENT TO THE ADMISSION OF CERTAIN COUNTIES INTO THE NEW STATE OF WEST VIRGINIA UPON CERTAIN CONDITIONS, AND WITHDRAWING CONSENT TO THE TRANSFER OF JURISDICTION OVER THE SEVERAL COUNTIES IN EACH OF SAID ACTS MENTIONED. PASSED DECEMBER 5, 1865.

Whereas it sufficiently appears that the conditions prescribed in the several acts of the general assembly of the restored government of Virginia, intended to give consent to the transfer, from this state to the state of West Virginia, of jurisdiction over the counties of Jefferson and Berkeley, and the several other counties mentioned in the act of February fourth, eighteen hundred and sixty-three, hereinafter recited, have not been complied with; and the consent of congress, as required by the constitution of the United States, not having been obtained in order to give effect to such transfer; so that the proceedings heretofore had on this subject are simply inchoate; and said consent may property be withdrawn; and this general assembly regarding the contemplated disintegration of the commonwealth, even if within its constitutional competency, as liable to many objections of the gravest character, not only in respect to the counties of Jefferson and Berkeley, over which the State of West Virginia has prematurely attempted to exercise jurisdiction, but also as to the several other counties above referred to:

1. Be it therefore enacted by the general assembly of Virginia, That the second section of the act passed on the thirteenth day of May, eighteen hundred and sixty-three, entitled an act giving the consent of the state of Virginia to the county of Berkeley being admitted into, and becoming part of the state of West Virginia, be and the same is, in like manner, hereby repealed.

2. And be it further enacted, That the act passed on the thirty-first day of January, eighteen hundred and sixty-three, entitled an act giving the consent of the state of Virginia to the county of Berkeley being admitted into, and becoming part of the state of West Virginia, be and the same is, in like manner, hereby repealed.

3. And be it further enacted, That the act passed on the fourth day of February eighteen hundred and sixty-three, entitled an act giving consent to the admission of

certain counties into the new state of West Virginia upon certain conditions, be and the same is, in like manner, hereby repealed.

4. And be if further enacted, That all consent in any manner heretofore given, or intended to be given, by the general assembly of Virginia, to the transfer, from its jurisdiction to the jurisdiction of the state of West Virginia, of any of the counties mentioned in either of the above recited acts, be and the same is hereby withdrawn; and all acts, ordinances and resolutions heretofore passed, purporting to give such consent, are hereby repealed.

5. This act shall be in force from and after the passage thereof.

SUPREME COURT OF THE UNITED STATES
NO. 11—ORIGINAL

THE COMMONWEALTH OF VIRGINIA, COMPLAINANT,

VS.

THE STATE OF WEST VIRGINIA

This defendant by protestation, not confessing or acknowledging all or any of the matters and things in the said complainant's bill to be true in such manner and form as the same are therein, doth demur thereto, because the complainant hath not in and by her said bill made or stated such a case as doth or ought to entitle her to any such discovery or relief as is thereby sought and prayed for from or against this defendant; and for cause of special demurrer this defendant states, first, that in and by the acts of the general assembly of the said Commonwealth of Virginia, or January 31, 1863, and February 4, 1863, made exhibits to said bill, the governor of said Commonwealth was vested with the exclusive jurisdiction of deciding whether the election authorized by said acts was legally held, and his proclamation that it was is conclusive and cannot be reexamined by this court and secondly, because the said counties of Berkeley and Jefferson, mentioned in said bill, were thereby lawfully made parts of the State of West Virginia, and ever since been so treated by said state.

Wherefore this defendant demands the judgment of this honorable court whether she shall be compelled to make any further or other answer to the said bill, or any of the matters and things therein contained, and prays to be hence dismissed, with the reasonable cost in this behalf sustained.

REVERDY JOHNSON,
Solicitor for Defendant

The undersigned counsel for the above-named defendant, certified that, in his opinion, the above demur is well founded in point of law.

REVERDY JOHNSON

Arthur J. Boreman, the governor of said State of West Virginia, makes oath that the foregoing demurrer is not intended for delay.

A. J. BOREMAN, Governor

Sworn before me, John S. Witcher, secretary of state of the said State of West Virginia, this 20th day of April, 1867; and I, the said secretary, hereby certify that I am authorized, by the laws of said State of West Virginia, to administer oaths in all cases there they may be lawfully taken.

In testimony whereof I have hereunto set my hand and affixed the seal of the said State, at the city of Wheeling, this 20th day of April, 1867

J. S. WITCHER,

Secretary of State

Filed 24th April, 1867.

The Supreme Court's Decision in *Virginia vs. West Virginia*

F OLLOWING are the majority and dissenting opinions of the United States Supreme Court in the case of *State of Virginia vs. State of West Virginia*, presented in their entirety. The footnotes are in the original opinion, and have not been added by us.

United States Supreme Court
STATE OF VIRGINIA v. STATE OF WEST VIRGINIA (1870)
Decided: December 1, 1870

ON original bill to settle the boundary line between the States of Virginia and West Virginia, the case as existing in well-known public history and from the record being thus:

A convention professing to represent the State of Virginia, which assembled in Richmond in February, 1861, attempted by a so-called "ordinance of secession" to separate that State from the Union, and combined with certain other Southern States to accomplish that separation by arms. The people of the northwestern part of the State, who were separated from the eastern part by a succession of mountain ranges and had never received the heresy of secession, refused to acquiesce in what had been thus done, and organized themselves to defend and maintain the Federal Union. The idea of a separate State government soon developed itself; and an organic convention of the State of Virginia, which in June, 1861, organized the State on loyal principles-"the Pierpont government"- and which new organization was acknowledged by the President and Congress of the United States as the true State government of

Virginia-passed August 20th, 1861, an ordinance by which they ordained that a new State be formed and erected out of the territory included within certain boundaries (set forth) including within those boundaries of the proposed new State: the counties of, &c. [thirty-nine counties being named]. These counties did not include as within the proposed State the counties of either Greenbrier, Pocahontas, Hampshire, Hardy, Morgan, Berkeley, or Jefferson; but the third section of the ordinance enacted that the convention might change the boundaries described in the first section of the ordinance so as to include within the proposed State the counties of Greenbrier and Pocahontas, or either of them, and also the other counties just above named, or either of them, "and also all such other counties as lie contiguous to the said boundaries or to the counties named," if the said counties to be added, or either of them, by a majority of the votes given, & c., should declare their wish to form part of the proposed State, and should elect delegates to the said convention, &c. The name of the new State as ordained by the ordinance was Kanawha.

The convention provided for by the ordinance met in Wheeling, November 26th, 1861, and made a "Constitution of West Virginia." Certain counties named, forty-four in number, "formerly part of the State of Virginia," it was ordained should be "included in and form part of the State of West Virginia." No one of the counties of Pendleton, Hardy, Hampshire, Morgan, Berkeley, or Jefferson, were among these forty-four. The constitution proceeded, in a second section:

> And if a majority of the votes cast at the election or elections held as provided in the schedule hereof, in the district composed of the counties of Pendleton, Hardy, Hampshire, and Morgan, shall be in favor of the adoption of this constitution, the said four counties shall be included in and form part of the State of West Virginia; and if the same shall be so included, and a majority of the votes cast at the said election or elections, in the district composed of Berkeley, Jefferson, and Frederick, shall be in favor of the adoption of this constitution, then the three last-named counties shall also be included in and form part of the State of West Virginia.

All through the constitution, as, ex. gr., in the fixing of senatorial and representative districts, and of judicial circuits, provision was made for the case of these two sets of counties coming in, or of one set coming in without the other. A separate section ordained that—

> Additional territory may be admitted into, and become part of this State, with the consent of the legislature.

And it provided for the representation in the Senate and House of Delegates of such new territory.

By the terms of this constitution it was to be submitted to a vote of the people on the first Thursday in April, 1862; and on a vote then taken it was ratified by the people of the forty-four counties first named, and by those of Pendleton, Hardy, Hampshire, and Morgan. But no one of the counties of Berkeley, Jefferson, or Frederick, apparently, voted on the matter; owing, as was said by the defendant's counsel at the bar, to the fact, "that, from the 1st of June, 1861, to the 1st of March, 1862; during which time these proceedings for the formation of a new State were held, those counties were in the possession, and under the absolute control, of the forces of the Confederate States; and that an attempt to hold meetings in them to promote the formation of the new State would have been followed by immediate arrest and imprisonment."

All this being done, the legislature of Virginia, as reorganized, passed, on the 13th May, 1862, an act, in title and body, thus:

An Act giving the consent of the Legislature of Virginia to the formation and erection of a new State within the jurisdiction of this State.

1. Be it enacted by the General Assembly, That the consent of the legislature of Virginia be, and the same is hereby given to the formation and erection of the State of West Virginia, within the jurisdiction of this State, to include the counties of Hancock, &c. [forty-eight counties being named (being the forty-four first mentioned, with Pendleton, Hardy, Hampshire, and Morgan), but the counties of Berkeley, Jefferson, or Frederick, not being included], according to the boundaries and under the provisions set forth in the constitution for the said State of West Virginia and the schedule thereto annexed, proposed by the convention which assembled at Wheeling on the 26th day of November, 1861

2. That the consent of the legislature of Virginia be, and the same is hereby given, that the counties of Berkeley, Jefferson, and Frederick, shall be included in and form part of the State of West Virginia WHENEVER the voters of said counties shall ratify and assent to the said constitution, at an election held for the purpose, at such time and under such regulations as the commissioners named in the said schedule may prescribe.

3. That this act shall be transmitted by the Executive to the senators and representatives of this Commonwealth in Congress, together with a certified original of the said constitution and schedule, and the said senators and representatives are hereby requested to use their endeavors to obtain the consent of Congress to the admission of the State of West Virginia into the Union.

4. This act shall be in force from and after its passage.

Under this act, no elections apparently were held; and on the 31st December, 1862[1], Congress passed

An Act for the admission of the State of 'West Virginia' into the Union, and for other purposes.

---

1 12 Stat. at Large, 633.

Whereas, The people inhabiting that portion of Virginia known as West Virginia, did by a convention assembled in the city of Wheeling, on the 26th November, 1861, frame for themselves a constitution with a view of becoming a separate and independent State; and whereas, at a general election held in the counties composing the territory aforesaid, on the 3d of May last, the said constitution was approved and adopted by the qualified voters of the proposed State; and whereas, the legislature of Virginia, by an act passed on the 13th day of May, 1862, did give its consent to the formation of a new State within the jurisdiction of the said State of Virginia, to be known by the name of West Virginia, and to embrace the following named counties, to wit [the forty-eight counties mentioned in the above-quoted Virginia act of May 13, 1862, were here set forth by name, and not including Berkeley or Jefferson]; and whereas, both the convention [78 U.S. 39, 44] and the legislature aforesaid have requested that the new State should be admitted into the Union, and the constitution aforesaid being republican in form, Congress doth hereby consent that the said forty-eight counties may be formed into a separate and independent State; therefore,

Be it enacted, &c., That the State of West Virginia be, and is hereby declared to be one of the United States of America, and admitted into the Union on an equal footing with the original States, in all respects whatsoever, &c.

The act contained a proviso that it should not take effect until after the proclamation of the President of the United States, hereinafter provided for. It then proceeded to recite that it was represented to Congress that since the convention of 26th November, 1861, which framed and proposed the constitution for the said State of West Virginia, the people thereof had expressed a wish to change the 7th section of the 11th article of said constitution, by striking out the same, and inserting the following in its place. The article [on the subject of slavery] was then set forth. It was therefore further enacted that whenever the people of West Virginia should, through their said convention, and by a vote to be taken, &c., make and ratify the change aforesaid, and properly certify the same under the hand of the president of the convention, it should be lawful for the President of the United States to issue his proclamation stating the fact, and that thereupon this act should take effect, and be in force from and after sixty days from the date of the proclamation.

This proclamation President Lincoln did issue on the 20th April, 1863[2], reciting the act, with, however, a condition annexed; reciting that proof of compliance with the condition, as required by the second section of the act, had been submitted to him, and in pursuance of the act declaring and proclaiming that the act should take effect, and be in force from and after sixty days from his proclamation.

Next in the history came certain acts of the State of Virginia; among them one passed January 31, 1863, and which, with its title, ran thus:

---

2 13 Stat. at Large, 731.

An Act giving the consent of the State of Virginia to the County of Berkeley being admitted into, and becoming part of, the State of West Virginia.

Whereas, By the constitution for the State of West Virginia, ratified by the people thereof, it is provided that additional territory may be admitted into and become part of said State, with the consent of the legislature thereof, and it is represented to the General Assembly that the people of the county of Berkeley are desirous that said county should be admitted into and become part of the said State of West Virginia: Now, therefore,

1. Be it enacted by the General Assembly, That polls shall be opened and held on the fourth Thursday of May next, at the several places for holding elections in the county of Berkeley, for the purpose of taking the sense of the qualified voters of said county on the question of including said county in the State of West Virginia.

2. The poll-books shall be headed as follows, viz.: "Shall the county of Berkeley become a part of the State of West Virginia?" and shall contain two columns, one headed "Aye," and the other "No," and the names of those who vote in favor of said county becoming a part of the State of West Virginia shall be entered in the first column, and the names of those who vote against it shall be entered in the second column.

3. The said polls shall be superintended and conducted according to the laws regulating general elections, and the commissioners superintending the same at the court-house of the said county shall, within six days from the commencement of the said vote, examine and compare the several polls taken in the county, strike therefrom any votes which are by law directed to be stricken from the same, and attach to the polls a list of the votes stricken therefrom, and the reasons for so doing. The result of the polls shall then be ascertained, declared, and certified as follows: The said commissioners shall make out two returns in the following form, or to the following effect:

"We, commissioners for taking the vote of the qualified voters of BerkeleyCounty on the question of including the said county in the State of West Virginia, do hereby certify that polls for that purpose were opened and held the fourth Thursday of May, in the year 1863, within said county, pursuant to law, and that the following is a true statement of the result as exhibited by the poll-books, viz.: for the county of Berkeley becoming part of the State of West Virginia, _____ votes; and against it _____ votes. Given under our hands this ___ day of _____, 1863;"

which returns, written in words, not in figures, shall be signed by the commissioners; one of the said returns shall be filed in the clerk's office of the said county, and the other shall be sent, under the seal of the secretary of this commonwealth, within ten days from the commencement of the said vote, and the governor of this State, if of opinion that the said vote has been opened and held, and the result ascertained and certified pursuant to law, shall certify the result of the same under the seal of this State, to the governor of the said State of West Virginia.

4. If the governor of this State shall be of opinion that the said polls cannot be safely and properly opened and held in the said county of Berkeley, on the fourth Thursday of May next, he may by proclamation postpone the same, and appoint in the same proclamation, or by one to be hereafter issued, another day for opening and holding the same.

5. If a majority of the votes given at the polls opened and held pursuant to this act be in favor of the said county of Berkeley becoming part of the State of West Virginia, then shall the said county become part of the State of West Virginia when admitted into the same with the consent of the legislature thereof.

6. This act shall be in force from its passage.

Then followed, four days later, on the 4th of February of the same year, 1863, an act relating to the admission of several other counties, including Jefferson, thus:

An Act giving consent to the admission of certain counties into the new State of West Virginia upon certain conditions.

1. Be it enacted by the General Assembly of Virginia, That at the general election on the fourth Thursday of May, 1863, it shall be lawful for the voters of the district composed of the counties of Tazewell, Bland, Giles, and Craig to declare, by their votes, whether said counties shall be annexed to, and become a part of, the new State of West Virginia; also, at the same time, the district composed of the counties of Buchanan, Wise, Russell, Scott, and Lee, to declare, by their votes, whether the counties of the said last-named district shall be annexed to, and become a part of, the State of West Virginia; also, at the same time, the district composed of the counties of Alleghany, Bath, and Highland, to declare, by their votes, whether the counties of such last-named district shall be annexed to, and become a part of, the State of West Virginia; also, at the same time, the district composed of the counties of Frederick and Jefferson, or either of them, to declare by their votes whether the counties of the said last-named district shall be annexed to, and become a part of, the State of West Virginia; also, at the same time, the district composed of the counties of Clarke, Loudoun, Fairfax, Alexandria, and Prince William, to declare, by their votes, whether the counties of the said last-named district shall be annexed to, and become a part of, the State of West Virginia; also, at the same time, the district composed of the counties of Shenandoah, Warren, Page, and Rockingham, to declare, by their votes, whether the counties of the said last-named district shall be annexed to, and become a part of, the State of West Virginia; and for that purpose there shall be a poll opened at each place of voting in each of said districts, headed "For annexation," and "Against annexation." And the consent of this General Assembly is hereby given for the annexation to the said State of West Virginia of such of said districts, or of either of them, as a majority of the votes so polled in each district may determine; provided that the legislature of the State of West Virginia shall also consent and agree to the said annexation, after which all jurisdiction of the State of Virginia over the districts so annexed shall cease.

2. It shall be the duty of the governor of the Commonwealth to ascertain and certify the result as other elections are certified.

3. In the event the state of the country will not permit, or from any cause, said election for annexation cannot be fairly held on the day aforesaid, it shall be the duty of the governor of this Commonwealth, as soon as such election can be safely and fairly held, and a full and free expression of the opinion of the people had thereon, to issue his proclamation ordering such election for the purpose aforesaid, and certify the result as aforesaid.

4. This act shall be in force from its passage.

Under these two acts elections of some sort were held and the governor certified the same to the State of West Virginia, and that State thereupon extended her jurisdiction over the counties of Berkeley and Jefferson, and still maintained it.

Next came an act of the State of Virginia, passed December 5th, 1865:

An Act to repeal the second section of an act passed on the 13th day of May, 1862, entitled An act giving the consent of the legislature of Virginia to the formation and erection of a new State within the jurisdiction of this State; also, repealing the act passed on the 31st day of January, 1863, entitled An act giving the consent of the State of Virginia to the county of Berkeley being admitted into, and becoming part of, the State of West Virginia; also, repealing the act passed on the 4th day of February, 1863, entitled An act giving consent to the admission of certain counties into the new State of West Virginia, upon certain conditions, and withdrawing consent to the transfer of jurisdiction over the several counties in each of said acts mentioned.

Whereas, It sufficiently appears that the conditions prescribed in the several acts of the General Assembly of the restored government of Virginia, intended to give consent to the transfer, from this State to the State of West Virginia, of jurisdiction over the counties of Jefferson and Berkeley, and the several other counties mentioned in the act of February 4th, 1863, hereinafter recited, have not been complied with; and the consent of Congress, as required by the Constitution of the United States, not having been obtained in order to give effect to such transfer, so that the proceedings heretofore had on this subject are simply inchoate, and said consent may properly be withdrawn; and this General Assembly, regarding the contemplated disintegration of the Commonwealth, even if within its constitutional competency, as liable to many objections of the gravest character, not only in respect to the counties of Jefferson and Berkeley, over which the State of West Virginia has prematurely attempted to exercise jurisdiction, but also as to the several other counties above referred to:

1. Be it therefore enacted by the General Assembly of Virginia, That the second section of the act passed on the 13th day of May, 1862, entitled An act giving the consent of the legislature of Virginia to the formation and erection of a new State within the jurisdiction of this State be, and the same is hereby, repealed.

2. That the act passed on the 31st day of January, 1863, entitled An act giving the consent of the State of Virginia to the county of Berkeley being admitted into and becoming part of the State of West Virginia, be, and the same is, in like manner, hereby repealed.

3. That the act passed February 4th, 1863, entitled An act giving consent to the admission of certain counties into the new State of West Virginia upon certain conditions, be, and the same is, in like manner, hereby repealed.

4. That all consent in any manner heretofore given, or in tended to be given, by the General Assembly of Virginia to the transfer, from its jurisdiction to the jurisdiction of the State of West Virginia, of any of the counties mentioned in either of the above-recited acts, be, and the same is hereby, withdrawn; and all acts, ordinances, and resolutions heretofore passed purporting to give such consent are hereby repealed.

5. This act shall be in force from and after the passage thereof.

On the 10th of March, 1866[3], Congress passed a

Joint Resolution giving the consent of Congress to the transfer of the Counties of Berkeley and Jefferson to the State of West Virginia.

Be it resolved, &c., That Congress hereby recognizes the transfer of the counties of Berkeley and Jefferson from the State of Virginia to West Virginia and consents thereto.

In this state of things, the Commonwealth of Virginia brought her bill in equity against the State of West Virginia in this court on the ground of its original jurisdiction of controversies between States under the Constitution, in which it was alleged that such a controversy had arisen between those States in regard to their boundary, and especially as to the question whether the counties of Berkeley and Jefferson had become part of the State of West Virginia or were part of and within the jurisdiction of the Commonwealth of Virginia; and the prayer of the bill was that it might be established by the decree of this court that those counties were part of the Commonwealth of Virginia, and that the boundary line between the two States should be ascertained, established, and made certain, so as to include the counties mentioned as part of the territory and within the jurisdiction of the State of Virginia.

The stating part of the bill was largely composed of the substance of four acts of the General Assembly of the Commonwealth, already presented at large, in the statement, copies of them being made exhibits and filed with the bill.

The bill, in addition to the substance of these statutes, alleged that no action whatever was had or taken under the second section of the act of 1862[4], but that afterwards the State of West Virginia was admitted into the Union, under an act of Congress and proclamation of the President, without including either the counties of Berkeley, Jefferson, or Frederick.

It further alleged that an attempt was made to take the vote in the counties of Jefferson and Berkeley at the time mentioned in the acts of January 31st, and February 4th, 1863[5], but that, owing to the state of the country at that time, no fair vote could be taken; that no polls were opened at any considerable number of the voting places; that the vote taken was not a fair and full expression; all of which was well known to the persons who procured the certificate of such election. It also alleged that it having been falsely and fraudulently suggested, and falsely and untruly made to appear to the governor of the Commonwealth, that a large majority of the votes was given in favor of annexation, he certified the same to the State of West Virginia, and that thereupon,

3   14 Stat. at Large, 350.

4   Supra, p. 43.

5   Supra, pp. 45, 47.

without the consent of Congress, that State extended her jurisdiction over the said counties of Berkeley and Jefferson, and over the inhabitants thereof, and still maintained the same.

The State of Virginia, of course, in coming before this court with this case, relied upon that clause of the Federal Constitution which ordains that "no State shall, without the assent of Congress, enter into any agreement or compact with any other State," and that one also which ordains that "the judicial power shall extend . . . to controversies between two or more States."

To the bill thus filed the State of West Virginia appeared and put in a general demurrer. It was not denied that West Virginia had from the beginning continued her assent to receive these two counties.

The case was elaborately argued at December Term, 1866, by Messrs. B. R. Curtis and A. Hunter, in support of the bill, and by Messrs. B. Stanton and Reverdy Johnson, in support of the demurrer; and again at this term by Mr. Taylor, Attorney-General of Virginia, Messrs. B. R. Curtis, and A. Hunter, on the former side, and Messrs. B. Stanton, C. J. Faulkner, and Reverdy Johnson, contra.

In support of the bill it was argued, among other things, that a State was incapable under the Constitution of making any contract with another State; that States might negotiate with each other, might express a mutual willingness to do the same thing, but that this was all; that Congress by the act of 1862, assenting to the admission of a State composed of but forty-eight counties, had not given its assent to a State having in it the counties of Berkeley and Jefferson; that Congress had never assented to the admission of those counties until its joint resolution of 1866; that previous to that time Virginia had withdrawn, as she had a right to do, her once offered assent to what Congress could alone complete; that the transfer could exist only by the concurrent assent of all these parties; that therefore no transfer had been made by the joint resolution. Even if this were not so, and if fair elections under the acts of 1863 would be sufficient, the allegations of the bill as to the character of the elections relied on-allegations of partial and fraudulent elections-which allegations on a demurrer were to be taken as true-concluded the matter; for if no elections had ever taken place, then even the condition upon which as between the two States the counties were to pass to West Virginia, had never taken effect.

In support of the demurrer the principal points were, that although this court had jurisdiction over "controversies between two States," it was only over controversies in which some question in its nature judicial was involved. This court could not settle a controversy of arms, or force, such as came near arising between Ohio and Michigan, on the matter of their boundary; nor would it settle a political one. *Georgia v. Stanton*[6] decided that. Now, the main question here involved was the political jurisdiction over

6 Wallace, 50.

two counties, and their inhabitants. There was no land that Virginia claims as her individual land. The question then was a political question; one for Congress. Of the disputed questions of boundary which had arisen in this country, Congress had settled most.[7] In the few cases, where this court had acted, including the case of *Rhode Island v. Massachusetts*,[8] where there was an old colonial agreement of 1710, there had always been some proper subject of judicial action involved; a question of the specific performance of contract, a question of property, or the like. Even in the great English case of *Penn v. Lord Baltimore*, A. D. 1750[9], before Lord Hardwicke, to settle the lines between Delaware and Maryland, there was an agreement for settling the boundary; a proper head of equitable jurisdiction. The dicta and much of the argument of Baldwin, J., who gave the opinion in the Rhode Island case, were unnecessary to the judgment. Other cases have followed that.

In reply to the other side it was contended that the boundary, as contemplated both by the State of Virginia and the proposed State, was not confined to the limits specifically stated, but was capable of being opened, to the extent provided for, by the two bodies; that this capacity was inherent in the State as constituted; that Congress in 1862 received the State with this capacity; that the right of voting was subsequently exercised by the two counties under the Virginia acts of 1863; that the condition thus became executed, and the two counties transferred to the State of West Virginia; that the court could not go behind the official returns of the vote; and, finally, that the purpose of one of the clauses of the Constitution, relied on in the argument of the other side, was not to prevent the States from settling their own boundaries so far as merely affected their relations to each other, but to guard against the derangement of their Federal relations with the other States of the Union, and the Federal government, which might be injuriously affected if the contracting parties might act upon their boundaries at pleasure; and that in this case the boundary having been settled by themselves, between Virginia and the new body to which she was in 1862 assisting to give existence, Virginia could not subsequently revoke her assent against the wish of the other party.

Mr. Justice MILLER delivered the opinion of the court.

The first proposition on which counsel insist, in support of the demurrer is, that this court has no jurisdiction of the case, because it involves the consideration of questions purely political; that is to say, that the main question to be decided is the conflicting claims of the two States to the exercise of political jurisdiction and sovereignty over the territory and inhabitants of the two counties which are the subject of dispute.

7   8 Stat. at Large, 751, title, Boundary, in Index.

8   12 Peters, 724.

9   1 Vesey, 444.

This proposition cannot be sustained without reversing the settled course of decision in this court and overturning the principles on which several well-considered cases have been decided. Without entering into the argument by which those decisions are supported, we shall content ourselves with showing what is the established doctrine of the court.

In the case of *Rhode Island v. Massachusetts*[10], this question was raised, and Chief Justice Taney dissented from the judgment of the court by which the jurisdiction was affirmed, on the precise ground taken here. The subject is elaborately discussed in the opinion of the court, delivered by Mr. Justice Baldwin, and the jurisdiction, we think, satisfactorily sustained. That case, in all important features, was like this. It involved a question of boundary and of the jurisdiction of the States over the territory and people of the disputed region. The bill of Rhode Island denied that she had ever consented to a line run by certain commissioners. The plea of Massachusetts averred that she had consented. A question of fraudulent representation in obtaining certain action of the State of Rhode Island was also made in the pleadings.

It is said in that opinion that, "title, jurisdiction, sovereignty, are (therefore) dependent questions, necessarily settled when boundary is ascertained, which being the line of territory, is the line of power over it, so that great as questions of jurisdiction and sovereignty may be, they depend on facts." And it is held that as the court has jurisdiction of the question of boundary, the fact that its decision on that subject settles the territorial limits of the jurisdiction of the States, does not defeat the jurisdiction of the court.

The next reported case, is that of *Missouri v. Iowa*[11], in which the complaint is, that the State of Missouri is unjustly ousted of her jurisdiction, and obstructed from governing a part of her territory on her northern boundary, about ten miles wide, by the State of Iowa, which exercises such jurisdiction, contrary to the rights of the State of Missouri, and in defiance of her authority. Although the jurisdictional question is thus broadly stated, no objection on this point was raised, and the opinion which settled the line in dispute, delivered by Judge Catron, declares that it was the unanimous opinion of all the judges of the court. The Chief Justice must, therefore, have abandoned his dissenting doctrine in the previous case.

That this is so is made still more clear by the opinion of the court delivered by himself in the case of *Florida v. Georgia*[12], in which he says that "it is settled, by repeated decisions, that a question of boundary between States, is within the jurisdiction conferred by the Constitution on this court." A subsequent expression in that opinion shows that he understood this as including the political question, for he says "that a

10 12 Peters, 724.

11 7 Howard, 660.

12 17 Id. 478.

question of boundary between States is necessarily a political question to be settled by compact made by the political departments of the government. . . . But under our form of government a boundary between two States may become a judicial question to be decided by this court."

In the subsequent case of *Alabama v. Georgia*[13], all the judges concurred, and no question of the jurisdiction was raised.

We consider, therefore, the established doctrine of this court to be, that it has jurisdiction of questions of boundary between two States of this Union, and that this jurisdiction is not defeated, because in deciding that question it becomes necessary to examine into and construe compacts or agreements between those States, or because the decree which the court may render, affects the territorial limits of the political jurisdiction and sovereignty of the States which are parties to the proceeding.

In the further consideration of the question raised by the demurrer we shall proceed upon the ground, which we shall not stop to defend, that the right of West Virginia to jurisdiction over the counties in question, can only be maintained by a valid agreement between the two States on that subject, and that to the validity of such an agreement, the consent of Congress is essential. And we do not deem it necessary in this discussion to inquire whether such an agreement may possess a certain binding force between the States that are parties to it, for any purpose, before such consent is obtained.

As there seems to be no question, then, that the State of West Virginia, from the time she first proposed, in the constitution under which she became a State, to receive these counties, has ever since adhered to, and continued her assent to that proposition, three questions remain to be considered.

1. Did the State of Virginia ever give a consent to this proposition which became obligatory on her?

2. Did the Congress give such consent as rendered the agreement valid?

3. If both these are answered affirmatively, it may be necessary to inquire whether the circumstances alleged in this bill, authorized Virginia to withdraw her consent, and justify us in setting aside the contract, and restoring the two counties to that State.

To determine these questions it will be necessary to examine into the history of the creation of the State of West Virginia, so far as this is to be learned from legislation, of which we can take judicial notice.

The first step in this matter was taken by the organic convention of the State of Virginia, which in 1861 reorganized that State, and formed for it what was known as the Pierpont government-an organization which was recognized by the President and by Congress as the State of Virginia, and which passed the four statutes set forth as exhibits in the bill of complainant. This convention passed an ordinance, August 30,

13 23 Howard, 505.

1861, calling a convention of delegates from certain designated counties of the State of Virginia to form a constitution for a new State to be called Kanawha.

The third section of that ordinance provides that the convention when assembled may change the boundaries of the new State as described in the first section, so as to include the "counties of Greenbrier and Pocahontas, or either of them, and also the counties of Hampshire, Hardy, Morgan, Berkeley, and Jefferson, or either of them," if the said counties, or either of them, shall declare their wish, by a majority of votes given, and shall elect delegates to the said convention.

It is thus seen that in the very first step to organize the new State, the old State of Virginia recognized the peculiar condition of the two counties now in question, and provided that either of them should become part of the new State upon the majority of the votes polled being found to be in favor of that proposition.

The convention authorized by this ordinance assembled in Wheeling, November 26, 1861. It does not appear that either Berkeley or Jefferson was represented, but it framed a constitution which, after naming the counties composing the new State in the first section of the first article, provided, by the second section, that if a majority of the votes cast at an election to be held for that purpose in the district composed of the counties of Berkeley, Jefferson, and Frederick, should be in favor of adopting the constitution, they should form a part of the State of West Virginia. That constitution also provided for representation of these counties in the Senate and House of Delegates if they elected to become a part of the new State, and that they should in that event constitute the eleventh judicial district. A distinct section also declares, in general terms, that additional territory may be admitted into and become part of the State with the consent of the legislature.

The schedule of this constitution arranged for its submission to a vote of the people on the first Thursday in April, 1862.

This vote was taken and the constitution ratified by the people; but it does not appear that either of the three counties of Jefferson, Berkeley, and Frederick, took any vote at that time.

Next in order of this legislative history is the act of the Virginia legislature of May 13, 1862, passed shortly after the vote above mentioned had been taken.[14]   This act gives the consent of the State of Virginia to the formation of the State of West Virginia out of certain counties named under the provisions set forth in its constitution, and by its second section it is declared that the consent of the legislature of Virginia is also given that the counties of Berkeley, Jefferson, and Frederick, shall be included in said State "whenever the voters of said counties shall ratify and assent to said constitution, at an election held for that purpose, at such time and under such regulations as the commissioners named in the said schedule may prescribe."

---

14 Supra, p. 42.

This act was directed to be sent to the senators and representatives of Virginia in Congress, with instructions to obtain the consent of Congress to the admission of the State of West Virginia into the Union.

Accordingly on the 31st of December, 1862, Congress acted on these matters, and reciting the proceedings of the Convention of West Virginia, and that both that convention and the legislature of the State of Virginia had requested that the new State should be admitted into the Union, it passed an act for the admission of said State, with certain provisions not material to our purpose.

Let us pause a moment and consider what is the fair and reasonable inference to be drawn from the actions of the State of Virginia, the Convention of West Virginia, and the Congress of the United States in regard to these counties.

The State of Virginia, in the ordinance which originated the formation of the new State, recognized something peculiar in the condition of these two counties, and some others. It gave them the option of sending delegates to the constitutional convention, and gave that convention the option to receive them. For some reason not developed in the legislative history of the matter these counties took no action on the subject. The convention, willing to accept them, and hoping they might still express their wish to come in, made provision in the new constitution that they might do so, and for their place in the legislative bodies, and in the judicial system, and inserted a general proposition for accession of territory to the new State. The State of Virginia, in expressing her satisfaction with the new State and its constitution, and her consent to its formation, by a special section, refers again to the counties of Berkeley, Jefferson, and Frederick, and enacts that whenever they shall, by a majority vote, assent to the constitution of the new State, they may become part thereof; and the legislature sends this statute to Congress with a request that it will admit the new State into the Union. Now, we have here, on two different occasions, the emphatic legislative proposition of Virginia that these counties might become part of West Virginia; and we have the constitution of West Virginia agreeing to accept them and providing for their place in the new- born State. There was one condition, however, imposed by Virginia to her parting with them, and one condition made by West Virginia to her receiving them, and that was the same, namely, the assent of the majority of the votes of the counties to the transfer.

It seems to us that here was an agreement between the old State and the new that these counties should become part of the latter, subject to that condition alone. Up to this time no vote had been taken in these counties; probably none could be taken under any but a hostile government. At all events, the bill alleges that none was taken on the proposition of May, 1862, of the Virginia legislature. If an agreement means the mutual consent of the parties to a given proposition, this was an agreement between these States for the transfer of these counties on the condition named. The condition was one which could be ascertained or carried out at any time; and this was clearly the idea of Virginia when she declared that whenever the voters of said counties should ratify and consent to the constitution they should become part of the State; and her subsequent legislation making special provision for taking the vote on this subject, as shown by the acts of January 31st and February 4th, 1863, is in perfect accord with this idea, and shows her good faith in carrying into effect the agreement.

2. But did Congress consent to this agreement?

Unless it can be shown that the consent of Congress, under that clause of the Constitution which forbids agreements between States without it, can only be given in the form of an express and formal statement of every proposition of the agreement, and of its consent thereto, we must hold that the consent of that body was given to this agreement. The attention of Congress was called to the subject by the very short statute of the State of Virginia requesting the admission of the new State into the Union, consisting of but three sections[15], one of which was entirely devoted to giving consent that these two counties and the county of Frederick might accompany the others, if they desired to do so. The constitution of the new State was literally cumbered with the various provisions for receiving these counties if they chose to come, and in two or three forms express consent is there given to this addition to the State. The subject of the relation of these counties to the others, as set forth in the ordinance for calling the convention, in the constitution framed by that convention, and in the act of the Virginia legislature, must have received the attentive consideration of Congress. To hold otherwise is to suppose that the act for the admission of the new State passed without any due or serious consideration. But the substance of this act clearly repels any such inference; for it is seen that the constitution of the new State was, in one particular at least, unacceptable to Congress, and the act only admits the State into the Union when that feature shall be changed by the popular vote. If any other part of the constitution had failed to meet the approbation of Congress, especially so important a part as the proposition for a future change of boundary between the new and the old State, it is reasonable to suppose that its dissent would have been expressed in some shape, especially as the refusal to permit those counties to attach themselves to the new State would not have endangered its formation and admission without them.

It is, therefore, an inference clear and satisfactory that Congress by that statute, intended to consent to the admission of the State with the contingent boundaries provided for in its constitution and in the statute of Virginia, which prayed for its admission on those terms, and that in so doing it necessarily consented to the agreement of those States on that subject. There was then a valid agreement between the two States consented to by Congress, which agreement made the accession of these counties dependent on the result of a popular vote in favor of that proposition.

3. But the Commonwealth of Virginia insists that no such vote was ever given; and we must inquire whether the facts alleged in the bill are such as to require an issue to be made on that question by the answer of the defendant.

---

15 Supra, p. 42.

The bill alleges the failure of the counties to take any action under the act of May, 1862, and that on the 31st of January and the 4th of February thereafter the two other acts we have mentioned were passed to enable such vote to be taken. These statutes provide very minutely for the taking of this vote under the authority of the State of Virginia; and, among other things, it is enacted that the governor shall ascertain the result, and, if he shall be of opinion that said vote has been opened and held and the result ascertained and certified pursuant to law, he shall certify that result under the seal of the State to the governor of West Virginia; and if a majority of the votes given at the polls were in favor of the proposition, then the counties became part of said State. He was also authorized to postpone the time of voting if he should be of opinion that a fair vote could not be taken on the day mentioned in these acts.

Though this language is taken mainly from the statute which refers to Berkeley County, we consider the legal effect of the other statute to be the same.

These statutes were in no way essential to evidence the consent of Virginia to the original agreement, but were intended by her legislature to provide the means of ascertaining the wishes of the voters of these counties, that being the condition of the agreement on which the transfer of the counties depended.

The State thus showed her good faith to that agreement, and undertook in her own way and by her own officers to ascertain the fact in question. The legislature might have required the vote to have been reported to it, and assumed the duty of ascertaining and making known the result to West Virginia; but it delegated that power to the governor. It invested him with full discretion as to the time when the vote should be taken, and made his opinion and his decision conclusive as to the result. The vote was taken under these statutes, and certified to the governor. He was of opinion that the result was in favor of the transfer. He certified this fact under the seal of the State to the State of West Virginia, and the legislature of that State immediately assumed jurisdiction over the two counties, provided for their admission, and they have been a part of that State ever since.

Do the allegations of the bill authorize us to go behind all this and inquire as to what took place at this voting? To inquire how many votes were actually cast? How many of the men who had once been voters in these counties were then in the rebel army? Or had been there and were thus disfranchised? For all these and many more embarrassing questions must arise if the defendant is required to take issue on the allegations of the bill on this subject.

These allegations are indefinite and vague in this regard. It is charged that no fair vote was taken; but no act of unfairness is alleged. That no opportunity was afforded for a fair vote. That the governor was misled and deceived by the fraud of those who made him believe so. This is the substance of what is alleged. No one is charged specifically with the fraud. No particular act of fraud is stated. The governor is impliedly said to have acted in good faith. No charge of any kind of moral or legal wrong is made against the defendant, the State of West Virginia.

But, waiving these defects in the bill, we are of opinion that the action of the governor is conclusive of the vote as between the States of Virginia and West Virginia. He was in legal effect the State of Virginia in this matter. In addition to his position as executive head of the State, the legislature delegated to him all its own power in the premises. It vested him with large contro as to the time of taking the vote, and it made his opinion of the result the condition of final action. It rested of its own accord the whole question on his judgment and in his hands. In a matter where that action was to be the foundation on which another sovereign State was to act-a matter which involved the delicate question of permanent boundary between the States and jurisdiction over a large population-a matter in which she took into her own hands the ascertainment of the fact on which these important propositions were by contract made to depend, she must be bound by what she had done. She can have no right, years after all this has been settled, to come into a court of chancery to charge that her own conduct has been a wrong and a fraud; that her own subordinate agents have misled her governor, and that her solemn act transferring these counties shall be set aside, against the will of the State of West Virginia, and without consulting the wishes of the people of those counties.

This view of the subject renders it unnecessary to inquire into the effect of the act of 1865 withdrawing the consent of the State of Virginia, or the act of Congress of 1866 giving consent, after the attempt of that State to withdraw hers.

The demurrer to the bill is therefore sustained, and the

BILL MUST BE DISMISSED.

Mr. Justice DAVIS, with whom concurred CLIFFORD and FIELD, JJ., dissenting.

Being unable to agree with the majority of the court in its judgment in this case, I will briefly state the grounds of my dissent.

There is no difference of opinion between us in relation to the construction of the provision of the Constitution which affects the question at issue. We all agree that until the consent of Congress is given, there can be no valid compact or agreement between States. And that, although the point of time when Congress may give its consent is not material, yet, when it is given, there must be a reciprocal and concurrent consent of the three parties to the contract. Without this, it is not a completed compact. If, therefore, Virginia withdrew its assent before the consent of Congress was given, there was no compact within the meaning of the Constitution.

To my mind nothing is clearer, than that Congress never did undertake to give its consent to the transfer of Berkeley and Jefferson counties to the State of West Virginia until March 2, 1866. If so, the consent came too late, because the legislature of Virginia had, on the fifth day of December, 1865, withdrawn its assent to the proposed cession of these two counties. This withdrawal was in ample time, as it was before the proposal of the State had become operative as a concluded compact, and the bill (in my judgment) shows that Virginia had sufficient reasons for recalling its proposition to part with the territory embraced within these counties.

But, it is maintained in the opinion of the court that Congress did give its consent to the transfer of these counties by Virginia to West Virginia, when it admitted West Virginia into the Union. The argument of the opinion is, that Congress, by admitting the new State, gave its assent to that provision of the new constitution which looked to the acquisition of these counties, and that if the people of these counties have since voted to become part of the State of West Virginia, this action is within the consent of Congress. I most respectfully submit that the facts of the case (about which there is no dispute), do not justify the argument which is attempted to be drawn from them.

The second section of the first article of the constitution of West Virginia was merely a proposal addressed to the people of two distinct districts, on which they were invited to act. The people of one district (Pendleton, Hardy, Hampshire, and Morgan) accepted the proposal. The people of the other district (Jefferson, Berkeley, and Frederick) rejected it.

In this state of things, the first district became a part of the new State, so far as its constitution could make it so, and the legislature of Virginia included it in its assent, and Congress included it in its admission to the Union. But neither the constitution of West Virginia, nor the assent of the legislature of Virginia, nor the consent of Congress, had any application whatever to the second district. For though the second section of the first article of the new constitution had proposed to include it, the proposal was accompanied with conditions which were not complied with; and when that constitution was presented to Congress for approval, the proposal had already been rejected, and had no significance or effect whatever.

The Supreme Court's 1911 Decision in
Virginia vs. West Virginia

F OLLOWING is the opinion of the United States Supreme Court in the 1911 case of *Commonwealth of Virginia vs. State of West Virginia*, presented in its entirety, and our brief commentary on it.

Initially, we note that Oliver Wendell Holmes, Jr. penned the decision on behalf of a unanimous Court. Holmes was a badly wounded combat veteran of the Civil War who served in the Fourth Battalion, Massachusetts Militia, then received a commission as first lieutenant in the Twentieth Regiment of Massachusetts Volunteer Infantry.[1] He ultimately rose to the rank of lieutenant colonel, and received a brevet promotion to colonel in recognition of his services during the war.[2] Justice Holmes served as an Associate Justice of the Supreme Court of the United States from 1902 to 1932, and as Acting Chief Justice of the United States from January–February 1930.

The 1911 case laid out below was filed by the Commonwealth of Virginia against West Virginia, and deals primarily with "amount due to the former as the equitable proportion of the public debt of the original state of Virginia, which was assumed by

---

1 The 20th Massachusetts is often called the Harvard Regiment, because virtually all of its officers were recent graduates of Harvard College. For a regimental history of the 20th Massachusetts, see Richard F. Miller, *Harvard's Civil War: The History of the Twentieth Massachusetts Volunteer Infantry* (Boston: University Press of New England, 2005).

2 A brevet was a warrant giving a commissioned officer a higher rank title as a reward for gallantry or meritorious conduct but without conferring the authority, precedence, or pay of real rank. Those receiving brevets were entitled to be called by that honorary rank.

the state of West Virginia at the time of its creation as a state."[3] This unanswered question had lingered unresolved since the creation of West Virginia in 1863, and was not addressed at all in the 1871 decision.

The Court began its opinion by reviewing the bill filed by Virginia, which "alleges the existence of a debt contracted between 1820 and 1861 in connection with internal improvements intended to develop the whole state, . . . [and] then sets forth the proceedings for the formation of a separate state, and the material provisions of the ordinance adopted for that purpose at Wheeling on August 20, 1861, the passage of an act of Congress for the admission of the new state under a Constitution that had been adopted, and the admission of West Virginia into the Union."[4]

The Court then examined the portion of the West Virginia Constitution that addressed the pre-war outstanding debt of Virginia.[5] "Through this constitutional provision, West Virginia attempted to unilaterally determine the amount of public debt for which it was responsible."[6] Without analysis, the Court stated that the unilateral declaration constituted a binding agreement between Virginia ("the old state") and West Virginia ("the new state"), as the Court had "held in 1870 [in] . . . *Virginia v. West Virginia*, 11 Wall. 39, 20 L. ed. 67."[7] The Court noted that "the cause was referred to a master by a decree made on May 4, 1908 (209 U. S. 514, 534, 52 L. ed. 914, 915, 28 Sup. Ct. Rep. 614), which provided for the ascertainment of the facts made the basis of apportionment by the original Wheeling ordinance ."[8]

The Supreme Court never ruled on whether West Virginia had the right to resolve the dispute unilaterally, and instead chose to decide what would be an "equitable" division.[9] Generally, "the Court adopted a ratio determined by the Master's estimated valuation of the real and personal property of the two States on the date of separation, June 20, 1863."[10]

---

3   *Com. of Virginia v. W. Virginia*, 220 U.S. 1, synopsis (1911).

4   Ibid., 23.

5   Ibid., 25-26.

6   Carsten Thomas Ebenroth & Matthew James Kemner, "The Enduring Political Nature of Questions of State Succession and Secession and the Quest for Objective Standards," *Univ. Pa. Journal of Intl. Econ. Law* (1996), 787.

7   *Com. of Virginia v. W. Virginia*, 220 U.S. 1, 26 (1911).

8   Ibid., 27.

9   Ibid., 34.

10 William C. Coleman, "The State As Defendant Under the Federal Constitution; the Virginia-West Virginia Debt Controversy." *Harvard Law Review* 31 (1919), 238-239.

This case reflects the "exception to the general rule that the U.S. Judiciary is not involved in the resolution of the public debt apportionment question."[11] The Court reasoned that "[b]ecause of the 'quasi-international' flavor of the divisions of public debt following the American Civil War, U.S. courts were able to rule on the question of how to divide public debt."[12]

Relevant to our discussion in this book, the case is an after-the-fact confirmation of the constitutionality of the establishment of West Virginia as a state, and seems to put that question to rest for good. While the 1870 decision, discussed at length in this book, was understated in its confirmation of the constitutionality of the establishment of West Virginia as a state, this case settles the issue definitively, explicitly accepting its constitutionality.

United States Supreme Court

COMMONWEALTH OF VIRGINIA v. STATE OF WEST VIRGINIA.

No. 3, Original.

Argued January 20, 23, 24, 25, and 26, 1911. Decided March 6, 1911.

Synopsis

ORIGINAL BILL in equity, filed by the commonwealth of Virginia against the state of West Virginia, which seeks an adjudication of the amount due to the former as the equitable proportion of the public debt of the original state of Virginia, which was assumed by the state of West Virginia at the time of its creation as a state. Ratio determined according to valuation of the real and personal property of the two states on the date of their separation, excluding slaves.

---

11 Ebenroth & Kemner, *The Enduring Political Nature of Questions of State Succession*, 785.

12 Ibid., 785-86 (citing *Com. of Virginia v. W. Virginia*, 220 U.S. 1, 27 (1911)). Justice Holmes "appears to have been the first to coin" the term "quasi-international" but in reference to the Court's role in resolving disputes between States he stated:The case is to be considered in the untechnical spirit proper for dealing with a quasi-international controversy, remembering that there is no municipal code governing the matter, and that this court may be called on to adjust differences that cannot be dealt with by Congress or disposed of by the legislature of either State alone.Thomas H. Lee, "The Supreme Court of the United States As Quasi-International Tribunal: Reclaiming the Court's Original and Exclusive Jurisdiction over Treaty-Based Suits by Foreign States Against States." *Columbia Law Review* 104 (2004), 1885 (quoting *Virginia v. West Virginia*, 220 U.S. 1, 27 (1911)).

The facts are stated in the opinion.

Opinion

This is a bill brought by the commonwealth of Virginia to have the state of West Virginia's proportion of the public debt of Virginia, as it stood before 1861, ascertained and satisfied. The bill was set forth when the case was before this court on demurrer. 206 U. S. 290, 51 L. ed. 1068, 27 Sup. Ct. Rep. 732. Nothing turns on the form or contents of it. The object has been stated. The bill alleges the existence of a debt contracted between 1820 and 1861 in connection with internal improvements intended to develop the whole state, but with especial view to West Virginia, and carried through by the votes of the representatives of the West Virginia counties. It then sets forth the proceedings for the formation of a separate state, and the material provisions of the ordinance adopted for that purpose at Wheeling on August 20, 1861, the passage of an act of Congress for the admission of the new state under a Constitution that had been adopted, and the admission of West Virginia into the Union, all of which we shall show more fully a little further on. Then follows an averment of the transfer in 1863 to West Virginia of the property within her boundaries belonging to West Virginia, to be accounted for in the settlement thereafter to be made with the last-named state. As West Virginia gets the benefit of this property without an accounting, on the principles of this decision, it needs not to be mentioned in more detail. A further appropriation to West Virginia is alleged of $150,000, together with unappropriated balances, subject to accounting for the surplus on hand received from counties outside of the new state. Then follows an argumentative averment of a contract in the Constitution of West Virginia to assume an equitable proportion of the above-mentioned public debt, as hereafter will be explained. Attempts between 1865 and 1872 to ascertain the two states' proportion of the debt and their failure are averred, and the subsequent legislation and action of Virginia in arranging with the bondholders, that will be explained hereafter so far as needs. Substantially all the bonds outstanding in 1861 have been taken up. It is stated that both in area of territory and in population West Virginia, was equal to about one third of Virginia, that being the proportion that Virginia asserts to be the proper one for the division of the debt, and this claim is based upon the division of the state, upon the abovementioned Wheeling ordinance and the Constitution of the new state, upon the recognition of the liability by statute and resolution, and upon the receipt of property, as has been stated above. After stating further efforts to bring about an adjustment, and their failure, the bill prays for an accounting to ascertain the balance due to Virginia in her own right and as trustee for bondholders, and an adjudication in accord with this result.

The answer admits a debt of about $33,000,000, but avers that the main object of the internal improvements in connection with which it was contracted was to afford outlets to the Ohio river on the west and to the seaboard on the east for the products of the eastern part of the state, and to develop the resources of that part, not those of what is now West Virginia. In aid of this conclusion it goes into some elaboration of details. It admits the proceedings for the separation of the state, and refers to an act of May, 1862, consenting to the same, to which we also shall refer. It denies that it received property of more than a little value from Virginia, or that West Virginia received more than belonged to her in the way of surplus revenue on hand when she was admitted to the Union, and denies that any liability for these items was assumed by her Constitution. It sets forth in detail the proceedings looking to a settlement, but, as they have no bearing upon our decision, we do not dwell upon them. It admits the transactions of Virginia with the bondholders, and sets up that they discharged the commonwealth from one third of its debt, and that what may have been done as to two-thirds does not concern the defendant, since Virginia admits that her share was not less than that. If the bonds outstanding in 1861 have been taken up, it is only by the issue of new bonds for two thirds and certificates to be paid by West Virginia alone for the other third. Liability for any payments by Virginia is denied, and accountability, if any, is averred to be only on the principle of § 9 of the Wheeling ordinance, to be stated. It is set up further that under the Constitution of West Virginia her equitable proportion can be established by her legislature alone; that the liquidation can be only in the way provided by that instrument; and hence that this suit cannot be maintained. The settlement by Virginia with her creditors also is pleaded as a bar, and that she brings this suit solely as trustee for them.

The grounds of the claim are matters of public history. After the Virginia ordinance of secession, citizens of the state who dissented from that ordinance organized a government that was recognized as the state of Virginia by the government of the United States. Forthwith a convention of the restored state, as it was called, held at Wheeling, proceeded to carry out a long-entertained wish of many West Virginians by adopting an ordinance for the formation of a new state out of the western portion of the old commonwealth. A part of § 9 of the ordinance was as follows: 'The new state shall take upon itself a just proportion of the public debt of the commonwealth of Virginia prior to the 1st day of January, 1861, to be ascertained by charging to it all state expenditures within the limits thereof, and a just proportion of the ordinary expenses of the state government since any part of said debt was contracted; and deducting therefrom the moneys paid into the treasury of the commonwealth from the counties included within the said new state during the same period.' Having previously provided for a popular vote, a constitutional convention, etc., the ordinance in § 10 ordained that when the general assembly should give its consent to the formation of such new state, it should forward to the Congress of the United States such consent, together with an official copy of such Constitution, with the request that the new state might be admitted into the union of states.

A Constitution was framed for the new state by a constitutional convention, as provided in the ordinance, on November 26, 1861, and was adopted. By article 8, § 8, 'An equitable proportion of the public debt of the commonwealth of Virginia, prior to the first day of January in the year one thousand eight hundred and sixty-one shall be assumed by this state; and the legislature shall ascertain the same as soon as may be practicable, and provide for the liquidation thereof by a sinking fund sufficient to pay the accruing interest, and redeem the principal within thirty-four years.' An act of the legislature of the restored state of Virginia, passed May 13, 1862, gave the consent of that legislature to the erection of the new state 'under the provisions set forth in the Constitution for the said state of West Virginia.' Finally Congress gave its sanction by an act of December 31, 1862, chap. 6, 12 Stat. at L. 633, which recited the framing and adoption of the West Virginia Constitution and the consent given by the legislature of Virginia through the last-mentioned act, as well as the request of the West Virginia convention and of the Virginia legislature, as the grounds for its consent. There was a provision for the adoption of an emancipation clause before the act of Congress should take effect, and for a proclamation by the President, stating the fact, when the desired amendment was made. Accordingly, after the amendment and a proclamation by President Lincoln, West Virginia became a state on June 20, 1863.

It was held in 1870 that the foregoing constituted an agreement between the old state and the new (*Virginia v. West Virginia*, 11 Wall. 39, 20 L. ed. 67), and so much may be taken practically to have been decided again upon the demurrer in this case, although the demurrer was overruled without prejudice to any question. Indeed, so much is almost if not quite admitted in the answer. After the answer had been filed the cause was referred to a master by a decree made on May 4, 1908 (209 U. S. 514, 534, 52 L. ed. 914, 915, 28 Sup. Ct. Rep. 614), which provided for the ascertainment of the facts made the basis of apportionment by the original Wheeling ordinance, and also of other facts that would furnish an alternative method if that prescribed in the Wheeling ordinance should not be followed; this again without prejudice to any question in the cause. The master has reported, the case has been heard upon the merits, and now is submitted to the decision of the court.

The case is to be considered in the untechnical spirit proper for dealing with a quasi-international controversy, remembering that there is no municipal code governing the matter, and that this court may be called on to adjust differences that cannot be dealt with by Congress or disposed of by the legislature of either state alone. *Missouri v. Illinois*, 200 U. S. 496, 519, 520, 50 L. ed. 572, 573, 579, 26 Sup. Ct. Rep. 268; *Kansas v. Colorado*, 206 U. S. 46, 82–84, 51 L. ed. 956, 968, 969, 27 Sup. Ct. Rep. 655. Therefore we shall spend no time on objections as to multifariousness, laches, and the like, except so far as they affect the merits, with which we proceed to deal. See *Rhode Island v. Massachusetts*, 14 Pet. 210, 257, 10 L. ed. 423, 445; *United States v. Beebe*, 127 U. S. 338, 32 L. ed. 121, 8 Sup. Ct. Rep. 1083.

The amount of the debt January 1, 1861, that we have to apportion, no longer is in dispute. The master's finding was accepted by West Virginia, and at the argument we understood Virginia not to press her exception that it should be enlarged by a disputed item. It was $33,897,073.82, the sum being represented mainly by interest bearing bonds. The first thing to be decided is what the final agreement was that was made between the two states. Here again we are not to be bound by technical form. A state is superior to the forms that it may require of its citizens. But there would be no technical difficulty in making a contract by a constitutive ordinance if followed by the creation of the contemplated state. *Wedding v. Meyler*, 192 U. S. 573, 583, 48 L. ed. 570, 574, 66 L.R.A. 833, 24 Sup. Ct. Rep. 322. And, on the other hand, there is equally little difficulty in making a contract by the Constitution of the new state if it be apparent that the instrument is not addressed solely to those who are to be subject to its provisions, but is intended to be understood by the parent state any by Congress as embodying a just term which conditions the parent's consent. There can be no question that such was the case with West Virginia. As has been shown, the consent of the legislature of the restored state was a consent to the admission of West Virginia under the provisions set forth in the Constitution for the would-be state, and Congress gave its sanction only on the footing of the same Constitution and the consent of Virginia in the last-mentioned act. These three documents would establish a contract, without more. We may add, with reference to an argument to which we attach little weight, that they establish a contract of West Virginia with Virginia. There is no reference to the form of the debt or to its holders, and it is obvious that Virginia had an interest that it was most important that she should be able to protect. Therefore West Virginia must be taken to have promised to Virginia to pay her share, whoever might be the persons to whom ultimately the payment was to be made.

We are of opinion that the contract established as we have said is not modified or affected in any practical way by the preliminary suggestions of the Wheeling ordinance. Neither the ordinance nor the special mode of ascertaining a just proportion of the debt that it puts forward is mentioned in the Constitution of West Virginia, or in the act of Virginia giving her consent, or in the act of Congress by which West Virginia became a state. The ordinance required that a copy of the new Constitution should be laid before Congress, but said nothing about the ordinance itself. It is enough to refer to the circumstances in which the separation took place to show that Virginia is entitled to the benefit of any doubt so far as the construction of the contract is concerned. See opinion of Attorney General Bates to President Lincoln, 10 Ops. Atty. Gen. 426. The mode of the Wheeling ordinance would not throw on West Virginia a proportion of the debt that would be just, as the ordinance requires, or equitable, according to the promise of the Constitution, unless upon the assumption that interest on the public debt should be considered as part of the ordinary expenses referred to in its terms. That, we believe, would put upon West Virginia a larger obligation than the mode that we adopt, but we are of opinion that her share should be ascertained in a different way. All the modes, however, consistent with the plain contract of West Virginia, whether under the Wheeling ordinance or the Constitution of that state, come out with surprisingly similar results.

It was argued, to be sure, that the debt of Virginia was incurred for local improvements, and that in such a case, even apart from the ordinance, it should be divided according to the territory in which the money was expended. We see no sufficient reason for the application of such a principle to this case. In form the aid was an investment. It generally took the shape of a subscription for stock in a corporation. To make the investment a safe one, the precaution was taken to require as a condition precedent that two or three fifths of the stock should have been subscribed for by solvent persons, fully able to pay, and that one fourth of the subscriptions should have been paid up into the hands of the treasurer. From this point of view the venture was on behalf of the whole state. The parties interested in the investment were the same, wherever the sphere of corporate action might be. The whole state would have got the gain, and the whole state must bear the loss, as it does not appear that there are any stocks of value on hand. If we should attempt to look farther, many of the corporations concerned were engaged in improvements that had West Virginia for their objective point, and we should be lost in futile detail if we should try to unravel in each instance the ultimate scope of the scheme. It would be unjust, however, to stop with the place where the first steps were taken, and not to consider the purpose with which the enterprise was begun. All the expenditures had the ultimate good of the whole state in view. Therefore we adhere to our conclusion that West Virginia's share of the debt must be ascertained in a different way. In coming to it we do but apply against West Virginia the argument pressed on her behalf to exclude her liability under the Wheeling ordinance in like cases. By the ordinance, West Virginia was to be charged with all state expenditures within the limits thereof. But she vigorously protested against being charged with any sum expended in the form of a purchase of stocks.

But again, it was argued that if this contract should be found to be what we have said, then the determination of a just proportion was left by the Constitution to the legislature of West Virginia, and that, irrespectively of the words of the instrument, it was only by legislation that a just proportion could be fixed. These arguments do not impress us. The provision in the Constitution of the state of West Virginia that the legislature shall ascertain the proportion as soon as may be practicable was not intended to undo the contract in the preceding words by making the representative and mouthpiece of one of the parties the sole tribunal for its enforcement. It was simply an exhortation and command from supreme to subordinate authority to perform the promise as soon as might be, and an indication of the way. Apart from the language used, what is just and equitable is a judicial question similar to many that arise in private litigation, and in nowise beyond the competence of a tribunal to decide.

The ground now is clear, so far as the original contract between the two states is concerned. The effect of that is that West Virginia must bear her just and equitable proportion of the public debt, as it was intimated in *Hartman v. Greenhow*, 102 U. S. 672, 26 L. ed. 271, so long ago as 1880, that she should. It remains for us to consider such subsequent acts as may have affected the original liability, or as may bear on the determination of the amount to be paid. On March 30, 1871, Virginia, assuming that the equitable share of West Virginia was about one third, passed an act authorizing an exchange of the outstanding bonds, etc., and providing for the funding of two thirds of the debt, with interest accrued to July 1, 1871, by the issue of new bonds, bearing the same rate of interest as the old,—6 per cent. There were to be issued at the same time, for the other one third, certificates of same date, setting forth the amount of the old bond that was not funded, that payment thereof with interest at the rate prescribed in the old bond would be provided for in accordance with such settlement as should be had between Virginia and West Virginia in regard to the public debt, and that Virginia held the old bonds in trust for the holder or his assignees. There were further details that need not be mentioned. The coupons of the new bonds were receivable for all taxes and demands due to the state. *Hartman v. Greenhow, supra*; *McGahey v. Virginia*, 135 U. S. 662, 34 L. ed. 304, 10 Sup. Ct. Rep. 972. The certificates issued to the public under this statute, and outstanding, amount to $12,703,451.79.

The burden under the statute of 1871 still being greater than Virginia felt able to bear, a new refunding act was passed on March 28, 1879, reducing the interest, and providing that Virginia would negotiate or aid in negotiating with West Virginia for the settlement of the claims of certificate holders, and that the acceptance of certificates 'for West Virginia's one third' under this act should be an absolute release of Virginia from all liability on account of the same. Few of these certificates were accepted. On February 14, 1882, another attempt was made, but without sufficient success to make it necessary to set forth the contents of the statute. The certificates for balances not represented by bonds, 'constituting West Virginia's share of the old debt,' stated that the balance was 'to be accounted for by the state of West Virginia without recourse upon this commonwealth.'

On February 20, 1892, a statute was passed which led to a settlement, described in the bill as final and satisfactory. This provided for the issue of bonds for $19,000,000 in exchange for $28,000,000 outstanding, not funded, the new bonds bearing interest at 2 per cent for the first ten years and 3 per cent for ninety years; and certificates in form similar to that just stated in the act of 1882. On March 6, 1894, a joint resolution of the senate and house of delegates was passed, reciting the passage of the four above-mentioned statutes, the provisions for certificates, and the satisfactory adjustment of the liabilities assumed by Virginia on account of two thirds of the debt, and appointing a committee to negotiate with West Virginia when satisfied that a majority of the certificate holders desired it, and would accept the amount to be paid by West Virginia in full settlement of the one third that Virginia had not assumed. The state was to be subjected to no expense. Finally an act of March 6, 1900, authorized the commission to receive and take on deposit the certificates, upon a contract that the certificate holders would accept the amount realized from West Virginia in full settlement of all their claims under the same. It also authorized a suit if certain proportions of the certificates should be so deposited, as since then they have been,—the state, as before, to be subjected to no expense.

On January 9, 1906, the commission reported that, apart from certificates held by the state, and not entering into this account, there were outstanding of the certificates of 1871 in the hands of the public, $12,703,451.79, as we have said, of which the commission held $10,851,294.09, and of other certificates there were in the hands of the public $2,778,239.80, of which the commission held $2,322,141.32.

On the foregoing facts a technical argument is pressed that Virginia has discharged herself of all liability as to one third of the debt; that therefore she is without interest in this suit, and cannot maintain it on her own behalf; that she cannot maintain it as trustee for the certificate holders (*New Hampshire v. Louisiana*, 108 U. S. 76, 27 L. ed. 656, 2 Sup. Ct. Rep. 176); and that the bill is multifarious in attempting to unite claims made by the plaintiff as such trustee with some others set up under the Wheeling ordinance, etc., which, in the view we take, it has not been necessary to mention or discuss. We shall assume it to be true for the purposes of our decision, although it may be open to debate (*Greenhow v. Vashon*, 81 Va. 336, 342, 343), that the certificate holders who have turned in their certificates, being much the greater number, as has been seen, by doing so, if not before, surrendered all claims under the original bonds or otherwise against Virginia to the extent of one third of the debt. But even on that concession the argument seems to us unsound.

The liability of West Virginia is a deep seated equity, not discharged by changes in the form of the debt, nor split up by the unilateral attempt of Virginia to apportion specific parts to the two states. If one third of the debt were discharged in fact, to all intents, we perceive no reason, in what has happened, why West Virginia should not contribute her proportion of the remaining two thirds. But we are of opinion that no part of the debt is extinguished, and further, that nothing has happened to bring the rule of *New Hampshire v. Louisiana* into play. For even if Virginia is not liable, she has the contract of West Virginia to bear an equitable share of the whole debt,—a contract in the performance of which the honor and credit of Virginia is concerned, and which she does not lose her right to insist upon by her creditors accepting from necessity the performance of her estimated duty as confining their claims for the residue to the party equitably bound. Her creditors never could have sued her if the supposed discharge had not been granted, and the discharge does not diminish her interest and right to have the whole debt paid by the help of the defendant. The suit is in Virginia's own interest, none the less that she is to turn over the proceeds. See *United States v. Beebe*, 127 U. S. 338, 342, 32 L. ed. 121, 123, 8 Sup. Ct. Rep. 1083; *United States v. Nashville, C. & St. L. R. Co.*, 118 U. S. 120, 125, 126, 30 L. ed. 81, 83, 6 Sup. Ct. Rep. 1006. Moreover, even in private litigation it has been held that a trustee may recover to the extent of the interest of his cestui que trust. *Lloyd's v. Harper, L. R.*, 16 Ch. Div. 290, 315, 1 Eng. Rul. Cas. 686; *Lamb v. Vice*, 6 Mees. & W. 467, 472. We may add that in all its aspects it is a suit on the contract, and it is most proper that the whole matter should be disposed of at once.

It remains true, then, notwithstanding all the transactions between the old commonwealth and her bondholders, that West Virginia must bear her equitable proportion of the whole debt. With a qualification which we shall mention in a moment, we are of opinion that the nearest approach to justice that we can make is to adopt a ratio determined by the master's estimated valuation of the real and personal property of the two states on the date of the separation, June 20, 1863. A ratio determined by population or land area would throw a larger share on West Virginia, but the relative resources of the debtor populations are generally recognized, we think, as affording a proper measure. It seems to us plain that slaves should be excluded from the valuation. The master's figures without them are, for Virginia, $300,887,367.74, and for West Virginia, $92,416,021.65. These figures are criticized by Virginia, but we see no sufficient reason for going behind them, or ground for thinking that we can get nearer to justice in any other way. It seems to us that Virginia cannot complain of the result. They would give the proportion in which the $33,897,073.82 was to be divided, but for a correction which Virginia has made necessary. Virginia, with the consent of her creditors, has cut down her liability to not more than two thirds of the debt, whereas, at the ratio shown by the figures, her share, subject to mathematical correction, is about .7651. If our figures are correct, the difference between Virginia's share, say $25,931,261.47, and the amount that the creditors were content to accept from her, say $22,598,049.21, is $3,333,212.26; subtracting the last sum from the debt leaves $30,563,861.56 as the sum to be apportioned. Taking .235 as representing the proportion of West Virginia, we have $7,182,507.46 as her share of the principal debt.

We have given our decision with respect to the basis of liability and the share of the principal of the debt of Virginia that West Virginia assumed. In any event, before we could put our judgment in the form of a final decree, there would be figures to be agreed upon or to be ascertained by reference to a master. Among other things there still remains the question of interest. Whether any interest is due, and if due, from what time it should be allowed, and at what rate it should be computed, are matters as to which there is a serious controversy in the record, and concerning which there is room for a wide divergence of opinion. There are many elements to be taken into account on the one side and on the other. The circumstances of the asserted default and the conditions surrounding the failure earlier to procure a determination of the principal sum payable, including the question of laches as to either party, would require to be considered. A long time has elapsed. Wherever the responsibility for the delay might ultimately be placed, or however it might be shared, it would be a severe result to capitalize charges for half a century,—such a thing hardly could happen in a private case analogous to this. Statutes of limitation, if nothing else, would be likely to interpose a bar. As this is no ordinary commercial suit, but, as we have said, a quasi international difference, referred to this court in reliance upon the honor and constitutional obligations of the states concerned rather than upon ordinary remedies, we think it best at this stage to go no farther, but to await the effect of a conference between the parties, which, whatever the outcome, must take place. If the cause should be pressed contentiously to the end, it would be referred to a master to go over the figures that we have given provisionally, and to make such calculations as might become necessary. But this case is one that calls for forbearance upon both sides. Great states have a temper superior to that of private litigants, and it is to be hoped that enough has been decided for patriotism, the fraternity of the Union, and mutual consideration to bring it to an end.

Current Events Prove that These Questions Live On

T**HE** question of the dismemberment of the Commonwealth of Virginia remains relevant even in the year 2020. In 1862, Frederick County, Virginia was supposed to vote on the referendum that led to the secession of West Virginia, but it did not get the opportunity to do so. If West Virginia State Senator Charles S. Trump, IV, a Republican from Morgan County, gets his way, that omission will be righted. On January 13, 2020, the West Virginia State Senate passed State Concurrent Resolution 2, which provides:

> Requesting the citizens of Frederick County, Virginia, to consider becoming a part of the State of West Virginia.

Whereas, Frederick County, Virginia, was formed in 1743, and Hampshire County, Virginia, was formed in 1754. Most of what was originally Hampshire County, when it was formed in 1754, was territory that had been part of Frederick County. Berkeley County, Virginia, was formed from Frederick County in 1772; and

Whereas, The counties of Jefferson, Berkeley, Morgan, Hampshire, Mineral, Hardy and Grant counties in the State of West Virginia all contain territory that was once part of Frederick County, Virginia, such that Frederick County, Virginia, may truly be regarded as the mother of all seven of these West Virginia counties; and

Whereas, In addition to the historical connections between Frederick County, Virginia, and the seven counties in West Virginia, which are her children, there have always existed strong familial ties between and among the inhabitants of those counties, as well as ties of commerce, business, religion, education, arts, society, politics, travel, recreation, and connections of every possible kind. There remain, as there have always been, feelings of deep affection for Frederick County and for her inhabitants by and among the citizens of West Virginia, and in particular by and among the citizens of those counties in West Virginia which may be regarded as the children of Frederick County. In 1862, when the government of Virginia, meeting in Wheeling, took up the question of the formation of a new state, Frederick County was among those counties which were regarded as having a natural place within the new state. So strong was the desire to have Frederick County join the new state that the opportunity for her to do that was specifically provided for by an Act of the Legislature; and

Whereas, The Act of the Legislature of Virginia, passed May 13, 1862, giving the consent of the State of Virginia to the formation of the new State of West Virginia, provided as follows:

That the consent of the legislature of Virginia be, and the same is hereby, given that the counties of Berkeley, Jefferson, and Frederick shall be included in and form part of the State of West Virginia, whenever the voters of said counties shall ratify and assent to said constitution, at an election held for the purpose, at such time and under such regulations as the commissioners, named in said schedule, may prescribe; and

Whereas, Although the citizens of the counties of Berkeley and Jefferson thereafter voted to join the new state, the citizens of Frederick County have not yet done so; and

Whereas, By its decision in the case of *State of Virginia v. State of West Virginia*, 78 U.S. 39, 20 L.Ed.67, 11 Wall. 39 (1870), the United States Supreme Court recognized that the opportunity for Frederick County, Virginia, to transfer to and join the new State of West Virginia, was lawfully and permanently reserved unto her by the actions of Virginia and by the Congress of the United States, to be exercised whenever the voters of Frederick County might vote to join the new State of West Virginia, to-wit:

"The State of Virginia, in the ordinance which originated the formation of the new State, recognized something peculiar in the condition of these two counties, and some others. It gave them the option of sending delegates to the constitutional convention and gave that convention the option to receive them. For some reason not developed in the legislative history of the matter these counties took no action on the subject. The convention, willing to accept them, and hoping they might still express their wish to come in, made provision in the new constitution that they might do so, and for their place in the legislative bodies, and in the judicial system, and inserted a general proposition for accession of territory to the new State. The State of Virginia, in expressing her satisfaction with the new State and its constitution, and her consent to its formation, by a special section, refers again to the counties of Berkeley, Jefferson, *and Frederick*, and enacts that whenever they shall, by a majority vote, assent to the constitution of the new State, they may become part thereof; and the legislature sends this statute to Congress with a request that it will admit the new State into the Union. Now, we have here, on two different occasions, the emphatic legislative proposition of Virginia that these counties might become part of West Virginia; and we have the Constitution of West Virginia agreeing to accept them and providing for their place in the new-born State. There was one condition, however, imposed by Virginia to her parting with them, and one condition made by West Virginia to her receiving them, and that was the same, namely, the assent of the majority of the votes of the counties to the transfer. It seems to us that here was an agreement between the old State and the new that these counties should become part of the latter, subject to that condition alone. Up to this time no vote had been taken in these counties; probably none could be taken under any but a hostile government. At all events, the bill alleges that none was taken on the proposition of May 1862, of the Virginia legislature. If an agreement means the mutual consent of the parties to a given proposition, this was an agreement between these States for the transfer of these counties on the condition named. The condition was one which could be ascertained or carried out at any time; and this was clearly the idea of Virginia when she declared that *whenever* the voters of said counties should ratify and consent to the Constitution they should become part of the State; and her subsequent legislation making special provision for taking the vote on this subject, as shown by the acts of January 31st and February 4th, 1863, is in perfect accord with this idea, and shows her good faith in carrying into effect the agreement. But did Congress consent to this agreement? Unless it can be shown that the consent of Congress, under that clause of the Constitution which forbids agreements between States without it, can only be given in the form of an express and formal statement of every proposition of the agreement, and of its consent thereto, we must hold that the consent of that body was given to this agreement. The attention of Congress was called to the subject by the very short statute of the State of Virginia requesting the admission of the new State into the Union, consisting of but three sections, one of which was entirely devoted to giving consent that these two counties *and the county of Frederick* might accompany the others, if they desired to do so."; and

Whereas, With Frederick County, Virginia, in mind, Article VI, Section 11 of the West Virginia Constitution provides the mechanism for Frederick County to become part of the State of West Virginia, providing as follows:

"Additional territory may be admitted into, and become part of this state, with the consent of the Legislature and a majority of the qualified voters of the state, voting on the question. And in such case provision shall be made by law for the representation thereof in the Senate and House of Delegates, in conformity with the principles set forth in this constitution. And the number of members of which each house of the Legislature is to consist, shall thereafter be increased by the representation assigned to such additional territory"; and

Whereas, Upon joining the State of West Virginia, the citizens of Frederick County would be immediately entitled to all of the rights secured and protected by the West Virginia Constitution to the citizens of West Virginia, including not only the rights of free speech, freedom of the press, religious freedom, the right of peaceful assembly, the right to due process of law, but also the right to keep and bear arms without interference by the government; and

Whereas, upon joining the State of West Virginia, Frederick County, including the City of Winchester, contained therein, would be immediately entitled to at least six delegates in the West Virginia House of Delegates and two senators in the West Virginia Senate; and

Whereas, From the time of the admission of the State of West Virginia into the Union, the counties which are the children of Frederick County, and the citizens of those counties, have pined for reunion with their mother county and prayed that she might join them in the State of West Virginia; therefore, be it

Resolved by the Legislature of West Virginia:

That the citizens of Frederick County, Virginia, consider becoming a part of the State of West Virginia; and; be it

Further Resolved, That on behalf of the citizens of West Virginia, the Legislature of West Virginia does hereby remind the citizens and government of Frederick County, Virginia, of the invitation that was extended more than a century and a half ago, inviting Frederick County, Virginia to join the new State of West Virginia; and, be it

Further Resolved, That on behalf of the citizens of West Virginia, the Legislature of West Virginia assures the citizens and government of Frederick County, Virginia that the invitation extended in 1862 still stands, and that it stands as it was made, with the sincere and earnest hope of all of West Virginia that the invitation will one day be accepted by the citizens of Frederick County; and, be it

Further Resolved, That the 158 years which have elapsed since this invitation was first extended have not diminished the feelings of deep affection in which Frederick County and her citizens are held by the citizens of West Virginia; and, be it

Further Resolved, That at such time as the citizens of Frederick County may desire for Frederick County to become part of the State of West Virginia, the citizens of the Mountain State will welcome them with open arms and rejoice in the addition of Frederick County to the State of West Virginia; and, be it

Further Resolved, That the Clerk of the Senate is hereby directed to forward a copy of this resolution to the Board of Supervisors of Frederick County, Virginia.

Senator Trump, the Senate Judiciary Committee chairman, drafted the resolution and introduced it on January 10, 2020, meaning that it only took three days to pass after its introduction.

"I learned for the first time during West Virginia's 150th birthday celebration. As I read through some of the materials from the records—from the convention in 1862 that—there was an expressed invitation to Frederick County," Trump said. "I confess that before that I didn't know it—and it's been in the back of my mind for a number of years." He continued, "The main motivation was, actually, to bring people's attention to the history, which I think is fascinating. I didn't know—but in Wheeling in 1862, it was clearly contemplated that, 'Hey, Frederick County should be perhaps one of the counties that formed the new state of West Virginia'. That, plus just our common affinity, affection for the people and institutions of Frederick County, Virginia."[1]

Trump cited commonality as the reason for his resolution. "In addition to the historical connections between Frederick County and the seven counties of our Eastern Panhandle, there are strong bonds and ties of every kind among the citizens – family, business, education, culture, and commerce. We share common values,"

---

1 Dave Mistich, "West Virginia Senate Adopts Resolution Calling on Frederick Co., Virginia to Join Mountain State," https://www.wvpublic.org/post/west-virginia-senate-adopts-resolution-calling-frederick-co-virginia-join-mountain-state#stream/0

Senator Trump said. "Frederick County's residents have so much in common with West Virginia that our separation has never made sense."[2]

"I've heard mixed things," continued Trump when asked about the response from Frederick County. "I mean they've read it and they've said it's very touching. The resolution is really just an expression of our affection and a recognition of our joint history with Frederick County. So far, no one has taken offense to it at that they've expressed to me." He concluded, "I'm sure there will be lawyers all over this thing if the citizens of Frederick County decided they wanted to join (West Virginia). But there is a legal basis for the argument; it has been decided and already approved by Virginia and the Congress of the United States."[3]

The initial reaction to this resolution among elected officials of Frederick County leaves little room for hope for the county to secede from Virginia. "I can't speak for the rest of the people in the world," declared Bob Wells, a member of the board of supervisors of Frederick County. "You're wasting your time. I don't see Virginia, any portion of Virginia, joining West Virginia for any reason whatsoever."[4]

Not even Senator Trump expects much to come of his efforts. Even if the residents of Frederick County voted in support of the resolution, it would be a long and torturous path to secession of the county and its joining West Virginia. In short, it seems clear that this is a symbolic gesture at best. However, it nevertheless makes the obvious point that the question of secession remains an active and ongoing discussion. And it likewise demonstrates that the dismemberment of the Commonwealth of Virginia remains an issue of interest, more than 150 years after the fact.

2 Mike McCullough, "Resolution to add Frederick County, Va. to West Virginia passes Senate," http://wvmetronews.com/2020/01/13/resolution-passed-to-add-frederick-county-va-to-west-virginia/

3 Ibid.

4 Brad McIlhinny, "Local Leaders in Virginia Cast Doubt on Invitation, Even as Some W.Va. Lawmakers Cast a Broader Net," http://wvmetronews.com/2020/01/18/local-leaders-in-virginia-cast-doubt-on-invitation-even-as-some-w-va-lawmakers-cast-a-broader-net/?fbclid=IwAR3b9878N456jala4VF8ncPalBOUMrwHCzLtL4hgkJNo3jew8SzoOwnysRM.

BIBLIOGRAPHY

PRIMARY SOURCES

NEWSPAPERS

Alexandria Gazette
Alexandria Gazette and Virginia Advertiser
Baltimore Sun
Congressional Globe
Fairmont Free Press
Harper's Weekly
Jackson Clarion
Kanawha Valley Star
Kingwood Chronicle
Martinsburg Independent
The Morgantown Monitor
National Intelligencer (Washington, D.C.)
New Orleans Crescent
New York Daily Tribune
New York Times
Point Pleasant Register
Richmond Dispatch
Richmond Enquirer
Richmond Whig
The Crisis (Columbus, Ohio)
The Ohio Statesman (Columbus, Ohio)
Vicksburg Times
Wellsburg Herald
Wheeling Intelligencer
Wheeling Register

MANUSCRIPT MATERIALS

Census Bureau, Washington, DC:
>   1860 Census Results

Special Collections, Columbia University, New York, New York:
>   U. S. Supreme Court Archives
>>   Court files pertaining to Virginia v. West Virginia, including transcripts of arguments before the United States Supreme Court

Archives, Historical Society of Pennsylvania, Philadelphia, Pennsylvania:
>   Salmon P. Chase Papers

Manuscripts Division, Library of Congress, Washington, DC:
    Salmon P. Chase Papers
    Custis-Lee Family Papers
    Garrett Family Papers
    Abraham Lincoln Papers
    George B. McClellan Papers
    Samuel Freeman Miller Papers
Archives, Washington & Lee University, Lexington, Virginia:
    Robert E. Lee Papers
West Virginia Historical Archives and Manuscripts Collection, State Archives,
    Charleston, West Virginia:
    Laurane Boreman Papers
    Oath of Loyalty
    Francis H. Pierpont Papers
        "Address to the Reorganized Government of Virginia, May 6, 1861"
    Wheeling Artificial Collection
Archives, West Virginia Jesuit University, Wheeling, West Virginia:
    "List of Traitors in Wheeling"
    "List of Persons who Voted Direct for the Secession of the State of Virginia in
    Ohio County"
West Virginia & Regional History Collection, West Virginia University Libraries,
    Morgantown, West Virginia:
    Waitman T. Willey Papers
    Peter G. Van Winkle Papers

PUBLISHED SOURCES

"A Chapter of Inside History in Regard to the Admission of West Virginia Into the
    Union. Letter from Ex-Congressman Blair to Ex-Senator Willey," *Wheeling
    Intelligencer*, January 22, 1876.
*Acts of the General Assembly of the State of Virginia, Passed in 1861, in the Eighty-fifth Year of the
    Commonwealth*. Richmond: W. F. Richie, 1861.
*Acts of the General Assembly of the State of Virginia, Passed in 1865-66, in the Eighty-Ninth Year
    of the Commonwealth*. Richmond: Allegre and Goode, 1866.
"Alexander Hugh Holmes Stuart," *The Alumni Bulletin*, Vol. I, No. 3 (Charlottesville:
    University of Virginia, November, 1894): 59-68.
Basler, Roy, ed. *Collected Works of Abraham Lincoln*. 8 vols. New Brunswick, NJ: Rutgers
    University Press, 1953.
Beale, Howard K., ed. *The Diary of Edward Bates 1859-1866*. Washington, DC: U.S.
    Government Printing Office, 1933.
Blaine, James G. *Twenty Years of Congress: From Lincoln to Garfield*. 2 vols. Norwich, CT:
    The Henry Bill Publishing Co., 1884.
Carlile, John S. "Letter to the Editor," *National Intelligencer*, January 5, 1861.

"Carlile's Declaration," *Richmond Dispatch*, June 25, 1861.

"Charles Faulkner," *Martinsburg Independent*, November 8, 1884.

Curtis, Benjamin R. *A Memoir of Benjamin Robbins Curtis, L.L.D., with Some of His Professional and Miscellaneous Writings*. 2 vols. Boston: Little, Brown & Co., 1879.

Davis, Jefferson. *The Rise and Fall of the Confederate Government*. 2 vols. New York: D. Appleton, 1881.

"Documents Accompanying the Governor's Message," *Wheeling Intelligencer*, July 3, 1861.

Donald, David Herbert, ed. *Inside Lincoln's Cabinet: The Civil War Diaries of Salmon P. Chase*. New York: Longmans, Green & Co., 1954.

Edwards, William H. "A Bit of History." *The West Virginia Historical Magazine Quarterly*, vol. 2, no. 5 (July 1902): 59-66.

Fast, Richard Ellsworth. *The History and Government of West Virginia*. Morgantown, WV: The Acme Publishing Co., 1901.

Flournoy, Mary H. "The Secession of Virginia." *Confederate Veteran* 37 (1931): 332-334.

"Frank Pierpont's Speech," *Wheeling Intelligencer*, May 6, 1861.

"General News," *New York Daily Tribune*, August 10, 1863.

"Governor Letcher's Proclamation; His Reply to Secretary Cameron—State of Affairs at Norfolk." *New York Times*, April 22, 1861.

Greeley, Horace. *The Greeley Record: The Opinions and Sentiments of Horace Greeley*. Washington, DC: Union Republican Congressional Executive Committee, 1872.

Hall, Granville Davisson. *The Rending of Virginia. A History*. Chicago: Mayer & Miller, 1902.

"John S. Carlile and the New State," *Ritchie County Press*, reprinted in the *Wheeling Intelligencer*, July 28, 1862.

Journal of the Convention Assembled at Wheeling, on the 11th of June, 1861. Wheeling: Daily Press Book, 1861.

Journal of the House of Delegates, of the State of Virginia, 1864-1865. Alexandria, VA: D. Turner, 1865.

"Laid to Rest. Governor Pierpont's Funeral. The City Take a Half Holiday to Attend the Services. The People Were General Sad at the Death of the Grand Old Man Whom All Were Proud to Honor," *Fairmont Free Press*, March 30, 1899.

Lang, Theodore F. *Loyal West Virginia, 1861-1865*. Baltimore, MD: The Deutsch Publishing Co., 1895.

"Letter from General J. J. Jackson," *The Crisis*, May 14, 1862.

Lewis, Virgil A. *A History of West Virginia*. Philadelphia: Hubbard Brothers, 1889.

——, State Archivist, comp. *How West Virginia was Made: Proceedings of the First Convention of the People of Northwestern Virginia at Wheeling, May 13, 14 and 15, 1861, and the Journal of the Second Convention of the People of Northwestern Virginia at Wheeling, which Assembled, June 11, 1861*. Charleston, WV: News-Mail Co., 1909.

"Making New States: Speech of Hon. Martin F. Conway, of Kansas, Delivered in the House of Representatives, Tuesday, Dec. 9, 1862," *New York Times*, December 16, 1862.

McPherson, Edward. *A Political Manual for 1866 and 1867.* Washington, DC: U.S. Government Publishing Office, 1867.

"Military Despotism in Western Virginia—Free Speech and Free Discussion Not Allowed," *The Ohio Statesman,* March 18, 1863.

"Mr. Webster's Speech," *National Intelligencer,* July 5, 1851.

Munford, George W., comp. *Third Edition of the Code of Virginia: Including Legislation to January 1, 1874.* Richmond: J. Goode, 1873.

Nicolay, John G. *The Outbreak of Rebellion.* New York: Charles G. Scribner's Sons, 1882.

——. and John Hay, eds. *Abraham Lincoln Complete Works Comprising His Speeches, Letters, State Papers and Miscellaneous Writings.* 2 vols. New York: The Century Co., 1894.

"Northwestern Virginia. Great Movement in Harrison County for a Separate Organization of the Northwest from the Seceders," *Wheeling Intelligencer,* April 25, 1861.

"Note This," *Wheeling Intelligencer,* April 8, 1863.

Ordinances and Acts of the Restored Government of Virginia, Prior to the Formation of the State of West Virginia with the Constitution and Laws of the State of West Virginia, to March 2d, 1866. Wheeling: John Frew, 1866.

Parker, Granville. *The Formation of the State of West Virginia, and Other Incidents of the Late Civil War.* Wellsburg, WV: Glass & Son, 1875.

Pease, Theodore Calvin and James G. Randall, eds. *The Diary of Orville Hickman Browning.* 2 vols. Springfield, IL: Illinois Historical Society, 1925.

Pollard, Edward A. *The First Year of the War.* Richmond: West & Johnston, 1862.

"Public Meeting at Guyandotte—Flag of Virginia Hoisted," *Kanawha Valley Star,* April 30, 1861.

Reader Frank S. *History of the Fifth West Virginia Cavalry, Formerly the Second Virginia Infantry, and of Battery G, First West Va. Light Artillery.* New Brighton, PA: Daily News, 1890.

"Reverdy Johnson on Test Oaths," *New York Daily Tribune,* December 29, 1865.

Richardson, James D., comp. *A Compilation of the Messages and Papers of the Presidents, 1789-1897.* 11 vols. Washington, DC: U.S. Government Printing Office, 1897.

Rossiter, Clinton, ed. *The Federalist Papers.* New York: New American Library, 1961.

Rowland, Dunbar, ed. *Jefferson Davis, Constitutionalist, His Letters, Papers, and Speeches.* 9 vols. Jackson: Mississippi Dept. of Archives and History, 1923.

"Secession of Virginia," *Richmond Dispatch,* April 19, 1861.

Senate Misc. Doc. No. 98, 37th Congress, 2nd Session, 2-3.

Smith, William Prescott. *The Book of the Great Railway Celebrations of 1857.* New York: D. Appleton & Co., 1858.

Speech of the Hon. P. G. Van Winkle, of West Virginia, Delivered in the Senate, April 21, 1864. Washington, DC: Gibson Brothers Printers, 1864.

Statue of Governor Francis Harrison Pierpont. 61st Congress, 2d Session, Doc. No. 656 Washington, DC: USGPO, 1910.

"The Baltimore and Ohio Road," *Wheeling Intelligencer,* April 27, 1861.

"The Day We Celebrate," *Wheeling Intelligencer,* June 20, 1863.

"The Election for Senators Yesterday," *Wheeling Intelligencer,* July 10, 1861.

"The Election To-day," *Wheeling Intelligencer*, October 24, 1861.

"The Inauguration of the New State of West Virginia. Valedictory of Governor Pierpont. Inaugural of Governor Boreman. Speech of Ex-Senator Willey," *Wheeling Intelligencer*, June 21, 1863.

"The Last Formality Gone Through With," *Wheeling Intelligencer*, April 17, 1863.

"The Movement in Harrison County," *Wheeling Intelligencer*, April 25, 1861.

"The New Dred Scott," *Harpers Weekly*, January 19, 1867.

"The Northwest," *Richmond Dispatch*, June 26, 1861.

"The Pan Handle," *Richmond Dispatch*, May 14, 1861.

"The Proceedings of Congress," *New York Times*, July 2, 1862.

"The State Debt—West Virginia," *Richmond Dispatch*, December 20, 1866.

"The Virginia Secession Ordinance; An Ordinance," *New York Times*, April 28, 1861.

"The Vote for Secession in Virginia," *New York Times*, June 1, 1861.

The War of the Rebellion: A Compilation of the Official Records of the Union and Confederate Armies. 128 volumes in 3 series. Washington, D.C.: United States Government Printing Office, 1889.

"The West Virginia Case," *Alexandria Gazette and Virginia Advertiser*, March 7, 1871.

"The Wheeling Convention," *Wheeling Intelligencer*, June 14, 1861.

"The Working Men's Mass Meeting," *Wheeling Intelligencer*, March 23, 1863.

Thirty-fifth Annual Report of the President and Directors to the Stockholders of the Baltimore and Ohio Railroad Company, for the Year Ending September 30, 1861. Baltimore: William N. Innes, 1862.

Thirty-Seventh Annual Report of the President and Directors to the Stockholders of the Baltimore & Ohio R. R. Co., for the Year Ending September 30, 1863. Baltimore: J. B. Rose & Co., 1864.

Thorpe, Francis Newton. *The Federal and State Constitutions, Colonial Charters, and Other Organic Laws of the States, Territories and Colonies Now or Heretofore Forming the United States of America*. Washington, DC: United States Government Printing Office, 1909.

"To Lincoln Voters," *Wheeling Intelligencer*, November 5, 1860.

"To the People of North-Western Virginia," *Kingwood Chronicle*, May 25, 1861.

"Trials by Military Commissions—The Supreme Court Decision," *New York Times*, January 3, 1867.

Trowbridge, J.T. *The South: A Tour of its Battle-Fields and Ruined Cities*. Hartford: L. Stebbins, 1866.

Virginia v. West Virginia, 78 U.S. 39, 11 Wall. 39 (1871).

Virginia v. West Virginia, 220 U.S. 1 (1911).

"Virginia Convention Seventh Day," *Wheeling Intelligencer*, June 19, 1861.

"Virginian," "Letter to the Editor," *National Intelligencer*, October 20, 1860.

Welles, Edgar T., ed. *The Diary of Gideon Welles, Secretary of the Navy Under Lincoln and Johnson*. 3 vols. Boston: Houghton-Mifflin, 1911.

"West Virginia," *The Weekly Register*, June 25, 1863.

"Western Virginia," *New York Daily Tribune*, September 14, 1861.

"West Virginia—Free or Slave," *Wheeling Intelligencer*, February 12, 1862.

SECONDARY SOURCES

Aler, F. Vernon. *Aler's History of Martinsburg and Berkeley County, West Virginia.* Hagerstown, MD: The Mail Publishing Co., 1888.

Allardice, Bruce S. *Confederate Colonels: A Biographical Register.* Columbia: University of Missouri Press, 2008.

Amar, Akhil Reed. *America's Constitution; A Biography.* New York: Random House, 2005.

Ambler, Charles H. *Francis H. Pierpont: Union War Governor and Father of West Virginia.* Chapel Hill: University of North Carolina Press, 1937.

——. *History of West Virginia.* New York: Prentiss-Hall, 1930.

——. *Sectionalism in Virginia from 1776 to 1861.* Chicago: University of Chicago Press, 1910.

——. "The Cleavage Between Eastern and Western Virginia." *The American Historical Review* 15 (1910): 762-780.

——. *Waitman Thomas Willey, Orator, Churchman, Humanitarian.* Huntington, WV: Standard Print and Publishing Co., 1954.

Bailey, Kenneth R. "Test Oaths, Belligerent Rights and Confederate Money: Civil War Lawsuits before the West Virginia Supreme Court of Appeals." *West Virginia History,* Vol. 7, No. 1 (Spring 2013): 1-22.

Bogue, Allan G. *The Earnest Men: Republicans of the Civil War Senate.* Ithaca, NY: Cornell University Press, 1981.

Boney, F. N. *John Letcher of Virginia: The Story of Virginia's Civil War Governor.* Tuscaloosa: University of Alabama Press, 1966.

Braver, Joshua. "The Recurrent Myth of Court-Packing." Harvard Public Law Working Paper No. 19-44 (2019).

Burlingame, Michael. *Abraham Lincoln: A Life.* 2 vols. Baltimore: Johns Hopkins University Press, 2007.

Cain, Marvin R. *Lincoln's Attorney General: Edward Bates of Missouri.* Columbia: University of Missouri Press, 1965.

Callahan, James Morton. *Semi-Centennial History of West Virginia.* Charleston, WV: The Semi-Centennial Commission of West Virginia, 1913.

Coleman, William C. "The State As Defendant Under the Federal Constitution; the Virginia-West Virginia Debt Controversy." *Harvard Law Review* 31 (1919): 210-245.

Collins, Darrell. *The Jones-Imboden Raid: The Confederate Attempt to Destroy the Baltimore & Ohio Railroad and Retake West Virginia.* Jefferson, N.C.: McFarland & Co., 2007.

Cooling, Benjamin Franklin. *Monocacy: The Battle that Saved Washington.* Shippensburg, PA: White Mane, 2000.

Curry, Richard Orr. *A House Divided: A Study of Statehood Politics and the Copperhead Movement in West Virginia.* Pittsburgh: University of Pittsburgh Press, 1964.

——. "The Virginia Background for the History of the Civil War and Reconstruction Era in West Virginia: An Analytical Commentary," *West Virginia History* 20 (July 1989): 215-246.

Cutright, W. B. *The History of Upshur County, West Virginia From Its Earliest Exploration and Settlement to the Present Time.* Buckhannon, WV: privately published, 1907.

Davis, Madison. *The Public Career of Montgomery Blair, Particularly with Reference to His Services as Postmaster General of the United States.* Washington, DC: Columbia Historical Society, 1910.

Dickinson, Jack L. *Wayne County, West Virginia in the Civil War.* Salem, MA: Higginson Book Co., 2003.

Hon. Bernice Bouie Donald, "When the Rule of Law Breaks Down: Implications of the 1866 Memphis Massacre for the Passage of the Fourteenth Amendment," *Boston University Law Review,* Vol. 98 (2018): 1607-1676.

Ebenroth, Carsten Thomas and Matthew James Kemner. "The Enduring Political Nature of Questions of State Succession and Secession and the Quest for Objective Standards." *Univ. Pa. Journal of Intl. Econ. Law,* Vol. 17 (1996): 753-819.

Eckenrode. Hamilton. *The Political History of Virginia During Reconstruction.* Baltimore; Johns Hopkins University Press, 1904.

Fairman, Charles. "Reconstruction and Reunion, 1864-88," *History of the Supreme Court of the United States.* 9 vols. New York: Macmillan, 1971. Vol. 6.

Fansler, Homer F. *History of Tucker County West Virginia.* Parsons, West Virginia: McClain Printing Co., 1962.

Finkelman, Paul. *An Imperfect Union: Slavery Federalism, and Comity.* Chapel Hill: University of North Carolina Press, 1981.

Finn, John E. "Civil Liberties and the Bill of Rights," *The Teaching Company.* Part I: Lecture 4: The Court and Constitutional Interpretation, 2016.

Foner, Eric. *Reconstruction: America's Unfinished Business, 1863-1877.* New York, Harper Collins, 1988.

Freehling, William W. *The Road to Disunion, Vol. I: Secessionists at Bay, 1776-1854.* London and New York: Oxford University Press, 1990.

———. *The Road to Disunion, Vol. II: Secessionists Triumphant 1854-1861.* London and New York: Oxford University Press, 2007.

Freeman, Douglas Southall. *R. E. Lee.* 4 vols. New York: Doubleday, 1934-1935.

Gerhardt, Michael J. "The Constitutional Limits to Court Stripping." *Lewis and Clark Law Review,* Vol 9, No. 2 (2004): 347-361.

Goodwin, Doris Kearns. *Team of Rivals: The Political Genius of Abraham Lincoln.* New York: Simon & Schuster, 2005.

Grove, Tara Leigh. "The Exceptions Clause as a Structural Safeguard." *Columbia Law Review,* Vol. 113, No. 4 (2013): 929-1005

Guelzo, Allen C. *Abraham Lincoln: Redeemer President.* Grand Rapids, MI: Eerdmans, 2003.

———. *Reconstruction: A Concise History.* New York and London: Oxford University Press, 2018.

Harris, William C. *With Charity for All: Lincoln and the Restoration of the Union.* Lexington: University of Kentucky Press, 1997.

Hart, Albert Bushnell. *Salmon Portland Chase.* Boston: Houghton-Mifflin, 1899.

Heinman, Ronald. *Old Dominion, New Commonwealth: a History of Virginia, 1607-2007.* Charlottesville: University of Virginia Press, 2008.

Hesseltine, William B. *Lincoln and the War Governors.* New York: Alfred A Knopf, 1948.

Humbert, Archer Butler. *The Old National Road: A Chapter of American Expansion.* Columbus, OH: F. J. Heer, 1901.

Hyman, Harold. *A More Perfect Union; the Impact of the Civil War and Reconstruction on the Constitution.* New York: Knopf, 1973.

Kesavan, Vasan and Michael Stokes Paulsen. "Is West Virginia Unconstitutional?" *California Law Review,* Vol. 90, No. 2 (March 2002): 291-400.

Kneebone, John T., et al., eds. *Dictionary of Virginia Biography.* 3 vols. Richmond: The Library of Virginia, 1998.

Lankford, Nelson D. *Cry Havoc! The Crooked Road to Civil War, 1861.* New York: Penguin Books, 2007.

Lee, Thomas. "The Supreme Court of the United States As Quasi-International Tribunal: Reclaiming the Court's Original and Exclusive Jurisdiction over Treaty-Based Suits by Foreign States Against States." *Columbia Law Review.* Vol. 104 (2004): 1765-1888.

Lesser, W. Hunter. *Rebels at the Gate: Lee and McClellan on the Front Line of a Nation Divided.* Naperville, IL: Sourcebooks, 2004.

Marvel, William. *Lincoln's Autocrat: The Life of Edwin Stanton.* Chapel Hill: University of North Carolina Press, 2015.

McGregor, James C. *The Disruption of Virginia.* New York: MacMillan, 1922.

Miller, Richard F. *Harvard's Civil War: The History of the Twentieth Massachusetts Volunteer Infantry.* Boston: University Press of New England, 2005.

Moore, George E. *A Banner In The Hills: West Virginia's Statehood.* New York: Appleton-Century-Crofts, 1963.

Myers, Sylvester. *Myers' History of West Virginia.* 2 vols. Wheeling, WV: Wheeling News Lithograph Co., 1913.

Newton, J. H., G. G. Nichols, and A. G. Sprankle, comps. *History of the Pan-Handle; Being Historical Collections of the Counties of Ohio, Brooke, Marshall, and Hancock, West Virginia.* Wheeling, WV: J. A. Caldwell, 1879.

Nicoletti, Cynthia. *Secession on Trial.* Cambridge: Cambridge Univ. Press, 2017.

Niven, John. *Gideon Welles: Lincoln's Secretary of the Navy.* New York and London: Oxford University Press, 1973.

——. *Salmon P. Chase: A Biography.* New York and London: Oxford University Press, 1995.

Oakes, James. *The Radical and the Republican; Frederick Douglas, Abraham Lincoln, and the Triumph of Antislavery Politics.* New York: W.W. Norton, 2008.

Owens, Richard H. *Rogue State: The Unconstitutional Process of Establishing West Virginia Statehood.* Lanham, MD: University Press of America, 2013.

Randall, James Garfield. *Constitutional Problems Under Lincoln.* 2d ed. Champaign: University of Illinois Press, 1951.

Reizenstein, Milton. *The Economic History of the Baltimore & Ohio Railroad 1827-1853.* Baltimore: Johns Hopkins University Press, 1897.

Reynolds, William L. and Gordon G. Young, "Equal Division in the Supreme Court: History, Problems, and Proposals", *North Carolina Law Review*, Vol. 62, (1983): 29-56.

Riccards, Michael P. "Lincoln and the Political Question: The Creation of the State of West Virginia." *Presidential Studies Quarterly*, vol. 27, no. 3 (Summer 1997): 549-564.

Rice, Otis K. *A History of Greenbrier County.* Lewisburg, WV: Greenbrier County Historical Society, 1986.

Rice, Otis K. and Stephen W. Brown. *West Virginia: A History.* 2nd ed. Lexington: University Press of Kentucky, 1993.

Ross, Michael A. *Justice of Shattered Dreams: Samuel Freeman Miller and the Supreme Court During the Civil War Era.* Baton Rouge: Louisiana State University Press, 2003.

Sandberg, Carl. *Abraham Lincoln: The War Years.* 4 vols. New York: Harcourt, Brace & Co., 1939.

Sander, Kathleen Waters. *John W. Garrett and the Baltimore & Ohio Railroad.* Baltimore, MD: Johns Hopkins University Press, 2017.

Steiner, Bernard Christian. *Life of Reverdy Johnson.* Baltimore: The Norman, Remington Co., 1914.

Stewart, David O. *Impeached: The Trial of President Andrew Johnson and the Fight for Lincoln's Legacy.* New York: Simon & Schuster, 2009.

Summers, Festus P. *The Baltimore and Ohio in the Civil War.* New York: G. P. Putnam's Sons 1939.

Taylor, John M. *William Henry Seward: Lincoln's Right Hand.* Washington, DC: Brassey's, 1991.

"The Original Jurisdiction of the United States Supreme Court," *Stanford Law Review*, Vol. 11 (July 1959): 665-719.

Thomas, Emory M. *Robert E. Lee: A Biography.* New York: W.W. Norton, 1995.

Thomas, William G. *The Iron Way: Railroads, the Civil War, and the Making of Modern America.* New Haven: Yale University Press, 2011.

Toomey, Daniel Carroll. *The War Came by Train: The Baltimore & Ohio Railroad during the Civil War.* Baltimore, MD: B&O Railroad Museum, 2013.

Wagner, W.J. "Original Jurisdiction of National Supreme Courts." *St. Johns Law Review*, Vol. 32, No. 2 (May 1959): 217-248.

Wallenstein, Peter. *Cradle of America; A History of Virginia.* Lawrence: University of Kansas Press, 2007.

Warden, Robert Bruce. *An Account of the Private Life and Public Services of Salmon Portland Chase.* Cincinnati: Wilstach, Baldwin & Co., 1874.

Wellman, Judith. *The Road to Seneca Falls.* Champaign: University of Illinois Press, 2010.

Willey, William P. *An Inside View of the Formation of the State of West Virginia with Character Sketches of the Pioneers in that Movement.* Wheeling, WV: The News Publishing Co., 1901.

Wingerter, Charles A. *History of Greater Wheeling and Vicinity.* Chicago: Lewis Publishing Co., 1912.

Winters, John D. *The Civil War in Louisiana.* Baton Rouge: Louisiana State University Press, 1963.

Winthrop, William. *Military Law and Precedents*. 2nd ed. Washington, DC: U. S. Government Printing Office, 1920.

Wittenberg, Eric J. *The Battle of White Sulphur Springs: Averell Fails to Secure West Virginia*. Charleston, SC: The History Press, 2011.

Zimring, David R. "'Secession in Favor of the Constitution': How West Virginia Justified Separate Statehood During the Civil War." *West Virginia History*, New Series, Vol. 3, No. 2 (Fall 2009): 23-51.

WEBSITES

"Address of Hon. Waitman T. Willey," *Debates and Proceedings of the First Constitutional Convention of West Virginia*, February 12, 1863, www.wvculture.org/history/ statehood/cc021263.html

Arrington, Robert. "Pierpont's Bastille—The Trials of Judge Thompson," sites.google.com/site/wvotherhistory/pierpont-s-bastille-the-trials-of-judge-tho mpson

"Biography of Arthur Ingram Boreman," www.wvculture.org/history/government/ governors/ boreman.html

"Biography of John S. Carlile." www.encyclopediavirginia.org/Carlile_John_ S_1817-1878

Constitution of West Virginia, www.wvculture.org/history/statehood/ constitution. html

Debates and Proceedings of the First Constitutional Convention of West Virginia, December 11, 1861, www.wvculture.org/history/statehood.html

Gilot, Jon-Erik. "A Monumental Controversy." Web blog post, *Emerging Civil War*, 5 Sept. 2017. www.emergingcivilwar.com/2017/09/05/a-monumental-contro-versy/

McIlhinny, Brad. "Local Leaders in Virginia Cast Doubt on Invitation, Even as Some W.Va. Lawmakers Cast a Broader Net." http://wvmetronews.com/2020/01/18/ local-leaders-in-virginia-cast-doubt-on-invitation-even-as-some-w-va-lawmakers-cast-a-broader-net/?fbclid=IwAR3b9878N456jala4VF8ncPalBOUMrwHCzLtL 4hgkJNo3jew8SzoOwnysRM.

McCullough, Mike. "Resolution to add Frederick County, Va. to West Virginia passes Senate." http://wvmetronews.com/2020/01/13/resolution-passed-to-add-fred erick-county-va-to-west-virginia/.

Mistich, Dave. "West Virginia Senate Adopts Resolution Calling on Frederick Co., Virginia to Join Mountain State." https://www.wvpublic.org/post/west-virginia-senate-adopts-resolution-calling-frederick-co-virginia-join-mountain-state#strea m/0.

Proceedings of the Second Session of the Second Wheeling Convention, August 21, 1861, www. wvculture.org/history/statehood/wheelingconvention20821.html

Sayre, R. H. "An Important Contribution to the 'Missing Chapter' in the History of the Formation of West Virginia by an Eyewitness. Recollections and Narrative of a

Member of the May Convention of 1861, the Restored Government and the New State, West Virginia." *The Bar* (October 1913), found at www. wvculture.org/history/statehood/sayre.html

"Soldiers and Camplife", lva.virginia.gov/public/ guides/Civil-War/Soldiers.htm.

"Waitman T. Willey." *Biographical Directory of the United States Congress, 1774-Present.* bioguide.congress.gov/scripts/biodisplay.pl?index=W000484

Index

resume all rights and powers granted under said Constitution, 31; admitted into the Confederacy, 34; preamble and resolutions, 35; response to Virginia's Ordinance of Secession, 35; Bill of Rights of Virginia, 48; convention picks name for the new state, 68; voters approve a new constitution, 69; requirements for a state to be admitted into the union, 70; only males could vote, 73; required consent of Congress, 76; all slaves be freed immediately as condition of statehood, 78; statehood bill passed the House, 89; admitted to the union, 118; becomes the 35th state, 121; new challenges after the end of the war, 124; new government settles in, 124; 32,000 served in the Union Army, 134; what Virginia lost when it lost West Virginia, 134; new constitution approved in 1869, 142; passed legislation to transfer Berkeley and Jefferson Counties to West Virginia, 148; defends claim to Berkeley and Jefferson Counties, 151; Supreme Court, 157; *Virginia v. West Virginia*, 176; would not exist without Lincoln, 182

Westsylvania, State of (proposed), 5

Whaley, Kellian V., 75

Wheat, James, 52

Wheeling Intelligencer, 3, 10, 15, 16-16n, 22, 38, 52, 55, 62, 68, 109, 117, 121

Wheeling movement, 56

Wheeling suspension bridge, 38-38n

Wheeling, West Virginia, 9, 11, 16n, 17-19, 34, 36, 38, 44, 46, 57, 63, 67, 69, 73, 80, 82, 84, 136

Whig Party, 2, 27, 42, 83, 92n, 94n, 103n

Willey Amendment, 79, 111, 115, 117, 182

Willey, Senator Waitman T., 3, 6, 26-27, 42-43, 45, 53n, 66, 74-75, 76n, 78, 116n, 182; comments on the B&O, 64; submits petition for the admission of West Virginia, 76; amendment calls for emancipation of all slave children, 79-81; Willey Amendment, 116; eluded Confederate forces, 118; *photo*, 42

Willey, William J., 27, 43

Wirt, William, 92n

Wise County, Virginia, 114

Wise, Henry A., 26, 30; *photo*, 30

Wood County, West Virginia, 23

Wyoming County, West Virginia, 115

Yerger, 175

Yerger, Edward M., 172-174

Zane, Ebenezer, 37

Zinn, William B., 39

About the Authors

Eric J. Wittenberg is an accomplished American Civil War historian and author. An attorney in Ohio, Wittenberg has authored nearly two dozen books on various Civil War subjects, with particular focus on cavalry operations, as well as three dozen articles in popular magazines.

Edmund A. Sargus, Jr. serves as a Federal district judge in Columbus, Ohio, worked as the U.S. Attorney heading Federal prosecutions in the district from 1993 through 1996, and since 2005 has been an adjunct professor at the Moritz College of Law at The Ohio State University, where he teaches Trial Advocacy and an evidence seminar.

Penny L. Barrick graduated summa cum laude from The Ohio State University with a B.S. in history education and later with a J.D., with honors, from The Ohio State University College of Law. She is a senior lawyer with the U.S. District Court for the Southern District of Ohio. She has a love of Civil War history and particularly its intersection with constitutional law.